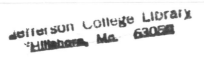

VICTOR P. MAIORANA

State University of New York at Farmingdale
Dowling College

How to Learn and Study in College

PRENTICE-HALL, INC., Englewood Cliffs, New Jersey 07632

Library of Congress Cataloging in Publication Data

Maiorana, Victor P
   How to learn and study in college.
   Includes bibliographical references and index.
   1. Study, Method of. I. Title.
LB2395.M34   378.1'7'02812   79-23527
ISBN 0-13-415059-7

Printed in the United States of America

10 9 8 7 6

Editorial/production supervision by Robert Hunter
Interior design by Emily Dobson
Cover design by Wanda Lubelska
Manufacturing buyer: Harry P. Baisley

PRENTICE-HALL INTERNATIONAL, INC., *London*
PRENTICE-HALL OF AUSTRALIA PTY. LIMITED, *Sydney*
PRENTICE-HALL OF CANADA, LTD., *Toronto*
PRENTICE-HALL OF INDIA PRIVATE LIMITED, *New Delhi*
PRENTICE-HALL OF JAPAN, INC., *Tokyo*
PRENTICE-HALL OF SOUTHEAST ASIA PTE. LTD., *Singapore*
WHITEHALL BOOKS LIMITED, *Wellington, New Zealand*

For Rosalie
For Daphne, Barbara, and Ann Camille
and for my
Mother and Father

CONTENTS

PREFACE

To The Student

By choosing to attend college you have said something good about yourself. You have decided to help yourself become all you are capable of being. Will college be difficult? Sometimes. Will it require hard work? Yes. Will you survive? Yes; especially if you first learn how to be a college student. Learning how to be a college student is what this book is about. This book has two basic purposes:

- The help you *achieve* the greatest amount of competency, awareness, and flexibility from your college experience.
- To help you *complete* your college course of study—whether day or evening and whether a certificate program, an associate's degree, or a bachelor's degree.

This is a study skills text. But knowing only how to study is not enough for college. Too many students drop out because they are bored with their course work. Others drop out because they don't know how to manage themselves in a college setting. As a college student you must also know how to handle these two concerns. Otherwise you may limit your chance for success. Unlike other texts on the subject, this one places learning, reading, and study skills in a system that will help assure the completion of your educational program. It provides the additional skills you need to survive in college.

The basic learning and study skills are: Establishing and using a study schedule, calling on others for help when necessary, understanding of the learning process, classroom listening and note taking, reading and studying textbooks and other materials, library use, and exam taking. If you are primarily interested in these skills, then the chapters to study are:

- Chapter 3 (Study Schedule)
- Chapters 6, 7 (Learning Skills and Techniques)
- Chapters 8, 9, 10 (Textbook Reading)
- Chapter 11 (Classroom Listening and Note Taking)
- Chapter 14 (People Who Can Help)
- Chapter 15 (Textbook Study Systems)
- Chapter 18 (Using The Library)
- Chapter 19 (Exams)

Other chapters include writing term papers (12), speaking in class (13), and studying math and science (16). Chapter 17 contains an alternate study method to use once the SCORE System described in Chapter 15 has been mastered. A feature of all chapters is their ability to actively engage you in thinking about and applying the material. You will have something to show for your efforts. In-chapter and chapter-end questions are included. You will find many of these questions interesting and rewarding to complete.

Chapters 1 and 2 place the above skills in a setting that help you obtain maximum benefit. They introduce you to a new approach to college going. The approach places you in a position to more firmly control the results you achieve in college. Do you want to reduce course boredom and maximize the chances of your surviving in college? These chapters will help:

- Chapter 4 (How To Manage Yourself)
- Chapter 5 (How To Make Every Course Interesting)

Learning and studying are obviously more interesting if you like the basic course material. The Appendix "Choosing Your Curriculum" will help you to choose or confirm your major field of study.

If you *want help now* on a problem that is troubling you, turn to Figure 4-1, page 40. There you will find quick passage to that chapter and page which will help most.

To The Instructor   This book is meant to be the basic text for the developmental student and the theme text for the remedial student. It is also aimed at those students, of whatever background, who simply feel a need to achieve more in college. Developmental and other students will be able to use the material directly. Remedial students will first need to possess basic reading ability. Regardless of initial abilities there is a growing realization in the basic skills field (see for example, *AAHE-ERIC Higher Education Research Report No. 1 1978; Journal of Developmental and Remedial Education Spring 1978;* discussion questions 4 and 5, pages 89 and 90) that high drop out rates and subject matter disinterest on the part of students can not be attributed solely to lack of basic arithmetic, grammar and reading skills or to a lack of developmental skills. Many students who already possess these skills don't survive in college. That part of the student who needs help with reading and study skills needs just as much attention as that part who is bored with course material and who doesn't know how to manage the new freedom and personal responsibility that comes with college. In addition, today's college student faces more severe economic, social and career preparation pressures than existed even five years ago. It is because of the impact that basic skills programs are having and can have on providing educational opportunity—as well as sustaining college careers that would otherwise wither—that the basic skills field has arrived as a valid part of the college curriculum. The enlarged scope of the basic skills teacher's responsibility brings with it a need for instructional materials that will improve the chance of student success. Today's basic skills teacher needs materials that address the total student. And they need them in a form that is simple and adaptable.

This text, while emphasizing traditional study skills, also introduces new ones that will help the student operate in the cognitive, affective, and behaviorial domains. The simplicity and adaptability to a variety of study skill requirements make this book particularly useful to the remedial and developmental student. All chapters have either in-chapter progress-check exercises or chapter-end questions (or both) that allow the student to demonstrate material competency. You will find the questions different from those in other texts. Their number and variety and their emphasis on providing learning experience will allow you to choose learning options to meet individual and class needs. Each part stands by itself as do most of the chapters within. As organized, the chapters follow the "management system" described in Chapters 1 and 2, and a course can be taught by taking each chapter in turn. However, you may prefer another sequence. Depending on available time and your assessment of student and class needs you can tailor a course, mini-course or workshop to fit situational requirements. For example, the study skill "core" chapters can be considered to be Chapters 3, 7, 8, 9, 10, 11, 15, 18 and 19. Chapters 2, 5 and 6 will help promote affective (attitudinal) awareness. Chapters 2, 4, 5 and 14 address behavioral areas. Specific concerns can be emphasized as follows:

Reading Emphasis
Chapters 7, 8, 9, 10, 18

Study Emphasis
Chapters 3, 6, 7, 15, 16, 17

Behavioral Emphasis
Chapters 2, 3, 4, 5, 14

Affective Emphasis
Chapters 2, 3, 5, 6, 11

Performance Emphasis
Chapters 4, 11, 12, 13, 15, 18, 19

There are many other arrangements that will work well. It is not expected that in a particular course every chapter will be used, every technique discussed, every in-chapter exercise completed or every chapter-end question assigned. However, experience in the basic skills field makes it evident that teachers prefer flexibility and variety in material and assignments to meet varying needs. This book has been written with these requirements in mind and you will be able to operate accordingly and, it is hoped, successfully.

The concept for this book came as a result of teaching, observation, research and discussion with students of varying backgrounds, ages and educational goals. Their desire to do well in college and their struggles to adapt to the new demands of college, both personal and educational, led to a new "Total Student" approach to college going and study skills. Appreciation is extended to those students and colleagues who suggested and/or reviewed portions of the manuscript.

VICTOR P. MAIORANA
JANUARY 1980

PURPOSE OF THE BOOK

You have just completed high school. Now you are about to start college. You have heard it will not be easy. You wonder if you will adapt. Questions remain. "What should be my major? How am I going to keep up with all the reading and studying?" You wonder what it means to be a college student. Yes, you can adapt. You can be a college student. And this book will help.

You have just read the same sentence for the fifth time in a row. You stop reading. You blink blankly at the page. Your head hurts, your right foot is numb, and your legs are itchy. You can't recall a thing you have read. You're not even sure you care. You leave the text open at the unread page. You spend the next five hours and twenty-five minutes with friends. The crowd breaks up and you return to your room. You switch on the light. As if drawn by an optical magnet, your eyes fix on the opened text, and they remain on the page you stopped reading hours ago. The headache and the itchy legs return. You slam the book shut and fall into bed. Another wasted day, another day behind. If you are like most students, you have probably had a similar experience. Studying may not be one of your favorite activities. You wonder if you can change it, if you can feel it's worthwhile. Yes, you can change. You can make it worthwhile. And this book will help.

You had wondered about college. But then you met and married college graduate Paul. Now the children are all grown or nearly so. You're beginning to think about college again. But you worry. "Can I ever hope to really be a college student? Maybe all I'll ever be is a grandparent." The answer is yes, you can be a college student. And this book will help.

You are a grandparent. As you enter class you almost drop your bifocals when you notice that the *teacher* looks about as old as your first grandchild. It's been forty years since you've been in a classroom. Then you notice a Septemberish person two rows in front of you and another to your right and still another to your left. You've got company. "Maybe we can show these folks a thing or two." You can, and they will benefit. And this book will help show you how.

You're a secretary. You actually run the office but get little notice and less pay. You're tired of doing your boss's job at your salary, tired of a job that asks less than your potential. But you are not sure about college. Can you really do college work? Will you really get that degree? That job you're capable of handling? The pay that goes with it? The answer is yes. And this book will help.

You are a descendant of a family whose roots in this country go back over 300 years. In all that time, first because of laws that prevented it and then because of thoughts that did the same, none of your family ever attended college. Then came you. You feel the word descendant doesn't quite fit you. You're not descending at all. You think you're ascending. Your thinking is right on target. And this book will help keep you there.

You've been promoted. You've also been told this is the last step unless you obtain more education. You resent having been pressured into attending evening courses. But much to your surprise you find yourself stimulated. As a supervisor you know how important it is to operate efficiently and effectively. You want to achieve the same for your college efforts. This book will help.

You're a student who usually does well. But you wonder, "Am I getting the most out of college? Are there approaches to studying that will challenge me intellectually?" If you are concerned with these kinds of questions, this book will help.

You dropped out when you couldn't see any purpose to school. Now it's ten years later. All those new graduates, both men and women, are getting hired into those management positions you really want. You think, "Am I too old?" Then you remember hearing that one-third of all college students are over 25 and the percentage is growing. You sign up for one course. Will it be better this time? The answer is almost certainly yes, because your viewpoint is different. Will you make it through this time? Yes again, and this book will help.

You're anyone who has decided that education is not merely preparation for living, it *is* living. You recognize that formal education is probably the best method of improving your situation. But you wonder—all those courses with all those teachers in all those classrooms with all those textbooks, and all the studying required—can you really manage it all? The answer is yes.

An Experiment

Let's try this little experiment and see what happens. What do you like to do? Do you like dancing? Playing basketball? Volleyball? Tennis? Skydiving? Sailing? Bowling? Talking? Spelunking? Listening to music? Playing music? Skiing? Reading? . . . *Reading?* Wait—did you say you like to read? The thing you do when trying to understand something that's been printed? Oh? You didn't mean *that* kind of reading. But then what did you mean? Oh, the kind of reading you do when you read the sports page or your favorite magazine or newspaper. Well, okay, we can use that kind of reading in our experiment. Now what is it about that kind of reading that makes it fun? Can you list the reasons? Let's imagine what your list might look like.

- You make the decision about what to read.
- You make the decision about when to read.
- You make the decision about how much time you spend reading.
- You make the decision about whether you should read more on the same subject.

Our experiment is over. It looks successful. You have found the reasons why the things you like to do are fun. Look at the list again. Substitute anything you like to do. You will find the list holds up. You have discovered the management conditions that exist when you are doing something you consider enjoyable or worth your time doing. The next idea has probably already leaped out at you: "If only these conditions applied to college and studying."

The question is not whether these conditions apply to college. They do. The question is *how* do they apply? In other words, how can you approach college and studying so that you are in fact in charge? Here is an answer.

How to Survive in College: A Basic Approach

This book uses a management approach to college. You will get much more from the book, and from college, if you understand the term *management*. For the moment let's define management as "efficiently accomplishing what you want to do." That is a simple enough definition. But it contains a few hooks. First it means that you must know, rather clearly, what you want to do. Second, it means that you *actually accomplish* your intent. Last, the idea of efficiency requires that you accomplish your intent with little wasted effort. Here are the major activities that take place when you manage something:

- *Planning*. This simply means deciding in advance what you want to do. It also includes identifying the conditions under which you will work and preparing a work schedule.
- *Organizing*. This involves identifying those activities necessary to accomplish your intent. It also involves figuring out how these activities relate to each other, how they should go together.
- *Staffing*. This activity is concerned with identifying people who will help you achieve your intent. This includes you as the major member. It also includes your teachers, librarians, and counselors.
- *Directing*. This refers to getting the most effort from people while keeping them reasonably happy. In college the main person doing the directing is you. The main person being directed is also you. This is an interesting relationship that you can take advantage of.
- *Evaluating*. This is keeping account of what you said you would do in relation to what you actually did. It is comparing result with intent and taking steps to narrow any difference.

These activities are used by all managers. If you use them, you will avoid many problems related to college. Using these activities puts you in charge of your college education. The following section relates the management activities to some basic college concerns. It also describes how each part of this book will help you act on your concerns.

What You Can Expect from This Book   Look at the following groups of items. Check all the statements that represent your feelings. Those you check will reveal your basic concerns with college. They will also show which part of the book will help you most. Remember to check *all* those that apply to you.

Group I. These Items Concern Planning

1. _____You are not sure what interests you.

2. _____You would like a method for selecting a major.

3. _____ You choose electives quickly and because you think the course is easy.

4. _____ Studying takes time away from other things.

5. _____ You would like to have time for studying and a part-time job.

6. _____ Sometimes you feel pressured to study.

7. _____ Studying puts a kink in your social life.

8. _____ You have heard it's a good idea to establish a study schedule but you feel it's not really important.

9. _____ You would rather be working full-time than attending college.

10. _____ You feel the things you study will never again be used in life.

11. _____ You would like to know how to make every college course interesting.

12. _____ After twenty minutes studying becomes boring.

Checked items in this group may mean you are not sure why you are in college. You are not sure which major field to study. Courses hold little interest. Their value is vague.

Many students feel this way. It is not unusual. It may even be common. But what can be done about it, especially if you actually feel this way all the time? That "all the time" is important. It is not reasonable to expect that everything will be exciting all the time. There are highs and lows in everything. So being sometimes bored with an activity (including college and studying) is to be expected. However, if these feelings persist, then a real problem exists.

The sorts of concerns listed above are hardest to solve. Since not solving them makes the rest of this book almost pointless, they are given special attention. In Part I, Planning Your Education, you will learn how to get off to a good start in college. If you have already started, Part I will help you recognize, maintain, or rekindle your interest in college and studying.

Group II. These Items Concern Organizing

1. _____ You believe that learning is mostly memory work.

2. _____ You feel only really smart students can get through college.

3. _____ If someone were to ask you to define studying, your definition would include the word memorizing.

4. _____ You would like to know techniques for logical thinking.

5. _____ You don't know the difference between textbook reading and textbook studying.

6. _____ You dislike reading.

7. _____ Your reading ability is not so great and you get bored fast.

8. _____ You believe speed reading is necessary for survival in college.

9. _____ The classroom makes you nervous.

10. _____ You think listening in the classroom is basically a matter of paying attention.

11. _____ Term papers are boring to research and a pain to write.

12. _____ You never or hardly ever ask a question in class.

Organization helps get things done. If you owned your own business, you would be concerned with making sure the office work was well organized. As a student, you have an "office" that includes your classroom, your textbooks, your library, and your place of study. That is where you perform your work. If you can learn to organize your efforts in these areas (or see the organization that is already present), then your effectiveness as a manager of learning will be multiplied. Part II, Organizing Your Learning, concerns thinking, reading, listening, writing, and speaking. These are the skills you need to organize your learning.

Group III. These Items Concern Staffing

1. _____ You would like to know what else there is to college other than teachers, textbooks, and tests.

2. _____ You would like to know what teachers expect of college students.

3. _____ If you have any questions, there is no one to help you out.

4. _____ You would like to know what the college thinks is important for success in college.

5. _____ You believe that asking a teacher for help is really a sign of weakness.

6. _____ When on campus you go only to class meetings.

7. _____ You would like to know how to evaluate your teachers.

8. _____ You want to know why the college wants your opinions.

9. _____ You are not a member of a college club.

10. _____ You don't know what student services are available at your college.

11. __ You feel going to college is basically a matter of attending class.

12. _____ You would like to know how a college is organized.

Your most important resource is yourself; the second most important is those who can help you help yourself. Part III, Your Learning Staff, will help you find answers to the items checked above. Part III will help you discover the people, conditions, and skills that will allow you to achieve the most from college.

Group IV. These Items Concern Directing

1. _____ It takes too long to study.

2. _____ You don't like studying when you have a lot of it to do.

3. _____ You would like to know how to study subjects you are not interested in.

4. _____ You go through the material and get nothing from it.

5. _____ Going over and over the same material until you understand it is boring and tiring.

6. _____ If you don't understand something at the beginning, it gets more confusing.

7. _____ You would like to know how to study math and science.

8. _____ The place where you study is too noisy.

9. _____ You would like to learn interesting methods of study.

10. _____ Studying is very aggravating.

11. _____ When you think of the library you think of books.

12. _____ The library is a place you visit only when you have a term paper assignment.

Let's assume studying is not one of your favorite activities. Do you know why? Here are some reasons to consider:

- There is no immediate connection between studying and any identifiable result. You finish studying, shrug your shoulders, and go on to something else. Consider other activities you engage in. If you turn on a television set, it sparks to life. If you swing a tennis racket, a ball changes direction. If you play a tape recorder, the tape spins out the sound. When the music is good you may start dancing. For every action a reaction. All these kinds of reactions come to a screeching halt when you pick up a textbook. There is no real result to which you can point. If there is any connection at all, it's possibly four or five weeks later when you are tested on all the material that someone said you should learn. And then, unfortunately, you may proceed to show how much you haven't learned.

- You don't know how to study even when you want to. Your intentions are good but your study methods are poor.

Part IV, Directing Your Learning, will show you several interesting and rewarding study methods which cover different study situations. You will be able to choose the method that best fits your assignment. Part IV also discusses the different learning experiences a library can provide.

Group V. These Items Concern Evaluation

1. _____ You would like to know what to do when exam results are poor.

2. _____ You get nervous when taking exams.

3. _____ Essay questions give you the most trouble.

4. _____ Other than looking at them, you usually do nothing with exam scores.

5. _____ You believe that exam scores are the only measure of your college performance.

6. _____ You usually prepare for exams at the last moment.

7. _____ You would like to know how to prepare for and take an exam.

8. _____ You believe an open book test is easy.

9. _____ You would like to know how to answer essay questions.

10. _____ You would like to know what to do when exam results are good.

11. _____ You believe exam taking is of little value.

12. _____ You believe success in college means success in your career.

Exams measure the results of your learning efforts. They allow you to evaluate your performance as a manager. Exams signal where you've been and where you must now go.

For these signals to be useful they must be timely. They must accurately represent what you have learned. Part V, Evaluating Your College Experience, will show you how to prepare for, take, and use the results of exams.

Now that you have completed checking off items in the above groups, look at the number of check marks in each area. Notice the nature of the checked items. You should be able to obtain a rough idea of which management area interests you most or which you feel you need the most help with. By looking at the table of contents you can locate the chapters relating to each area. These are the chapters you may want to look at first or pay special attention to.

Summary

Attending college becomes an exciting activity when these conditions exist:

- You have an understanding of what it means to be a college student.
- You are interested in the courses you take.
- You know how to study.

Those are the things this book is about. The fact that you are reading this book is an extremely good sign. It indicates your desire to meet the challenges presented by college. And they are challenges worth meeting. The people, activities, and materials available in today's colleges are so varied, interesting, and rewarding that once you start college you will wonder why you ever doubted or waited to attend.

College is much different from your previous school experiences. But how is it different and what can you do about it? Well, you might try reading Chapter 2. It discusses some of the differences as well as an approach for handling them. Good luck.

CHAPTER 2

A STUDENT-ORIENTED APPROACH TO COLLEGE

BASIC IDEAS
- Effective managing requires knowing what needs to be done.
- Good managers make use of available help.
- Good management practice matches result with intent.

KEY POINTS
- What are the big differences between school and college?
- What are you expected to accomplish in college?
- What does a student manager's view of college look like?

There you are, a little three-foot character out of a cartoon strip. People are all around. Your mother is fixing your new pink dress (the one with the little flowers on it) or tucking in your new green shirt (the one with the double pockets). You stand there looking up and around at all the activity. Your little brother or sister is crawling around on the floor and is now biting your ankle. Maybe your father is snapping a picture, perhaps your mother is crying a little. What's all the fuss about? It's your first day of school.

You arrive at school and sit at a table. You have books to look at. That big person up front is called teacher. You soon come to know teachers teach you interesting things. You begin to like the idea of schools, teachers, and friends. You find things highly organized. Your teacher always has something for you to do. Your teacher plans the material to be covered, organizes the material, directs you in performing it, and marks or grades you in order to evaluate what you learn. You really have very little to say about any of this. (The "teacher said" and you did. Just like "Mommy said" or "Daddy said" and you did.) You come to accept the idea that you learn things by listening to big people.

This habit of leaning on others for your learning and your daily activities involved more than real people. It's possible that when your parents or your teachers were not keeping you busy, television was. Once again what and how you learned was decided by somebody else. Once again you were conditioned to be more or less a spectator. And once again your dependence on others stopped you from developing your own learning independence.

The Way It Was

Years of sitting in classrooms with teachers may have resulted in an unconscious assumption on your part. It goes something like this: "When I go to school, I sit in a classroom. That's where the teacher is. That's where I will learn whatever it is I'm supposed to learn. That's where I'm tested. As far as formal educational schooling is concerned, the classroom is it. When class ends, learning ends." You believe this because it reflects reality. Do you recall seeing, in newspapers and on television, small kids being let out of school in June? School has ended. No more teachers, no more books, no more classrooms and . . . of course . . . no more learning.

Did you also notice that as you advanced through the grades, less and less attention was paid you as an individual? In your early school years you were given grades for basic subjects such as reading, mathematics, English, spelling and handwriting, social studies and science; you were also evaluated on such items as attentiveness, completion of class work, completion of homework, courtesy, respect for rights and property of others, dependability, cooperation, and on and on. It seems everything was on your report card except lunch. Teachers even wrote little personal comments on your report card: "It has been a pleasure to have Ann as a student this year. Have a wonderful summer." Teachers actually knew enough about you and took time to make personal observations. As you went from grade school to junior high school to high school, this kind of evaluation decreased. In your last two years of high school, you could sense that things were definitely changing. In your final year you spent less time in class, you had more free time, and your school day was shorter.

The above experiences have probably resulted in your holding certain ideas, which can be summarized as follows:

- Other people (parents, teachers, administrators) decide what, when, and how you learn.
- These people keep after you to attain some minimum performance.
- Learning takes place only in the classroom.
- The higher you climb the academic ladder, the less there is demanded of you and the less you have to do to satisfy requirements.

Now all of the above is the result of a necessary, logical, and comfortable system—a system with which you were more or less successful. A system you may still be following. It's also a system that's practically worthless on the college level.

Does it surprise you that about eight out of ten junior college students never graduate? That the majority of *all* students who start college never finish? Would it further surprise you to know that it hasn't much to do with ability? That it has more to do with understanding the new demands that college makes? That those who apply their old and comfortable school ideas are following a system that will not work at the college level? That, most of all, they underestimate the new central managerial role they must play in their own learning?

The Way It Is

Figure 2–1
Time Spent in Class

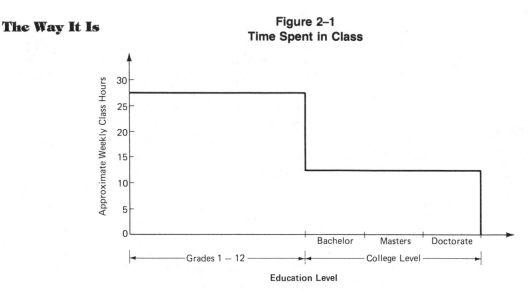

Undergraduate college requires classroom time of about 12-15 hours per week. This works out to about 4% of all the time in your college years. If you assume learning takes place only in the classroom, you are staking your future competence on less than 4% of the time you spend in college. Do you want to base your future competence on this assumption? Can you identify reasons why the assumption that learning takes place only in the classroom is a poor one for college level work?

Look at Figure 2–1. It shows that as your education progresses you spend a lot less time in class. Less time in class means:

- Less coverage and explanation of material
- Less teacher contact

These two conditions affect you as follows:

• Since you are a college student, most of your learning is expected to take place outside the classroom. This means you will have to develop methods of studying on your own. You will have to create your own classroom, a classroom in which you manage the conditions of learning.

• It is hard to obtain an unbiased view of your progress as a student and scholar. In school this sort of evaluation is built into the system, but in college there is less planned contact with your teachers. Your personal progress is less closely watched, so you will have to learn how to watch yourself.

Now look at Figure 2–2. Notice how the decision making regarding your learning shifts. It shifts from your teacher and school to you as you move through school and college.

When you were between 6 and 18 years old your major learning experiences were managed by your teachers and the school system. Look at what happens in the college years. Your teachers and the school system are no longer available to manage your learning. You might say: "My college teachers and the college system will take over where the others left off. They will still decide and control what I do. Won't they?" For most colleges the answer is no. You may see your

Figure 2–2
Who's in Charge?

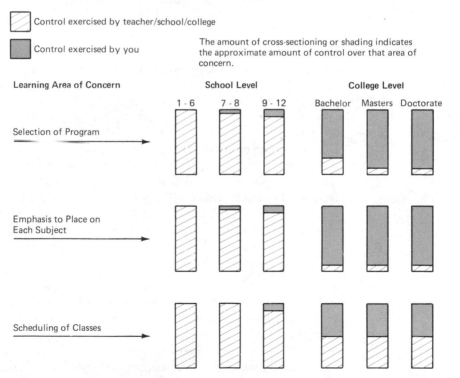

The higher the level of education, the more you the student assume responsibility for managing the learning process. In the three important areas of selection, subject emphasis, and class scheduling, teachers and administrators play less and less a role. Notice the sudden and dramatic change that takes place when you leave high school (grade 12) and start college. It's equivalent to skydiving. One moment you are in a nice warm, relatively safe airplane, the next you are falling through space. Are you ready for this sudden college change? Will your parachute open?

college teachers only once or twice a week. The meetings will most likely be rather formal and your teachers are apt to be unforgiving of poor work. In college you will find that people (especially teachers) will respond to you if you respond to yourself. What that means is, if you seem to care about what you are doing and are willing to take responsibility for your own actions, then there will be a lot of help to be had. But no one will go after you in college to perform. Once in a while you will find a teacher who may take an interest and try to "push" you a little. But not often. If you want the benefit of additional teacher contact, you will usually have to make the first move. When you do ask for assistance or just want to talk, you will be surprised at how willing and how very much they will help. As far as a control system in college goes, forget it. There is none. Your college teachers and administrators have no control over whether or not you select your courses, register for them, show up for classes, keep up with assignments, or take your exams. There is a law that says you must go to grade school. But there is no law that says you must go to college. You are now a free agent.

Look again at Figure 2–2. The control has shifted. You are now in charge. You are now responsible for your learning. You are solely responsible. Look at the figure again. It won't change. It doesn't change. But there is someone who must change. You.

RECOGNIZING

In college you won't be given grades for respecting the rights of others, being courteous or cooperative, or other similar school considerations. You will be evaluated on performance based on test results. There will be very few "judgment grades." Sounds harsh? Sorry. It's a new condition you have to handle. You must perform. No one will do it for you.

How can you relate to this new academic environment? Recognize that moving from school to college is the same as learning how to walk without outstretched hands around to catch you if you fall. Recognize that teachers and others will play a relatively small part in determining which subjects you take and when you take them. Recognize that your college learning doesn't end when you leave the classroom; it begins. Recognize that no longer will others keep after you to perform.

ADAPTING

It is not just the conditions of learning that change. The methods and techniques of learning also change. You learn by reading and observing and by listening and questioning. The best system of learning includes an effective combination of participation, organization, and persistence. Your experiences to date have most likely led you to rely primarily on memorizing. But college work is more demanding and there is more of it. You will need to adapt to new learning conditions. These conditions will require you not only simply to recall information, but to apply, analyze, and evaluate what you hear and see as well.

MANAGING

As you can see, things will be quite different in college. For the first time you will be academically (and perhaps personally) on your own. This independence will require that you be effective. It will require that you be efficient. It will require that you take on responsibilities previously held by others. It will require that you become a reasonably good manager of your learning and other activities. The next section discusses how the five management functions of planning, organizing, staffing, directing, and evaluating apply to you as a college student. These functions are placed in a framework that will allow you to appreciate, maybe for the first time, the exciting and varied experiences that college provides. You will see the central management role you must play.

How to Manage Your College Career

All good managers soon learn that questions are more important than answers. Why? (See, you are already becoming a good manager.) Well, answers to unimportant questions are of little value. Answers can usually be found. But it is not always easy to hit upon the right questions. Good management is often a matter of knowing the right questions. Consider these questions as they relate to your college career:

- What am I doing here and what should I be trying to accomplish?
- Do I know how to select a major course of study that reflects my interests and aptitudes?
- What will people expect from me?
- What is important to know?
- How much time should I spend studying?
- What skills do I really need?
- What are good methods of studying?
- How should I relate to teachers?
- What specific courses should I take?
- How should I relate to other students?
- How can I handle all this new-found freedom I suddenly have?
- Why are exam scores and grades important?
- What problems can I expect?
- Where is the money coming from?

You may be asking yourself these and other questions. They seem widely unrelated. But there are connections. And a method of connecting them is to employ a (self)-management approach to college.

The Management Connection

Figure 2–3 shows how the five basic management functions—planning, organizing, staffing, directing, and evaluating—have been joined into a systems view of college. This figure is a picture, or model, of management as it applies to a college student. Notice that the model has three basic elements:

- *Input:* What you start with
- *Process:* The skills, techniques, and concepts you apply
- *Result:* Your intended objective

It is especially important to see that the model applies to many types of students. It applies whether you are just fresh from high school with six courses, a laboratory, and a part-time job, or whether you are a continuing student struggling to keep up. It applies whether you are attending part-time or whether you are taking your first course in evening college. You and others who attend college all have at least one thing in common. You are students—no, you are college students. As such, regardless of age and background, you can benefit by becoming a better manager of your own education. Whether 18 or 68 years old, whether taking 3 credits or 18, the management concept applies.

Student Management of College: What It Means

Let's analyze the elements that appear in Figure 2–3.

INPUT

From a management standpoint you now know you are in charge. You are your own basic resource. You must supply most of the work. That's why you're at the top of the list.

But you're not alone. Other people can help you be more efficient and effective. Teachers, authors, librarians, and counselors all can help. They can save you time by explaining things and by helping you find and use library material. Maybe members of your family can help from time to time. Good managers call on other people. These other people can't do the actual work for you, but they certainly can help.

If your work is to be meaningful, you must be motivated. Otherwise you will just be going through motions, without interest and with little learning. Most students who leave college do so because they are bored. Therefore, finding *self-derived* as opposed to catalog-dictated reasons for taking a course becomes a matter of serious concern. Good managers know how to motivate.

Figure 2-3
A College Student Management Model

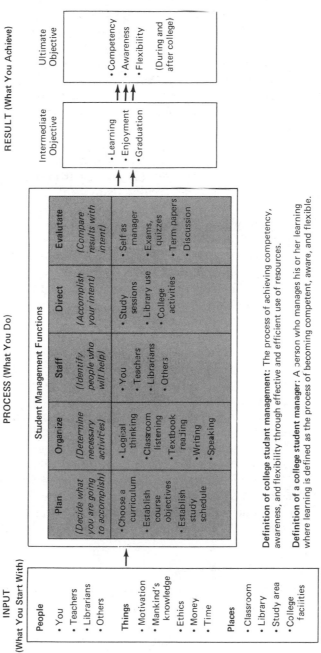

INPUT (What You Start With)

People
- You
- Teachers
- Librarians
- Others

Things
- Motivation
- Mankind's knowledge
- Ethics
- Money
- Time

Places
- Classroom
- Library
- Study area
- College facilities

PROCESS (What You Do)

Student Management Functions

Plan	Organize	Staff	Direct	Evalutate
(Decide what you are going to accomplish)	*(Determine necessary activities)*	*(Identify people who will help)*	*(Accomplish your intent)*	*(Compare results with intent)*
• Choose a curriculum • Establish course objectives • Establish study schedule	• Logical thinking • Classroom listening • Textbook reading • Writing • Speaking	• You • Teachers • Librarians • Others	• Study sessions • Library use • College activities	• Self as manager • Exams, quizzes • Term papers • Discussion

RESULT (What You Achieve)

Intermediate Objective
- Learning
- Enjoyment
- Graduation

Ultimate Objective
- Competency
- Awareness
- Flexibility

(During and after college)

Definition of college student management: The process of achieving competency, awareness, and flexibility through effective and efficient use of resources.

Definition of a college student manager: A person who manages his or her learning where learning is defined as the process of becoming competent, aware, and flexible.

17

Mankind's accumulated knowledge refers to all the things that the human race has gotten to know since people started telling each other stories and writing things down. But which part should you attempt to know? And how do you go about finding out which part it's to be? If you err in deciding what to study, you might be wasting your time. But then you have heard people say that college can be good for you no matter what you study. Which is right? Are they both right?

Having ethics means doing the right thing. For example, if you break the law, that's wrong. But then how does the American Revolution fit into that concept? Obviously there are some exceptions. Also there are a lot of situations that law doesn't cover, such as most personal relationships with other people. Anyway, what has all this to do with college? There have been professors who were accused of falsifying their records. They made it look like they had taken some college courses they really hadn't taken. That surely is unethical. Maybe that's how ethics relates to college. If a student takes credit for something he or she hasn't done, that's unethical. If the whole point of going to college is to become competent socially and intellectually, then it's only the student him or herself who can demonstrate that accomplishment. Consider, for example, taking exams or writing term papers. They must reflect individual efforts. A student can't use someone else's competence to demonstrate his or her own.

You will need money to operate. A part-time job will help but that may not be possible or desirable. As a good manager you should check out all possible sources of aid through your college's financial aid office. Another basic resource is time. Time is really the most important asset you have. As a manager you need to make sure time works for and not against you.

That you should have a place to attend (with classrooms, a library, learned people, and social facilities), all of it dedicated to helping you, is really quite remarkable. Your college represents a collection of people, places, and things all aimed at helping you achieve competency, awareness, and flexibility. You are a free agent living in a free society. You can come and go as you please. You can decide to attend or not attend college. You can also decide to get the most out of attending through effective management.

PROCESS

In Chapter 1 management was defined as "efficiently accomplishing what you want to do." This definition is adequate, but it may leave the impression that managing is something you do at 2:30 P.M. Tuesday and then not again for another week. Perhaps a better definition is that shown in Figure 2–3: the process of achieving competency, awareness, and flexibility through effective and efficient use of resources. Notice at least three things about this definition:

- Management is objective or result oriented.
- Management is a continuing activity with identifiable elements. All effective management starts with a plan and ends with an evaluation of whether the plan has been accomplished. In other words, management is a process that allows you systematically to pursue an objective. This concept of management is flexible. You can apply it to a study session, to the writing of a term paper, or to a two-year, four-year, or longer college career.
- Management implies the actual accomplishment of all important objectives. It means, for example, actually achieving learning and being efficient with the use of time.

These three points form the basics of management. The activities, skills, and responsibilities associated with being a college student all fit into the management framework.

The list of questions at the beginning of this section appear unrelated. But this model shows they are very much related through the five management functions. To plan, organize, staff, direct, and evaluate means to use the process of management. And the process of management, as applied to the college student, is what this book is all about.

RESULT

The last part of the model shows what will result when you draw on available inputs and use them in an effective and efficient manner. If you can become a fairly good college manager, you will attain a sense of learning, get reasonably good grades, and also enjoy yourself. These sound like pretty good things to have. If you're persistent, then after two or four years (or maybe more if you go on to graduate school), you will graduate. You will have achieved a measure of competency in a field of study, awareness of other people and ideas, and flexibility to move widely. You will be a different person than you were two or four years before. You will be in a better position to get a good job. With the flexibility to move within a company or to another company or career. You'll have more opportunities. You'll be operating at a higher level. You'll be more competent than you were, and probably more competent professionally, intellectually, and socially than most others. You'll be more aware, in a better position to form your own conclusions about things. You'll be able to give more to people you come in contact with and give more to your family. You'll have put yourself in a better position to enjoy life and the people in it. You will have started toward the point of feeling things are worthwhile, of feeling you're accomplishing something, of feeling fulfilled.

Can college really do all that for you? Well, maybe not by itself. But it can sure help get you started. But then again none of this may happen unless—*unless* you recognize that while people may call you a college student, you're really a manager. A manager of you.

Exercise 2–1. Is It Interesting to Be a College Student?

What do the following jobs have in common: assembly line worker, highway toll collector, car watcher in a tunnel, pool typist, bank guard, copy-machine operator, and automatic elevator operator? They are all rated as boring jobs. On a scale of 0 to 100 they would all score less than 25. Has anybody done anything about making jobs more interesting? Can you design a job as you would an automobile or a dress? The answer to both questions is yes. Back in 1965 a group of people got together and created a list of conditions that, if met, would result in interesting jobs. (R. E. Emery, E. Thorsud, and K. Lange, *The Industrial Democracy Project, Report No. 2,* Trondheim Institute for Industrial and Social Research, Technical University of Norway, 1965.) A summary of these conditions appears in Table 2–1. (Note that pay is not included in the list of conditions since a job may pay well and still be boring.) Analyze your present part-time or full-time job or your last job by doing the following: (a) First estimate your job's interest level and enter an arrow on the job interest scale in the table. Mark this arrow "Job Estimate." (b) Now complete the rest of table and determine your job's actual score by adding up the value of all check marks. Mark a second arrow "Job Actual."

How do you think the activity of being a college student scores on this test? Repeat (a) and (b) above for the activity of being a college student. This time use a symbol other than check marks to avoid confusion. Most students will find their actual college score exceeds their college estimate and their job scores by a wide margin. Actual college scores will average about 80. Why? Well, look at the list of items in the table. All the elements for interesting work are present in college activities. All the elements that make managing interesting are also present.

As you can see, being a college student is in itself interesting. One important objective you have as a college student is to make sure it stays interesting. Staying interested through managing is something you must do for yourself. It will allow you to get in touch with the best that is in yourself. Figure 2–3 provides a framework and this book provides help for managing your college career so you can sustain and promote the interesting activity of being a college student.

Summary

This chapter stresses a basic theme. The theme is that in your precollege days you had very little to do with what and how you learned. That was managed initially by your parents and later by your teachers. Now you are doing college work, and things are organized differently. You must manage your own college learning activities. No one else will. No one else really can.

Managing your college career means planning, organizing, staffing, directing, and evaluating your own learning efforts. Figure 2–3 gives the activities necessary for success in college. It shows how they fit within the management system. Knowledge and application of this system will help you achieve the greatest amount of competency, awareness, and flexibility. It will help ensure that you complete your college program.

Table 2–1

Job Interest Scale

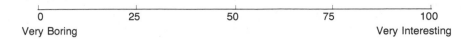

0 25 50 75 100	
Very Boring	Very Interesting

How Interesting is Your Job?

(If your job meets the stated condition to a very high degree then check off scale value ten; if to a very small degree then check off zero; if somewhere in between then check off estimated position.)

Job Conditions	0.0	2.5	*Scale* 5.0	7.5	10.0
1. Does the job include a variety of tasks? Does the job allow you to go from demanding tasks to less demanding tasks and back again?					
2. Does the job stretch your capabilities?					
3. Does the job have a meaningful pattern of tasks? Does doing one task make it easier to do the next task?					
4. Does the job have a reasonable work cycle? Is there a satisfying pattern or rhythm to the job?					
5. Does the job allow you to set some standards regarding how much you accomplish?					
6. Do you get feedback on how well you are doing your task?					
7. Does the job allow you to prepare beforehand? Does it allow you to inspect completed work?					
8. Does the job allow you to sometimes work in groups?					
9. Does the job include care, skill and knowledge that is worthy of other peoples respect?					
10. Does the job contribute to the well-being of yourself and society?					

Manager	Plan	Direct
Management	Organize	Evaluate
College inputs	Staff	College results

REVIEW QUESTIONS

---

1. Describe each of the key terms above.
2. Define management: (a) in general terms, (b) as related to a college student.
3. Define managers: (a) in general terms, (b) as related to a college student.
4. What recognition must be made before effective management can take place?
5. Identify the college learning activities associated with each of the five management functions.
6. With the aid of a dictionary, describe the difference between a pupil and a student.
7. Investigate the words *study, student,* and *college* in a dictionary. Write a paragraph that relates the three words.
8. For each of the following items identify the difference between college and your previous school experiences: (a) choice of subjects studied, (b) time spent in classrooms, (c) amount of supervision received.

APPLICATION QUESTIONS

---

1. Assume it is several months before you are starting your first college term or assume it is a period between terms.
   a. Identify which management function might be most important at this time.
   b. List three reasons for your choice.
2. Assume the term has just started.
   a. Identify which management function you think is now most important.
   b. What kinds of activities might be associated with this function?
3. In the section How to Manage Your College Career there is a list of questions. Now that you are familiar with the concept of management, can you place these questions within the Figure 2–3 framework? Does knowing how the questions relate to each other allow you to see a systematic approach to answering them?
4. Below are the first two lines of a poem. Complete this poem. Don't be concerned as to whether your lines rhyme.

   If a college student I would be
   There are some things that I should see

Planning Your Education

OBJECTIVES FOR PART I

When you complete this part you should be able to:
1. Create and follow a weekly study schedule.
2. Apply the self-management method to special college situations.
3. Know how to make every course interesting.

PREVIEW OF CHAPTERS

Chapter 3, Now Is the Time to Prepare a Study Schedule, includes a short story concerning reasons why students may dislike studying and the relationship it has to time. In this chapter you will learn how to schedule your activities. You will find that everything important to you *can* be done, even if you hold a part-time job and a full course schedule. That doesn't sound possible? Read the chapter and find out for yourself.

Chapter 4, How to Manage Yourself, features suggestions for dealing with special study problems. It shows how to increase study time, divide study time among your several courses, use exam results to improve your future performance, and keep track of exam grades so you can estimate your grade point average.

Chapter 5, How to Make Every Course Interesting, includes a play which shows that boredom and the apparent aimlessness of college work are more a result of attitude than reality. The Management-By-Motivation system is then presented. MBM provides an interesting approach for turning every course you take into learning experiences that will help you achieve the three ultimate aims of college: (1) competency in a field of your choosing, (2) awareness of people different from you and ideas different from yours, and (3) flexibility in thinking, language, and job skills.

CHAPTER 3

NOW IS THE TIME TO PREPARE A STUDY SCHEDULE

BASIC IDEAS
- There is no printing press for time.
- You can use time only in the present.

KEY POINTS
- How can I make efficient and enjoyable use of time?
- What *is* time?

You may think no great skill or effort is required to create a study schedule. You make a chart showing days and hours. Then you pencil in some study periods throughout the week. No big deal. Maybe because it's rather easy to establish a schedule, many people ignore it. The fact is that when you want to establish a study program, the last thing to do is actually establish the schedule. Why? Well, for a study schedule to have real meaning, the following conditions should exist:

- You should have some concept about the nature of time and what it may mean to you.
- You must identify the amount of time in hours that you can reasonably expect to devote to studying.

The chances are you will attach meaning to a schedule only if you attach meaning to time itself. Did you ever think about what time actually is? The following is a story about two college students who tried to answer the question: What is time?

24   PLANNING YOUR EDUCATION

THE STAR TREK WEIGHT-REDUCTION COMPANY

Ronnie placed the pen on the table and picked up the letter he had just written. "Dear Mr. Bruno," it began, "I am writing about the advertisement you placed in the classified section of the November issue of *Rainbow* magazine. The ad indicates that for 25¢ you will, by return mail, tell me about a mysterious secret which people keep losing and finding. Here's 25¢. Please send the information."

"Here, look at this," Ronnie said to Daphne, who was sitting next to him. "What do you think?"

Daphne read the letter and said, "It's okay, but why did you pick this ad?"

Ronnie flipped to the back of the magazine and said, "Well, there are others. Here's one on getting your legs waxed, another on Transback Biomedifeed. It says, 'If you could hear your own brain waves, would you like the tune? Check us out. Send 50¢ for more information.' And here's one that reads, 'Star Trek Weight-Reduction Company—blast your fat into outer space. Send 25¢ for details.'"

Ronnie and Daphne were in Professor Whipple's philosophy class. Try as they might, they just couldn't zero in on a good term paper topic. Professor Whipple had said that they should try to select something about the nature of life, something for which there was no pat answer, maybe something subject to wide interpretation. When they last spoke to him he had suggested reading classified ads. "If you are stuck for ideas," he said, "reading the classified ads could be helpful and enjoyable." Until then they had thought the professor a pretty normal guy. Now they didn't know whether he was being serious or not. Sensing their confusion, he had smiled and said: "Sounds a little silly, doesn't it? But why not give it a try and see what happens?"

"Well what do you think? Should we mail it off?" asked Ronnie. Daphne nodded and said, "I hope we get an answer quickly. Time is running out and that paper is due pretty soon."

Eight days later Ronnie received an envelope in the mail. It bore nothing on the outside except his name and address and a large red B in the upper left-hand corner. He quickly opened the envelope and read:

Dear Mr. Darwin:

Thank you for your request. In my ad I promised to tell you about the mysterious secret that people keep losing and finding. I am now going to keep my promise.

You will find the information between Timbuktu and half again of what you're looking for. And it is not one thing but many.

Very truly yours,

California Bruno

The meaning of the message was not clear. He showed the letter to Daphne. She asked, "What's a Timbuktu?" Together they went to the dictionary and looked up the word. They quickly found the general area. As her fingers raced past the words, Daphne, barely audibly, repeated some of them: *Tihwa, Tilden, tile, timbre;* she finally found Timbuktu. The definition said it was a town in Africa. The next entry listed was "time," and the one after that was "time and a half." Ronnie referred back to the letter and said: "Hey, that must be it. The letter said we would find the information between Timbuktu and half again of what we're looking for. It must be the word "time". Bruno has directed us to the word "time." And look at all the different definitions of the word. There are over 60 of them. That's what he meant by there being many."

Daphne offered to spend the afternoon analyzing the many entries for the word "time." Then she and Ronnie would discuss the list and try to make some sense of it.

After patiently writing and arranging, she had her list. At the top of the sheet she had entered the general dictionary definition of the word "time." It read "a nonspatial continuum in which events occur in apparently irreversible succession from the past through the present to the future." What an awful definition, she had thought. Nonspatial continuum sounded like some kind of disease. What does all that mean? She thought it terribly unusual that such a small, familiar word should have such a vague, strange definition. Her list showed the following information:

- *Time as a measure*–years, months, days, minutes, seconds
- *Time as related events*–past, present, future
- *Time as occurrences*–a time of trouble, harvest time, bedtime
- *Time as a measured activity*–hired for full-time, marching in double time, time as a musical measure as in three-quarter time
- *Time in popular phrases*–behind the times, gain time, high time, in good time, in no time, make time

She looked over her list and was surprised that there were so many different interpretations for such a common word. The subject of time would certainly qualify as a valid term paper project. It certainly met Professor Whipple's requirement that the topic be "something that was subject to wide interpretation." She had a topic with over 60 interpretations. Daphne decided that time was certainly something you measured, but it obviously was also something else. Why else all those dictionary definitions? She tried to come up with her own definition. All she could say was that time was something measured by a clock. But she couldn't define that something. She decided not to feel too bad about it. After all, the people who wrote the dictionary needed half a page to define it. She turned to look out the window, and whatever time was, some of it had certainly passed.

The next day Ronnie couldn't define time either and so they decided to ask Professor Whipple for help.

As Ronnie and Daphne sat in his office, Professor Whipple was trying to define the word "time." Then a strange thing happened.

Professor Whipple started to sound just like the dictionary! He used phrases like "event juxtaposition" and "inverted perceptual algonisms" and the ever popular "nonspatial continuum." At that point Daphne exclaimed, "Oh no, not you too!" Professor Whipple didn't seem to know what the word meant either! He suggested that they write another letter to California Bruno. Maybe he would be willing to supply some more information.

That afternoon they sent off another letter asking for more information. They mentioned they were college students writing a term paper. A few days later they received this reply:

Dear Ronnie (and Daphne too):

So you're college students! If you mentioned that in your first letter I might have sent along some more information—for example, the attached, which is titled "Bruno's Study Time Anti–Ripoff Chart." If you fill it out (just follow the simple directions along the bottom), you can identify how much time per week you actually have for studying. By the way, since you are college students you might be interested in a talk I had the other day. Someone said to me, "I don't enjoy studying, so why spend time on it?" I said: "Did it ever occur to you that it might be the other way around? That you don't like to study precisely because you don't allow enough time? For example," I continued, "if you engage in an activity such as skiing (or golfing, bowling, tennis, etc.) and are not very good at it, you may get frustrated and become disappointed. Your feelings are directed not at your inability to perform that activity well, but at the activity itself. If you could perform well, the bad feelings would disappear. Don't you agree that if conditions surrounding the study situation were good, perhaps dislike for studying would decrease?" Well, the fellow agreed and at that point he was joined by some friends. (No—he wasn't coming apart.)

I told them that perhaps the reason some students dislike studying as an activity is that they don't allow themselves enough study time. They cram into the little time they have all that is expected of them and all they expect of themselves. Holding a part–time job and having family responsibilities make it harder. Since they have set an impossible task (trying to cram 3 hours of studying time into 30 minutes), failure follows. The failure is associated with studying, not with the insufficient time allowed. You end up by asking yourself what you are accomplishing by attending college. And the answer to this question is not helpful because it's the wrong question. Maybe a better question is, "How can I find enough time for studying so I really get something for it?"

At this point they said, "You're right Bruno, you're right, tell us more." Well Ronnie (and Daphne too), I said:

"There are basically three reasons why you may have little
or no study time. First, there are mandated things you
absolutely must do such as eating and sleeping. Second,
there are activities that are either important to you or
necessary. These include family obligations, a part-time
job, community service, and college service. Third, there
are activities such as being with friends, going out, engaging in hobbies, watching TV, and just plain fooling around."
I told them that there is little to be done about reducing
time for mandated activities, but it's possible that analysis of the time taken by other activities will reveal that
there is time left over—time that could be devoted to
studying.

Well, anyway, when I finished talking to the students, I
whipped Bruno's chart out and invited them to complete it
when they had some time. (Heh, heh)

It's sincerely mine,
but it's truly yours,

California Bruno

When Ronnie and Daphne completed reading this letter, they
became hysterical. There was absolutely no doubt that Bruno was a
certified brainbreaker. But there was no denying his chart. It looked
reasonable. And in the fifteen minutes it took to complete it, they
discovered that even though they both had part-time jobs, they did have
an unexpectedly large amount of study time available. After allowing for
all the things on Bruno's chart (including some he hadn't thought of),
Ronnie had 24 hours a week for studying and Daphne 21.

They then noticed the fourth instruction, on the bottom of the chart.
The line read, "Now that you have identified time as measured in hours,
do you know what time really is?" Ronnie said: "Hey, that's what we
asked him to tell us. He's helping us manage our time but he really
hasn't told us what time is. He's asked us the same question we asked
him."

Daphne, who had picked up the envelope, suddenly said, "Hey, look
at this tiny piece of neatly folded paper in the corner of the envelope."
When she unfolded the paper, it turned out to be surprisingly large and
she wondered how they could have missed something that was right
before their eyes. She read the note aloud.

P.S. I thought I should tell you two that my study time chart
relates only to clock time, the kind you can measure. There
are other ways of looking at the word "time." Say you get in
an argument with somebody. Instead of focusing on the problem, you focus on each other. The time used in this manner can
no longer be used to solve the problem. You're both angry and
you haven't accomplished anything. You've wasted some of

your precious time. This kind of time really has nothing to do with time as measured by a clock. But it has a lot to do with how you use such time.

The next point is so simple it's scary. If someone asked whether you lived in the past, present, or future, you might respond, "I remember the past, I can think about the future, but I guess I can actually live only in the present." And that's part of what time really is. You can only accomplish something now, right now, in the present.

One last thing, Ronnie (and Daphne too), I think I actually do know how to define time. But I can't no—I won't tell you. It's something each person has to figure out for him or herself. I can give you a hint, though. The answer can be found in the word "time" itself.

It's cordially theirs, very truly mine, and sincerely yours,

California Bruno

When Daphne had read the note, she placed it on the tabletop. She and Ronnie reread it.

"Time," said Ronnie. "Bruno said the answer is in the word itself." He opened his notebook to a blank page and wrote down the word "time." He looked at it. Stared at it. Turned it upside down. Put his head on the table and looked at it lengthwise. He tried rearranging the letters: he wrote *tmie, emit, etim, item, teim, eimt, mtie*. He put the letters back together again so that they once again spelled "time." He stared again at the word; stared at it until it blurred. He blinked it clear and after a few seconds the blur returned. Then a strange thing began to occur. And though Ronnie was doing the staring, Daphne also saw it happen. As he stared at the four letters, they all seemed to vibrate as if in a very slight tremble. Then two of the letters seemed to grow larger and larger and these two seemed to be vibrating at a greater pace. They grew still larger, and Ronnie, blinking and shaking his head to clear it, now saw exactly what was happening. The word no longer looked like "time" but "tiME." The last two letters seemed to be vibrating themselves loose. The word ME started to detach itself, and Ronnie, transfixed, watched as the word ME shook itself loose from the page and flew straight into his eyeballs and into the center of his brain. He jumped up from his chair. "I've got it, Daphne," he screamed. "I've got it, I've got it, I've got it. Time is me. Time can't exist without me. I can't exist without time. There is no way of separating us. Time is what I do, what I think, what I say. Time is what I use. And I am time. Time can't be anything or go anywhere without me. Don't you see? That's why time is hard to define. You can't define time until you define yourself. And when you have defined yourself, you've defined time. Oh, why didn't we see it before. It was right in front of us!"

Daphne, with shaking knees and tears in her eyes, stood up and they grabbed each other's arms. "Come on," she said, still frightened by their experience., "let's go see Professor Whipple. He won't believe any of this. I don't believe it myself and I saw it."

Well, as you might expect, they had a very excited conversation with Professor Whipple. He smiled when Daphne said she never thought she would be in a position to explain something to a professor, especially something so complex and important. When Ronnie and Daphne left, Professor Whipple took out his copy of *Rainbow* magazine. "Let's see," he said, "in the last issue I used the name California Bruno in my classified ad. What name should I use next time?"

Well, so much for what time may be. Whatever it is, time is certainly something you can use. And that's the subject of the next section.

Creating a Study Schedule

An effective study schedule can be created in three steps.

1. Identify nonstudy activities and the amount of time they use.
2. Determine how much time is then available for studying.
3. Complete a weekly activity chart which highlights periods of study.

The first item can be accomplished through a time audit, the second through use of the Study Time Anti-Ripoff (STAR) Chart, and the third through use of a weekly schedule.

Time Audit

A *time audit* is a record of how you use your time. There are several ways to audit your use of the 168 hours in each week: (1) have someone follow you around and record how you spend your time; (2) follow yourself around and make the recordings yourself; and (3) lacking (1) or (2), you can estimate the time.

Exercise 3–1. Auditing Your Time
Figure 3–1 will help you audit your time. When you have completed your audit (or have otherwise estimated how you spend your time), you are in a position to complete the Study Time Anti-Ripoff (STAR) Chart.

The STAR Chart

A completed chart is shown in Figure 3–2. This figure shows 27 hours available for study per week, but let's assume it shows 45 hours. Should you actually schedule 45 hours for studying? Generally speaking, and depending upon your year of college and the demands of your particular curriculum, the answer is probably no. How can you tell? Ask yourself the question, "Am I doing well in my courses?" If the

Figure 3–1
Personal Time Audit for a College Student

	Mandated Activities				Special Responsibilities			Leisure Activities				Other Activities		
	Eating	Sleeping	College Classes	Studying	Commuting	Working	College Service	Community Service	Socializing	Dating	Hobbies	College Clubs			
A.M.															
7:00 - 7:30															
7:30 - 8:00															
8:00 - 8:30															
8:30 - 9:00															
9:00 - 9:30															
9:30 - 10:00															
10:00 - 10:30															
10:30 - 11:00															
11:00 - 11:30															
11:30 - 12:00															
P.M.															
12:00 - 12:30															
12:30 - 1:00															
1:00 - 1:30															
1:30 - 2:00															
2:00 - 2:30															
2:00 - 0:00															
3:00 - 3:30															
3:30 - 4:00															
4:00 - 4:30															
4:30 - 5:00															
5:00 - 5:30															
5:30 - 6:00															
6:00 - 6:30															
6:30 - 7:00															
7:00 - 7:30															
7:30 - 8:00															
8:00 - 8:30															
8:30 - 9:00															
9:00 - 9:30															
9:30 - 10:00															
10:00 - 10:30															
10:30 - 11:00															
11:00 - 11:30															
11:30 - Midnight															
Daily Summaries															
1st Day		7													
2nd Day		7													
3rd Day		7													
4th Day		7													
5th Day		7													
6th Day		7													
7th Day		7													
Grand Totals for all seven days		49													

Instructions for Performing the Time Audit:

1. The chart assumes the period 12 midnight to 7 A.M. for sleep. Therefore, 7 hours has already been entered. Add any additional sleep time to this initial figure of 7.
2. For each half-hour period, lightly check off with a pencil that activity which used most of the time.
3. At the end of the first day calculate the time spent on each activity. Do this by multiplying each check mark by 0.5. Enter the first day's total time for each activity in the daily summary.
4. Now erase the penciled check marks. Repeat steps 2 and 3 for each succeeding day. Enter the daily activity time in the daily summary for each day as appropriate.
5. At the end of the seventh day add the daily times for each activity. Enter the resultant numbers in the Grand Total spaces. The Grand Total number for each activity represents the amount of weekly total time spent on that activity.

Figure 3–2
A Completed STAR Chart

Study Time
Anti-Ripoff Chart

	Time Used Per Week (Hours)	Time Left (Hours)
Hours in Week · 168		
Mandated Activities		
Eating	_14_	_154_
Sleeping	_56_	_98_
College Classes	_12_	_86_
Commuting	_8_	_78_
Special Responsibilities (As applicable)		
Part-time Job	_20_	_58_
College Service	_2_	_56_
Community Service	_2_	_54_
Leisure Activities (As applicable)		
Socializing	_8_	_46_
Dating	_5_	_41_
Hobbies	_2_	_39_
College Social Clubs	_1_	_38_
Other Activities		
Watching TV	_8_	_30_
Daydreaming	_3_	_27_

Time Left for Studying (is the last entry in the "Time Left" column)

· ·

Instructions for Completing Chart:
1. Mandated activities:
   a. Identify activities you must do and enter them in the blank spaces under the "mandated activities" column. Some basic activities have already been entered for you.
   b. Estimate the weekly time required for each activity and enter that time in the "Time Used Per Week" column. (Or obtain from time audit. See Fig. 3 - 1.)
   c. Subtract, in turn, each time entry from the previous time left and enter the remainder in the "Time Left" column.
2. Repeat steps 1a, 1b, and 1c above for Special Responsibilities, Leisure Activities, and Other Activities.
3. The last figure in the "Time Left" column is the amount of time you have per week for studying.
4. Now that you have identified time as measured in hours, do you know what time really is?

answer is yes (and only trial and error will tell), then reduce the 45 hours accordingly and use the time left over for other activities. Thirty to 35 hours a week for most daytime students with a full course schedule (15 to 18 credits) should be more than sufficient. Between 10 and 20 hours is probably a minimum if college is to be meaningful. If you are going to school part-time in the day or evening, you may want to consider using an old rule of thumb that says one should study 2 hours for every credit carried. This means that if you are taking two courses, each worth 3 credits, you should consider studying 12 hours per week. (Six credits times 2 hours equals 12 study hours.) But again, you must determine the amount of study time so it matches your own course requirements and academic performance.

Exercise 3–2. Available Study Hours

Complete the blank STAR Chart shown in Figure 3–3. Enter the weekly totals from Figure 3–1 according to the instructions given at the bottom of Figure 3–3. It is interesting to compare the amount of time you have actually spent studying (as revealed by your audit) to the amount of time actually available for studying (as shown by your completed STAR Chart).

If you are a full-time student and your chart shows 10 or fewer study hours per week, it is more than likely your performance will suffer. What should you do? Look over your other activities and determine where you can cut back. Then add the saved time to your study time. A full-time day college student should probably study about 15 hours per week. You can, of course, study less and still get by. Whether as a manager of your learning this is what you should do is something only you (and your grades) can answer. It really is your time.

Scheduling Your Week's Study Time

A sample weekly schedule is shown in Figure 3–4.

Exercise 3–3. Establishing Your Study Schedule

Figure 3–5 is a blank study schedule form. Your objective is to create a study schedule similar to Figure 3–4 but one that reflects your particular situation. Here are instructions for completing Figure 3–5.

   a. Look at your completed Study Time Anti-Ripoff Chart. Identify the time allotted for each mandated activity. Block in and label this time in your schedule. (As a minimum this includes eating, sleeping, and attending classes.) Next, block in the identified time for special responsibilities; these may include a part-time job, family obligations, and others as appropriate. Now check that the time shown on your schedule for each activity matches the time you have allotted in your STAR Chart.

   b. Next, cross out blocks of time you are almost sure will not be used for studying because of competing activities. Friday and Saturday nights are examples of such time. There is a high chance that these and/or other time will be used for social or recreational activities. From a self-management standpoint this is a very important step. You do not want to set yourself up

Figure 3–3

Study Time
Anti-Ripoff Chart

	Time Used Per Week (Hours)	Time Left (Hours)
Hours in Week		168
Mandated Activities		
Eating	_____	_____
Sleeping	_____	_____
College Classes	_____	_____
Commuting	_____	_____
_____	_____	_____
Special Responsibilities		
(As applicable)		
Part-time Job	_____	_____
College Service	_____	_____
Community Service	_____	_____
_____	_____	_____
Leisure Activities		
(As applicable)		
Socializing	_____	_____
Dating	_____	_____
Hobbies	_____	_____
College Social Clubs	_____	_____
_____	_____	_____
Other Activities		
Watching TV	_____	_____
Daydreaming	_____	_____
_____	_____	_____
_____	_____	_____

Time Left for Studying (is the last entry in the "Time Left" column)

• •

Instructions for Completing Chart:
1. Mandated activities:
   a. Identify activities you must do and enter them in the blank spaces under the "mandated activities" column. Some basic activities have already been entered for you.
   b. Estimate the weekly time required for each activity and enter that time in the "Time Used Per Week" column. (obtain from time audit. See Fig. 3 - 1.)
   c. Subtract, in turn, each time entry from the previous time left and enter the remainder in the "Time Left" column.
2. Repeat steps 1a, 1b, and 1c above for Special Responsibilities, Leisure Activities, and Other Activities.
3. The last figure in the "Time Left" column is the amount of time you have per week for studying.
4. Now that you have identified time as measured in hours, do you know what time really is?

Figure 3–4
A Sample Activity and Study Time Schedule

	Monday	Tuesday	Wednesday	Thursday	Friday	Saturday	Sunday
7 - 8 A.M.							
8 - 9	Class		Class		Class	Job	
9 - 10	Study	Class	Study	Class	Study	Job	
10 - 11	Study	Class	Class	Class	Study	Job	
11 - 12	Class	Study		Study	Class	Job	
12 - 1 P.M.							
1 - 2	Class	Study	Class	Study	Study		
2 - 3	Class	Study	Class	Class	Study		
3 - 4							Study
4 - 5	Job	Job	Job	Job	Job		Study
5 - 6	Job	Job	Job	Job	Job		
6 - 7	Job		Job		Job		
7 - 8	Job		Job		Job		
8 - 9							
9 - 10	Study	Study	Study	Study			Study
10 - 11	Study	Study	Study	Study			Study
11 - 12							

for a failure in this area. Therefore, do not plan on studying at those times when other activities are likely to win out.

c. Now take the amount of time you have identified for studying and spread this time throughout the week. Enter the time where you believe the chances of studying are very good. Consider the following when spotting your study time:

- Determine when during the day you usually feel good and are mentally alert. Use this time for study.
- Avoid scheduling study periods longer than about two hours without stopping for about a half-hour break. Research shows that people are more effective using a work–break–work approach than just work–work–work.

Figure 3–5
Your Activity and Study Time Schedule

	Monday	Tuesday	Wednesday	Thursday	Friday	Saturday	Sunday
7 - 8 A.M.							
8 - 9							
9 - 10							
10 - 11							
11 - 12							
12 - 1 P.M.							
1 - 2							
2 - 3							
3 - 4							
4 - 5							
5 - 6							
6 - 7							
7 - 8							
8 - 9							
9 - 10							
10 - 11							
11 - 12							

- If you are going to study two subjects within a given block of time, try to schedule dissimilar subjects. The difference will heighten your interest and enhance your ability to retain what you have studied.
- Make a strong effort to place study periods directly after class meetings. Why? Well, the time immediately after class is a special time. Your mind is tuned to the subject, the discussion is fresh in your head, the explanation and examples are still clear. This mental state cannot be duplicated later in the day. It is prime study time. Seize it for study and homework. Make a strong effort especially to use such time for math and science. The formulas and techniques will be more easily remembered and applied. Understanding and retention will be promoted.

d. Complete your schedule by blocking in the remaining activities. Use the time crossed out in Step 2 above and any other time that remains.

Exercise 3–4. Keeping Track of Your Study Time

Prepare and use the following self-monitoring device to track the time you spend studying. Tack it on a wall where you study or place it in a notebook.

Date	Scheduled Study Hours (from Figure 3–5)	Actual Study Hours	Comments

Keep the chart for at least 3 weeks. Then answer these questions:

    a. Can you justify to yourself those instances during the day where you spent less time studying than you planned?

    b. Analyze the weekly time. Did you come close to your plan?

    c. Did the weekly time improve in the second and third week?

Keeping the above chart can help you develop the habit of studying in certain time periods.

A View of Schedules

Chances are the first schedule you create will have to be changed. The actual experience of using the study schedule will show the need for adjustments. It's to be expected. If experience shows your schedule to be unrealistic or if your activities and responsibilities change, then change your schedule. When midterms or finals or special assignments approach, you may want to alter your schedule. It's your schedule and you should make it work for you.

It is important to remember that your completed schedule should serve as a guide. While it can be extremely beneficial to acquire the habit of studying at certain times, you should retain flexibility. If the desire or need to study occurs at an unscheduled time, then of course go ahead and study.

One last point. Despite schedules and good intentions, sometimes you will be just unable to work. Your motivation will be gone, the term will still have seven weeks to go, and graduation will be a long way off. At these times you may want to talk to friends or listen to music. If so, do these things and enjoy them. If an activity comes up (including studying) that you don't want to do, then postpone it or just don't do it. You are the one who's managing you. You know what is necessary.

Summary

The poet William Yeats wrote that time was a song. With your college time you can write a song that may be especially meaningful. It is your time . . . and it will be your song.

Identifying how much time you can actually spend studying is the key to establishing a usable study schedule. A study time schedule may be established by performing a time audit, identifying how much time is available for studying, and then writing out a schedule.

A schedule is something you create and something you can change. It should work for you. A realistic schedule will help make college exciting and rewarding.

KEY TERMS

| Time | STAR Chart | Monitoring |
| Audit | Schedule | |

REVIEW QUESTIONS

1. Describe each of the key terms above.
2. Age, duration, and succession are synonyms for the word "time." (a) Identify three other words and (b) refer to a dictionary to determine whether the definition of any of these words helps in understanding the word "time."
3. Analyzing opposites can also be helpful in determining meanings. (a) Try to think of or find antonyms for the word "time." (b) What conclusions can you draw?
4. What three steps are necessary for creating a study schedule?

DISCUSSION QUESTIONS

1. The average lifetime of someone living in the United States is about 70 years. Approximately 23 of these will be spent sleeping. Another 12 will be spent growing up and going to grade school. This leaves 35 years. If you spend the equivalent of 4 years in college and average a total of 25 hours a week attending class and studying, then you will have spent 0.9 percent of your time directly preparing for your career and future life. If you complete two years, the figure is 0.45 percent.
   a. How do you feel about the idea of so small an amount of time largely determining your future?
   b. What is the implication regarding the time you spend in class and the time you spend studying?
2. Your college experiences require a lot of work in a short amount of time. This requires that you become an effective student as soon as possible. What can you do to help ensure that the time as represented by the numbers .9 percent and .45 percent is used effectively?

CHAPTER 4

HOW TO MANAGE YOURSELF

BASIC IDEAS
- If you know where you're going, you'll know if you've arrived.
- Self-evaluation helps you achieve competency.
- You are primarily responsible for what you achieve or don't achieve in college.

KEY POINTS
- What are you trying to accomplish in college?
- How do you know if you are accomplishing it?
- If you are not, what can you do about it?

Can you answer these questions? Do I know, rather clearly, what I want to accomplish in college? Am I aware enough of my actions so I can identify and resolve problems that prevent me from accomplishing my intent? Unless you know the answers to these questions you cannot really say you are in control of your college education. And if you're not in control, no one else is. The purpose of this chapter is to help make sure you accomplish your basic educational intent.

The basic intent of a college education is to achieve competency, awareness, and flexibility. Figure 4–1 shows these three general aims of education in more detailed terms. It also shows measurement, evaluation, and control procedures you can use to achieve your intent. Here is what these three terms mean:

- A *measurement* is any procedure that applies numerals to persons, places, or things. For example, a graph that plots the amount of time you spend studying or the scores you attain on examinations are results of measurements.
- An *evaluation* is a value judgment based in whole or part on available measurements. A teacher can use exam scores (meas-

Figure 4-1
A Guide to Managing Your College Career

EDUCATIONAL AIM AND LIST OF COLLEGE CONCERNS FOR WHICH YOU MAY WANT HELP OR INFORMATION:	WHERE TO FIND HELP IN THIS BOOK:		HOW TO MEASURE, EVALUATE, OR CONTROL YOUR PERFORMANCE		PERSON IN BEST POSITION TO:		
	Chapter	Page	Chapter	Page	Measure	Evaluate	Control
1. Competency as a Self-Directed College Student (Managing your personal choices and yourself)							
• Managing Your Choices							
Choosing a curriculum	Appendix	290	Appendix	295	You/Counselor	You/Teacher	You
Choosing electives	Appendix	296	Appendix	296	You/Counselor	You/Teacher	You
Making each course interesting	5	66	5	72	You	You	You/Teacher
• Managing Yourself							
Finding time to study	3	30	4	51(Ex4-2)	You	You	You
Creating a study schedule	3	33	4	51(Ex4-2)	You	You	You
Increasing the length of study sessions (read this if you find yourself unable to study for more than 15 minutes at a time)	4	47	4	51(Ex4-2)	You	You	You
Asking and answering questions in class	13	180	13	182	You	You	You
Scheduling term papers (see below for writing term papers)	12	177	12	177	You	You	You
What teachers will expect of you	14	195	19	270	Teacher	Teacher	You

Amount of study time for each course	4	51	4	53(Ex4-5)	You	You	You
2. Competency in Course Material Achieved through:							
• Recognition of How Learning Takes Place							
How your previous experiences can prevent learning	6	82	6	91	You	---	You
How important is IQ?	6	84	---	---	---	---	You
How important is note taking?	6	88	11	166	---	---	You
Why underlining may hurt you	6	90	15	209	---	---	You
How to use the classroom to advantage	11	160	11	161	---	---	You
What you can expect from your teachers	14	197	---	---	You	You	Teacher
• Acquiring Learning Skills							
Thinking logically	7	97	15	209	Teacher	Teacher	You
Becoming a good class listener	11	163	11	168(Ex11-4)	Teacher	Teacher	You
Taking class notes	11	166	See Chapters 4, 19				
How to understand words	8	117					
How to read a text	9	126			Teacher/You	Teacher/You	You
How to mark a text	10	152					
How to use the SCORE study system	15	209					

Figure 4-1 (continued)

EDUCATIONAL AIM AND LIST OF COLLEGE CONCERNS FOR WHICH YOU MAY WANT HELP OR INFORMATION:	WHERE TO FIND HELP IN THIS BOOK		HOW TO MEASURE, EVALUATE, OR CONTROL YOUR PERFORMANCE		PERSON IN BEST POSITION TO:		
	Chapter	Page	Chapter	Page	Measure	Evaluate	Control
How to study math and science	16	227	See Chapter 4, 19		Teacher/You	Teacher/You	You
Studying difficult subjects	15	224					
How to be a creative studier	17	236					
(Be sure to master Chapter 15 before trying Chapter 17)							
How to use the library	18	253	4	53	You	You/Librarian	You
3. Ability to Show Competency through:							
• Examination Management							
How to prepare for exams	19	271	3 / 15	30 / 209	You	You	You
The type of exam questions to expect	19	273	---	---	---	---	---
How to answer essay questions	19	275	---	---	Teacher	Teacher	You
How to use exam results to improve future scores	19	284	4	53(Ex4-6)	You	You	You

• Term Paper Management						
How to write a good term paper (see above for scheduling term papers)	12	173	12	177	Teacher	Teacher	You
• Discussions						
Talking with teachers	13	184	---	---	Teacher/You	Teacher/You	You
Studying with other students	15	219	---	---	You	You	You
Asking/answering questions in class	13	180	13	182	Teacher/You	Teacher/You	You
4. Achieving Awareness	5	66	4	56	You	You	You
5. Achieving Flexibility	5	66	4	57	You	You	You

urements) together with other things (i.e., class participation, progressive improvement) as a means of evaluating your overall course performance and establishing a course grade.

- *Control* refers to the ability to (usually) change something as a result of measurements and/or evaluations. If a measurement or evaluation shows poor results, a decision is made to take some action so that future results will be better.

Facts (the actual record) help you manage. The statement "I think I study enough" when an actual record would show 2½ hours studied for all of last week represents a situation you can't control. Telling yourself that you really know the course material when the record shows an exam average of 62 is another example. In the absence of data that support your case, how do you know your evaluation is valid? How do you know what control decisions to make?

Exercise 4–1. Are You in Control?

Answer the following questions. They will help you decide whether you are in control of your college education. Check the left-hand column if the statement describes you and the right-hand column if the statement does not describe you.

Yes   *No*

1. ____ ____ I haven't given serious thought to selecting a curriculum.

2. ____ ____ I usually select elective courses on the spur of the moment.

3. ____ ____ I hardly ever know why I take a particular course.

4. ____ ____ I usually don't take advantage of campus activities.

5. ____ ____ I have never tried to schedule and control my study time.

6. ____ ____ I think I can do better in college.

7. ____ ____ I want to speak in class but I am afraid.

8. ____ ____ I want to study but find it boring.

9. ____ ____ After a few minutes studying I get anxious, restless, or upset.

10. ____ ____ Other things always seem to interfere with studying.

11. ____ ____ I almost never say no when asked to join friends.

12. ____ ____ I fall asleep a lot when studying.

13. ____ ____ I almost always put off assignments.

14. ____ ____ I don't feel I accomplish something when I study.

15. _____ _____ Studying is really difficult for me.

16. _____ _____ I am easily distracted in my place of study.

Did you answer yes to any of these questions? If you did, you must now ask yourself this question: "Am I prepared to give or am I now giving myself a fair chance at college?" Many students are not fair with themselves. They do not establish conditions that let them do well or improve their college performance. For many students it is not a matter of difficult courses, it is difficulty in controlling personal behavior as it relates to their college career. Unless you can first recognize that this problem may exist and then act to solve the problem, you may never realize your true academic potential.

Answering yes to any of these questions means *you* have provided *yourself* with a signal that something is probably wrong with your study program. But take heart. You can most likely solve these problems by yourself. How? By systematically employing programs of self-management. Such programs allow you to identify what you want to change and help you achieve change. Before discussing such programs, you should be aware of the following.

Some problems associated with college and studying are not really college or study problems at all. For example: (1) The inability to read, to write, or to do basic math is not a study problem but a problem in academic preparation. A student must get separate and special help (through tutoring, special remedial classes, learning laboratories) to resolve this kind of problem. (2) Some students may quite honestly dislike college and attend because of parental or other types of pressure. They have a strong feeling they would be better off doing something else. The result is often poor academic performance that is unrelated to ability or studying. This is not a study problem but a conflict of wills. Students in this situation must either accept it, change it by asserting their position, or reach some compromise. Here, too, professional help may be needed. (3) Other nonstudy problems are those dealing with physical or psychological disorders. In such cases professional help is necessary. If your problems don't fall into any of these categories, then the following discussion will prove helpful—provided you want to change.

Some of the sixteen situations listed in Exercise 4–1 can be resolved by obtaining and using available information. For example:

• *Right Curriculum?* Here are some questions to consider when trying to evaluate whether you have selected the right field of study: (1) Was your selection carefully considered and based on good information about yourself and your major? (2) Do you find yourself in the library doing unassigned research? (3) Are you curious about your major? (4) Is your interest in your major growing? (5) Do you look forward to the next sequence of courses? (6) Is there a portion of your major that is particularly interesting? Positive answers are, of course, a good sign. Negative answers may signal the need for another look on your part. To select a curriculum or make sure your present one is still good for you, see the Appendix.

• *Interesting Courses?* Most students leave college because they are bored with their course work. If a student leaves college because of boredom or lack of direction, it's not because the college hasn't made it interesting, it's primarily because he or she hasn't made it interesting. As a manager of your learning you can't rely only on others to make college interesting for you.

The fact that most students instinctively ask the question, "Why am I taking this course and what does it mean to me?" is an indication of the instinct for management that most students have. That this question is asked shows a natural desire to control the conditions that surround educational efforts. A way of exerting such control, and of answering this question, is to establish reasons (objectives) for taking each of your courses. Chapter 5 will show you how to do this.

The Self-Management Technique

Some problems listed in Exercise 4–1 may require a special effort to fix. But here is some interesting news. The same Chapter 2 management process used to guide your overall college career can be used to help resolve some of the self-control problems you may have checked off above. Here are how the steps apply:

• *Planning.* Decide in advance what you want to do or accomplish. For a self-management program you must decide, *rather specifically,* what end behavior you want to achieve. The end behavior will allow you to stop doing too much of one thing and not enough of another.

• *Organizing.* Use methods that will help you shape or model your behavior to achieve your intent. Organizing includes looking at your behavior through use of graphs, charts, and self-awareness.

• *Staffing.* You, of course, are the main participant.

• *Directing.* Help yourself to achieve your objective through a combination of behavior change techniques.

• *Evaluating.* Analyze your actions and take steps to control future behavior.

A Sample Application of the Self-Management Approach

Let's suppose you want to establish a study schedule. With all good intentions, and following the Chapter 3 directions, you complete and post your study schedule. It reflects 22 hours set aside for study spotted over six days in the week (or less time, perhaps over fewer days, if you are attending college part-time). You now sit down to study. After ten minutes you somehow find yourself either talking on the phone, watching television, reading a magazine, raiding the refrigerator, or perhaps sleeping. Now such things will probably happen once in a while. But if they seem always to happen, then you might consider trying the following.

PLANNING

It is possible to complete and follow a study schedule with little or no trouble. But what if you have never studied more than one or two hours a week? Suddenly trying to study 22 hours a week, despite your good intentions, can be self-defeating. It is just too much to accomplish in one great leap. You can and will accomplish it—but at the outset you must avoid making sweeping demands of yourself. You have to make ripples before you can make waves. Here is what is meant by establishing reasonable initial goals. The author of this book once decided to improve his ability to shoot a basketball from the foul line. A goal of 10 baskets in a row was initially established. It proved too much. Just getting one in a row was a problem. Two in a row were hard to come by. The goal was reset to 3 baskets. When this was achieved, it was set to 5, then 10, then 15. Today it is not uncommon for him to make 20 baskets in a row. In fact once consistency was achieved, setting higher, seemingly difficult, goals—like 20 in a row—seemed to improve performance. (Thirty-one is the present record.) But what would have happened if a goal of 10 or 20 was initially established and then not changed to reflect reality? Probably frustration and defeat. Small steps that built skill and confidence were necessary. The same principle applies in self-management projects:

• *Start small, build skill and confidence, and then finish big.*

In the case at hand, telling yourself at the outset, "I am going to spend 22 hours a week studying" is equivalent to stepping to the foul line and saying, "I am going to make 20 baskets in a row." It's better to identify the 22 hours as an ultimate goal but in the meantime establish more realistic, immediately *achievable* goals. For example, and depending upon how severe your situation is, you might establish a goal such as, "I am going to study 20 minutes each day for the next five days." When you are capable of consistently achieving this goal, you can consider increasing the time. For the moment let's assume that 20 minutes a day is the goal.

ORGANIZING

Now you arrange your surroundings and activities to support your goal. To achieve studying 20 minutes a day, consider doing the following:

- Clear your desk of nonstudy items (magazines, radio, photographs) that compete for your attention.
- Face your desk away from your bed. (One student who felt sleepy when she studied was advised to change her 40-watt lamp and replace it with a 100 watt one and to position her desk so that it faced away from her bed. This was part of a program that increased her study time from 10 minutes a day to 3 hours a day.[1])
- Use your desk *only* for studying. If you are going to snack, read a magazine, or write a letter, do it elsewhere.
- Prepare and post a self-monitoring chart similar to that shown in Figure 4–2. Note that the vertical axis can be marked to reflect any time goal you want to achieve. (Figure 4–2 assumes a goal of 3 hours a day.) Both practical experience and controlled research have shown that the act of self-monitoring *by itself* may be all that is necessary for you to achieve your goal.
- Use a system of study that in itself is interesting, a system that causes you to participate in and organize the study material. Self-monitoring together with a system that allows you to forget about yourself and concentrate on the material can be a powerful team in helping to change study behavior. You may be interested to know that many of the case studies and research programs dealing with improving study behavior center around the use of systematic study systems. The study system *itself* helps achieve the desired behavior. (See Chapters 15 and 17 for study systems you can use.)

STAFFING

You are your own staff. The best thing you can do for yourself is to make a solid self-commitment to change. You might consider writing your target behavior ("I definitely want to study 20 minutes a day") in large letters and posting it in your study place. Other actions you can take to help yourself are described under Directing.

---

[1]Israel Golddiamond, "Self-Control Procedures in Personal Behavior Problems," in *Behavior Change Through Self-Control,* ed. Marvin E. Goldfried and Michael Merbaum (New York: Holt, Rinehart & Winston, 1973).

Figure 4-2
How to Record Time Spent Studying

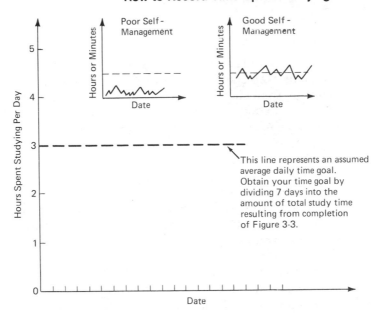

This line represents an assumed average daily time goal. Obtain your time goal by dividing 7 days into the amount of total study time resulting from completion of Figure 3-3.

Prepare this graph. Then plot the daily time spent studying. Consistently falling below your target line is a signal either to: (1) restrict your other activities and be firm with yourself and possibly your friends since it may be the only way of achieving your study time or goal, or (2) recompute your target line since it may represent an unreasonable goal; before making such an adjustment, you must be open with yourself. Are you sure you are trying hard enough to meet your original goal?

DIRECTING

This activity concerns keeping yourself motivated so you can obtain the best effort from yourself. Consider doing the following:

• If you have an activity you like (listening to music, watching TV, talking with friends), do not engage in such activity until you *first* complete your studying. Such activities can then serve as rewards for your study efforts. In other words, you can motivate yourself by first working and then playing.

• Reward yourself in other ways:

— Verbally encourage yourself.

— Allow yourself to have a candy bar or some other reward.

— Stop studying (wherever you are in the 20 minutes) whenever you feel uncomfortable. Do something else away from your desk; go for a walk, stare out the window, talk to yourself. When the feeling passes, return to your desk. If possible, before you stop, try completing the immediate paragraph.

This will help provide study continuity and keep you from giving in too easily to negative impulses.

EVALUATING

Identify and record your progress by making daily entries in your self-monitoring chart (see Figure 4–2). If you do not consistently meet your goal, then make sure the organizing and directing steps discussed above are being fully used. If you do experience trouble, it may be because you have set too high a goal. Or maybe you haven't given yourself enough time to become familiar with the self-monitoring procedure or the study systems described in Chapters 15 and 17. A sufficient trial period is always necessary in self-management programs. You will need at least two weeks before you can expect to see increases in your study time. Don't be impatient with yourself. If you are persistent, you will see results. Consistently meeting your goal will signal two things:

- That you have in fact achieved your planned objective (you should feel pretty good about that).
- That you are now in a position to proceed to a still more significant study time achievement. Now that you've made a ripple, you can start making waves.[2]

In summary, you can achieve control of your study actions by employing the techniques of self-management. Self-management as it relates to studying is basically the systematic removal of those things and activities that compete with your effort to study. Here is a list that will help you minimize or remove such competition:

- Study at one place only. Use this place only for studying.
- Establish an initial study schedule that you know you can maintain. You can build from there.
- Reward yourself.
- Employ enjoyable and rewarding study systems.
- Establish reasonable goals for grade achievement.
- Learn to say no when friends want you to interrupt your studying.
- Choose supportive study partners.
- Use active self-monitoring.

[2]If you are interested in finding out more about self-management procedures, these books will help: Robert L. Williams and James D. Long, *Toward a Self-Managed Life Style* (Boston: Houghton Mifflin, 1975); Jerry A. Schmidt, *Help Yourself: A Guide to Self-Change* (Champaign, Ill.: Research Press, 1976).

Exercise 4–2. Managing Your Study Time

Establish and maintain a time-spent studying program. Use a chart similar to that shown in Figure 4–2.

Other Self-Manage-ment Applications

A term paper assignment is probably the one activity that allows you to show your overall skills as an effective college student. Information on how to write and manage a term paper is presented in Chapter 12.

If fear of speaking out is holding you back from asking and answering class questions, see Chapter 13.

You can establish other programs for yourself by completing Exercises 4–3 and 4–4.

Exercise 4–3. Selecting Self-Management Programs

Refer to the list in Exercise 4–1. Then (a) select three yes-checked items that most concern you, (b) list the three items in order of importance, and (c) establish a self-management program for the one at the top of the list. Use the sample application discussed above as a guide. Establish similar programs for the other itoms on your lict.

Exercise 4–4. Joint Identification of Programs

Form a group of four students. Make a list of six (or more) things that prevented the people in the group from studying in high school or from trying to do well. What specific things can be done to improve personal habits or abilities?

Evaluating Your Competency in Course Material

Once you have resolved problems that deal with personal habits, you can begin to concentrate on fulfilling your academic potential. Here are methods of measuring, evaluating, and therefore controlling your degree of achievement in course competency.

Classroom Listening, Textbook Reading, Studying, Exam Taking

The evaluation step you perform as part of the study systems described in Chapter 15 will tell whether you are studying effectively. If you cannot change the material you study into your own words, in a manner that provides you with a record for later exam review, then your study techniques need revision. Understanding and using the ideas and systems described in Chapters 3 through 19 will also allow you to exert control over your study and learning activities.

Time Devoted to Studying Individual Courses

What is most important is what you have learned, not necessarily what exam score or course grade you are assigned. Your post-college career success will be based on job performance, not previous exam performance. Exam scores and course grades have meaning only to the extent that they reflect your ability to later apply what you have

Figure 4-3
Establishing Course Study Time

Course name and number	Your estimated degree of course interest (use scale of 1 to 10)	Your estimated degree of course difficulty (use scale of 1 to 10)	Add interest and difficulty scale points	Percent of total points for each course	Approximate number of hours per week to spend studying each course
American Literature 100	10	5	15	15/53 x 100 = 28%	28% of 21½ = 6
Math 121	1	10	11	11/53 x 100 = 21%	21% of 21½ = 4½
Macroeconomics 156	2	5	7	7/53 x 100 = 13%	13% of 21½ = 3
Principles of Sociology 140	7	4	11	11/53 x 100 = 21%	21% of 21½ = 4½
English Composition 110	5	4	9	9/53 x 100 = 17%	17% of 21½ = 3½
Total Scale Points			53	100%	(The number 21½ is an assumed total weekly study hour figure that might result from using Figure 3-3. Final figures are rounded to the nearest half hour)

learned. The amount of time spent in effective study can be as important as any exam or course grade. It is, therefore, important that study time be properly spread among your subjects. Here is how to make sure each course receives the study time it needs.

Assume you are taking five courses this term. Assume also that you have identified 17.5 hours per week as study time. The question that presents itself is, "How can I distribute the 17.5 hours (control the time) among the five courses?" You could, for example, simply decide to spend 3.5 hours studying each course (17.5 divided by 5). While this is not a bad initial approach, there is a better method of controlling the time and it is described in Figure 4–3.

Exercise 4–5. How Much Study Time Per Subject?

Prepare a blank table similar to Figure 4–3. Now, using figure 4–3 as a guide, determine how much time to spend studying each subject by completing the table. When estimating the degree of interest and difficulty, use past experience with similar subjects or make the best guess you can. Avoid overuse of the number five, since it will neutralize distinctions between courses. The completed chart will help you avoid spending more time on subjects you like at the expense of other subjects that may require more of your attention. In Figure 4–3 note that the least liked and most difficult subject is assigned 21 percent of the total study time available. How are you treating your least liked and most difficult subject? A time analysis such as this can help you better control your initial assignment of study time.

When you start to receive information from other sources (e.g., class discussions, exams) regarding your competency, you can then adjust the time spent studying each course. This approach to using study time will help you manage that area of college effort that is most directly responsible for achieving course competency—the amount of time spent in effective systematic study.

Use of the Library

The question here is a simple one: Can you find what you need in minimum time and with minimum help? The material in Chapter 18 will help you answer yes to this question. Establish a specific amount of weekly library time (at least one hour per week). Then select a certain day and time to use that hour (e.g., Tuesdays at 3 p.m.). This routine will allow you to control your use of the library.

Grade Estimation

Since course grades are received at the end of the term, you might question how they can help control study efforts during the term. The answer is that you employ a three-part program as follows: (1) monitor your exam results, (2) then estimate each final grade, and (3) estimate your final grade point average. The following exercises will help you perform these three steps.

Exercise 4–6. Tracking Your Exam Scores

Prepare and post a series of graphs as shown in Figure 4–4.

Figure 4–4
How to Graph Exam Results

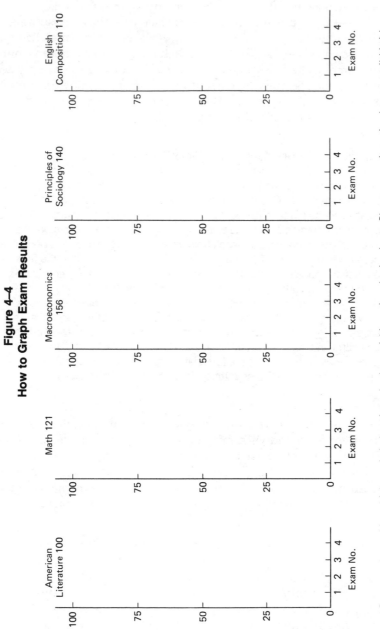

American Literature 100

Math 121

Macroeconomics 156

Principles of Sociology 140

English Composition 110

Prepare and post this multiple graph. It doesn't need to be much bigger than the size shown. Plot exam results as they become available (also enter other marks such as term papers, graded homework, and quizzes). It is especially important to plot marginal or low scores. Adjust your study program to reflect emerging patterns. Keeping a chart such as this can have a positive effect on your motivation to study and achieve.

Figure 4–5
How to Estimate Grade Point Average

(1) Name and Number of Course	(2) Number of Credits	(3) Estimated Course Grade		(5) Column 2 Multiplied by Column 4
		Letter Grade	Corresponding Point Grade	
American Literature 100	3	A	4	12
Math 121	3	C	2	6
Macroeconomics 156	3	C	2	6
Principles of Sociology 140	3	B	3	9
English Composition 110	3	B	3	9
Totals	15			42

Estimated GPA = Column 5 Total/Column 2 Total
= 42/15
EGPA = 2.8

To get the most from these graphs, post them in your study place so you can easily see them. They will serve as a constant reminder of your progress. They will stimulate your desire for systematic study and remind you of those subjects which may need special attention. They will allow you to control your study program. Downward sloping curves can have a remarkable impact on your study program. When you have entered at least one exam result for each course, proceed to Exercise 4–7.

Exercise 4–7. Estimating Your Grade Point Average
Prepare and complete a table similar to Figure 4–5. Here are directions:

a. Enter course names and numbers in Column 1.
b. Enter corresponding number of credits each course is worth in Column 2. Most college courses are worth 3 credits. Check your college course catalog.
c. Estimate your final course grades, basing your estimates on the first series of exams, and enter them in Column 3. If you received first exam marks of 92 (A), 71 (C), 81 (B), and 80 (B), then assume they represent your ultimate term average and enter the appropriate letter grade. The usual relationship between number grades and letter grades is as follows: 90 to 100 is equal to A, 80 to 89 is equal to B, 70 to 79 is equal to C, 60 to 69 is equal to D, and below 60 is an F.

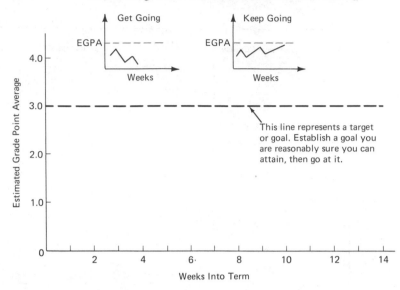

Figure 4–6
Monitoring Your Estimated Grade Point Average

Establish a target GPA that you believe is realistic but yet causes you to stretch your capacity. Estimate your GPA as often as you like and enter the results. In most instances you will find that regardless of the direction of the curve you will probably be motivated to keep or change its direction. If the curve is going down, you will work to bring it up. If it is already up, you will work to keep it there.

d. Change the letter grade into its corresponding grade point value and enter the point value in Column 4. The usual relationship is: A is equal to 4 grade points, B is equal to 3, C is 2, D is 1, and F is 0.

e. Divide the total of Column 5 by the total of Column 2. The result is your estimated GPA. The estimated GPA will vary as your average in each course varies. To keep track of what your final GPA is likely to be, complete Exercise 4–8.

Exercise 4–8. Monitoring Your Estimated Grade Point Average
During the term periodically estimate your GPA by completing Exercise 4–7. Then plot the result in a graph similar to that in Figure 4–6. Post this graph next to the one showing your exam scores.

Evaluating Awareness   Awareness is the ability to be sensitive, receptive, and responsive to ideas and people. It is the most difficult of the educational aims to measure and evaluate. There is no test for awareness. You can't assign a number; you can only attempt to get a rough idea. Ask yourself the following kinds of questions: Do I sometimes strike up conversations with people I don't know? Can I sense when a friend is in need of help? Do I let others complete their conversation before starting mine? Can I tolerate points of view different from mine? Can I appreciate a painting, a poem, a bird in flight? Can I spot an inference passed off as a fact? Have I made a new friend lately? Can I stop thinking only of myself and my needs? Participation in the kinds of activities described in Chapter 14 will help you answer these questions positively. You will start to acquire awareness when you find yourself appreciating ideas and people not because they are the same as you but because they are different from you.

Evaluating Flexibility

Being flexible means achieving general language skills in reading, writing, speaking, and listening. Flexibility also includes developing a capability in more than one field of study. How can you measure and control your efforts at achieving flexibility? Here are some activities to consider:

- Take advantage of the out-of-classroom activities available on campus. Such activities not only are fun, they also help you develop the ability to meet and communicate with new people, something you will be doing after you leave college.
- Take advantage of term paper assignments to explore new fields and develop new interests. Don't select the same old topics that bore not only you but your teacher as well.
- Use the library.
- Make a conscious effort to recognize and apply what you are learning to the job you may have.
- Don't use the dart-against-the-wall method of selecting electives. Choose courses that interest you and that also can serve as future areas of competence. Allow yourself to take special advantage of the time spent in class and in studying.

Summary

Knowing you are the manager of your college education is one thing; doing something about it is another.

In order to accomplish the basic educational aims of competency, awareness, and flexibility, you must develop the ability to measure, evaluate, and control your own actions.

There are three areas that concern your competency as a college student. Competency is necessary: (1) in managing your personal choices and habits, (2) in course material, and (3) in showing what you've learned. Research shows that self-monitoring of your actions and accomplishments together with a systematic approach to studying enhance achievement. This chapter includes a self-management approach for increasing your study time. Also discussed are how much time to spend studying each course, identifying and monitoring exam results, and estimating your grade point average.

To gain the most from college, the qualities of awareness and flexibility must be developed. The chapter closes by suggesting several methods for assessing your progress in these two areas.

KEY TERMS

Measure	Self-management	Flexibility
Evaluate	Competency	Study time
Control	Awareness	Grade point average

REVIEW QUESTIONS

1. Describe each of the above key terms.
2. After defining the terms *measure, evaluate,* and *control,* show an example of each.
3. What does self-management mean as applied to a college student?
4. Identify and describe the five elements in a self-management program.
5. Identify three self-management activities that can improve your (a) competency as a manager of your college education, and (b) competency in learning course material.

CHAPTER 5

HOW TO MAKE EVERY COURSE INTERESTING

BASIC IDEAS
- Knowing how to study is helpful, but it may not be enough for good academic performance unless motivation is present.
- If college is to have real meaning, you have to make your own motivation.

KEY POINTS
- What should be the main focus of your day-to-day college efforts?
- How can your courses provide motivation?

"The best way to make college valuable is to show the students that they will get something out of the work they do. Have them set some sort of goal to work for. Show the student that he or she is going somewhere. I can't relate to a lot of the courses I take and I don't know how to make myself relate. This is why a lot of people drop out—and this is why I am dropping out." This statement was made by a student who considered leaving after one semester. Quite simply he was bored. And studies show that boredom is a major reason for dropping out.

People who have a clear idea of what they want are usually in a much better position to stay in and do well in college. Success in college does not result simply because one has good study habits and applies good study techniques. Something quite different may account for success. There is reason to believe that good college performance is not just a function of study skills.[1] An interest in courses and the ability to

---

[1] Research results, reported in the Questions section of this chapter, suggest that even when given the chance to acquire study skills, students may refuse the opportunity. Those who do acquire study skills *may* improve their academic performance but not solely because their study skills improved.

see things through may be more important. Certainly study skills can help, but if you don't want to apply them what good are they? You will want to study if you have sufficient reason.

The management approach can be applied to almost any activity. Successful application requires knowledge of who you are and what you want to accomplish. An interesting benefit of knowing these two things is that you become better motivated. You begin to identify solid reasons for doing your college work. A good manager asks, "Who am I and where am I going?" The search for the answer helps provide motivation. Fortunately, as a college student, you can ask (and get some answers) to that question on at least two levels of concern. These are:

The college level. As a college student, how might I think of myself? What does it mean to be a college student?
The specific course level. How can I get myself more interested in my courses? What specific things can I do?

This chapter covers both these points. What now follows is written in the form of a play. It might be helpful now to imagine yourself sitting in a familiar theatre or auditorium. Now imagine the theatre is filled with people. The lights slowly start to dim and the audience stirs in anticipation. The curtain is rising. Enjoy yourself.

THE WINGS OF CHANGE

CHARACTERS

Adam
Dick
Mark
Professor Catherine Goodbooks

The action takes place at a college some-where in the United States. The time is the present.

SCENE I

The scene opens in the campus library. The top half of one wall is all window, which at the moment reveals dark and ominous clouds. Each library table has its own lamp. Upon entering, one is struck with its safe, timeless atmosphere.

It is late afternoon and Adam is sitting in the library. His elbows are on the tabletop, his hands on top of his head. His head is bent over and he is staring down glumly and blankly. Dick enters, sees Adam, and sits down next to him. Seated at the end of the table is an older man writing on a pad.*

DICK
Hey, why so glum? Are you coming to the gym or not?

ADAM
I got the exam results today. I just skinned by two of them and failed the math test. Even when I got the right answer, the teacher put me down for not writing clearly.

DICK
Hey, don't be tragic. Don't you know that college is a game? You're not going to apply what you're studying anyhow, so why get uptight?

ADAM
What do you mean it's a game?

DICK
Listen, most students are in college because they haven't anything better to do. Also, I read that if all college students suddenly quit and tried to get a job, this country would really be in trouble. Why get bothered? You only have to attend a few classes a week. Anyway, you're only here to get a degree so you can make more money.

ADAM
Baloney. You don't need a college degree to make good money. These days working for the government as a policeman, fireman, or garbage man can pay you well. And if you're a member of a strong union, forget it—some of those old guys never graduated high school and they make a lot of money.

DICK
Yeah, when they can find jobs.

ADAM
You know, I'm surprised to hear you say all this. I mean, I like to have fun, too. Just look at my marks and you can tell where I've been spending my time. But you—you don't seem to care about learning at all.

DICK
Why should I? Most of the courses we take mean nothing. The chances of getting a job that relates to your studies are zero. So who's kidding who? C'mon, you comin' or not?

ADAM
No, I don't think so. I've got problems. You go on anyway.

DICK
Okay, catch you later.

End of Scene I

SCENE II

Dick leaves. As he exits stage right, the man at the table stops writing, looks up, and says to Adam:

MAN AT TABLE
Pretty sure of himself, isn't he?

ADAM
Huh? You talking to me?

MAN AT TABLE
Your friend. He seems to have all the answers.

ADAM
Dick? It sure seems that way. Wish I was as sure of things.

MAN AT TABLE
By the way, my name is Mark.

ADAM
Mine's Adam. Do you work here?

MARK *(smiling)*
No, I'm a student. One of those old people you mentioned before.

ADAM *(embarrassed)*
Oh hey—gee—I didn't mean . . .

MARK
Forget it.

ADAM
I wish I could forget college. I don't think I can handle it.

MARK
Don't feel too bad. Asking questions is usually a good sign.

ADAM
Yeah, but I need answers.

MARK
Welcome to the club. But do you know what I think? I think the key is in what you are doing now, today.

ADAM
Are you saying that many college students have problems because they don't know what it means to be a college student?

MARK
Adam, it seems to me that college is not just the process of becoming, it's also the process of being. So for now you know who you are. You are a college student. Recognize it, accept it. Enjoy it. I wish I had originally.

ADAM

But how?

MARK

By recognizing that college gives you a chance to change, and most important, it gives you the chance to shape that change. That's what brought me back to school. I had no sense of control. Other people were deciding things for me. If you use college for career preparation and for growing into an aware, self-directed, thinking person, then you will minimize frustrations. College provides the chance for your life to be more than just long.

ADAM

You sound pretty sure for a guy who never went to college.

MARK

Who says you have to go to college to know things? And anyway, when you get to be as old as I am, you do get to learn a few things.

ADAM

Zap! Okay, I see what you mean, but how do I stay interested when I'm in the middle of reading a boring chapter?

MARK

Well, now you're asking, "How can a student stay interested in college?" That's a different question than recognizing why you are a college student.

ADAM

Well?

MARK

Well what?

ADAM

Aren't you going to help me answer this new question?

MARK *(standing as if to leave)*

Haven't I said enough?

ADAM

Hey, no way. Where are you going? Hey, Mark, don't leave. I was just starting to understand.

MARK

You can find out more.

ADAM

How?

MARK

The way I've found out about most things. By reading, thinking, and talking with others. I'm sorry but I really must leave. I've got to go to work. Goodbye.

Mark now has his coat on. Adam stands, and in doing so he knocks a book off the table. He stoops to get it and as he does Mark quickly exits stage right. Adam straightens up—looks around—and heads for the exit.

End of Scene II

SCENE III

It is 10 A.M. the next morning. Adam is again in the library. It is raining outside. He is taking off his wet jacket and is looking around when he sees Professor Catherine Goodbooks, whom he knows. He goes over to talk to her.

ADAM

Hello, Professor Goodbooks. What are you doing here? I thought teachers knew everything.

GOODBOOKS *(mockingly serious)*

Adam, admitting one's ignorance is the first step in gaining knowledge.

ADAM

And I've sure got a lot of admitting to do. I only wish I could get more interested in my courses. I was talking to a fellow named Mark here yesterday. He said some good things but then he had to leave. Do you know him?

GOODBOOKS

No, I don't. But maybe I can help. What courses are you taking?

ADAM

American Literature, Math, Macroeconomics, Sociology, and English.

GOODBOOKS

Adam, I think I know what may be bothering you. Do you feel that your reason for attending college has practically nothing to do with the subjects you study and assignments you're given?

ADAM

Sort of. I keep thinking, what's the point of all this work? How do I get interested in it? I really don't see how most subjects I take relate to me now.

GOODBOOKS

Well, it seems to me that you have to do two things if your day-to-day college career is to have meaning and be interesting. First you have to achieve motivation and second you have to have a decent study program.

ADAM

What do you mean by study program?

GOODBOOKS

Well, you should schedule your time, organize your class and study activities, learn study techniques and know how to use the college resources to your advantage. The ability to manage your college work will help you in managing your career work.

ADAM

Are you saying that one way to keep interested in something is to try to become good at it?

GOODBOOKS

Yes.

ADAM

Okay, I guess that makes sense, but getting to be good at something doesn't mean you will like doing it. I could be an excellent bricklayer but that doesn't mean I like the job.

GOODBOOKS

You're absolutely right, and that brings me to motivation. You have to find or establish reasons for taking your courses—even the courses you think are boring.

ADAM

What if I find most all my subjects boring? I really don't, but what if I did? How do I handle that?

GOODBOOKS

By looking at college as more than just a place to prepare for a career, meet people, and have

fun. You have to have enough imagination to see that everything you study, even subjects you think boring, can develop your ability to think things through and come to a reasonable solution—or at least to identify the right question. This is a skill an educated person must develop regardless of the particular job.

ADAM

But aren't you asking me to take an awful lot on faith, that somehow almost all the things I study will eventually be useful?

GOODBOOKS

If you adopt the attitude that there really is something to get out of a particular course, you will begin to find reasons why a course can or will be useful, not reasons why it's not. You have to try. You can't expect the subject matter or your teachers always to do it for you.

ADAM

But how do I go about it?

GOODBOOKS

Well, one way is to establish a purpose, a goal, or an objective for any course you take. Tell yourself in advance what it is you want to get out of the course. Identify a reward for yourself.

ADAM

But doesn't that mean I first have to know something about the course?

GOODBOOKS

To some degree yes. But you can start with any goal—like trying to see how a course could improve your ability to identify problems or improve your writing skills, or how it relates to a job you may have. If you have a reason for doing something now, you won't be overly concerned with long-term goals.

ADAM

Isn't it a long-term goal to graduate?

GOODBOOKS

Yes. But if you identify something specific now, it will give an overall direction to your college career and put you more at ease. It will help remove the "I don't see where I'm going" feeling. There is one last thing I think is really important.

ADAM

What's that?

GOODBOOKS

Altruism. It would be a pretty sad and pretty cold world if people always acted only because they saw a reward in it for themselves.

ADAM

Is that what altruism is? You do things just because—just because—

GOODBOOKS

Just because you're human, because you're a person. And helping others, even in very simple, seemingly trivial ways, is an expression of that humanness.

Adam leans back with his hands on his head, staring at the ceiling as if summarizing in his mind all that's been said.

ADAM

You know I've kind of felt, "Oh, what's the use, what difference does anything make."

GOODBOOKS

It's a normal reaction. Things used to be relatively simple years ago. Studying and working today is much more complex. It's much harder to find out where and how you fit into things. But it is really ever so much more exciting.

ADAM

I guess it really is. Having so much to choose from can be confusing but it also makes it possible that I will hit on something I really like.

GOODBOOKS

And college is probably the one place where you can start taking hold of your own destiny and have a say in shaping it. It's a place where you can help yourself become aware of the world around you.

ADAM

I think I see what you mean. I was a pupil before, but now I'm a student—a college student. When I entered college, I thought I really didn't have a good reason. Well, maybe all along I did have a reason but wasn't able to express it so it made sense. Maybe I was really saying, "Hey, I want to be someone, I want to understand, I want to think and act for myself. I want to be better able to help myself and those around me. I want to use my head in life." Maybe that's what I was really saying. Well, you know something, Professor Goodbooks? I'm tired of hanging around and feeling sorry for myself. An apple hangs and it eventually drops to the ground. I don't want to drop. I want to fly—to soar; I want my head to have wings. I want to make a difference. I want to be of some significance.

Adam is now sitting up straight in his chair, his head tilting up slowly. He is looking out the great glass wall watching the clouds move away.

THE CURTAIN FALLS

EPILOGUE: What Now? If someone said to you, "Paint this house and I will pay you two or four years from now," you would find it very difficult to accept the offer. Your motivation for accepting is most likely zero. The relationship between performance (your doing the job) and reward (your getting paid) is too far apart. A college degree is also a deferred reward. This fact accounts, in part, for the large number of students who start but don't complete college. The attraction of immediate results for their actions (i.e., some money-making job) lures them away from college. Such an attraction may also lock them into a track that's hard to get off, a track that can reduce future opportunities and rewards. Adam's concerns are at one time or another shared by most college students, regardless of age. You may feel your resolve for college sometimes weakening. But the question really is: What can you do about it? What about the reality of day-to-day college work? How can you stay interested and motivated? What can you actually do to implement Professor Goodbook's suggestions? Well, let's examine why you are in college.

It's already been said that the reasons for college are to gain increased competency, awareness, and flexibility. *Competency* is the ability to discuss a given body of knowledge or to perform adequately in a given activity. As used here it refers primarily to courses that are directly related to your major field or courses that may prepare you to eventually enter a major field. If you have *awareness,* you have achieved the ability to place your studies and actions in a wider world context. Awareness is related to developing thoughtfulness about things, ideas, and people. *Flexibility* means developing general skills in reading, writing, speaking, listening, and thinking logically. Flexibility also means developing special skills in other fields of interest.

These objectives do not lend themselves to exact mathematical calculation. And certainly you don't magically achieve these college objectives because you receive good course grades or because you eventually receive your college diploma. The achievement of competency, awareness, and flexibility in college is a collective process. They develop from all the courses you take and the experiences you have. Each course makes its contribution.

If you accept competency, awareness, and flexibility as the main college objectives, you will value those courses and experiences which help you attain these qualities. You will attach some value to courses that help get you where you want to go. You will see the logic of spending time on them. You will be motivated to study a course because you see some reward (objective) in doing so.

The next question has no doubt already occurred to you: "Just how do I attach value to the courses I take?" The answer is that you attach value by finding reasons for taking the courses. These reasons become your course objectives. They are the motivation on which you can draw every time you open a book or go to class. Such reasons help you manage. The course management-by-motivation system, described in the following sections, will help you establish reasons for taking each of your courses. This simple system will allow you to discover reasons for taking college courses—reasons you can establish by yourself.

The Course Management-By-Motivation (MBM) System

Motivation can be described as having a reason for doing something. It doesn't have to be any more complex a definition than that. You are motivated when you have a reason for doing something. If you establish the reasons yourself, your desire to follow through can be enhanced simply because it is your idea.

The something you are now doing is taking college courses. Therefore, establishing personal reasons (they can also be called objectives, motivators, or rewards) for taking your courses should prove very helpful. What should such motivators be? Another way of stating this question is: "Why am I taking this course and what can I get from it?" You may often ask this question. It shows your instinct for management. Here is a way of answering the question.

The reasons for taking a course are, not surprisingly, closely tied to the reason for getting educated in the first place. What are some of these reasons? How can they be classified? The following list, classifies reasons for education. The list provides a basis for general objectives which can enhance your competency, awareness, and flexibility.

Educational Aims

1. *Competency, acquired through:*
   a. *Knowledge*
   b. *Comprehension*
   c. *Application*
   d. *Specific skills*
   e. *Evaluation*
   f. *Analysis*
   g. *Synthesis*

2. *Awareness, acquired through:*
   a. *Receptiveness*
   b. *Responsiveness*
   c. *Attitude*

3. *Flexibility, acquired through:*
   a. *General language skills*
   b. *Specific interests*

Figure 5–1 summarizes the basic meaning of each of the three major educational aims and the following describes the meaning of each sub-aim listed above.

When I take a course I can gain *competency* in that course by mastering:

Figure 5–1
Educational Aims: Their Basic Meaning

| COMPETENCY | AWARENESS | FLEXIBILITY |

"Yes, I've considered that possibility. But the return on investment is marginal. And when one compares current bond rates with investment tax credits and the current rate of exchange, it becomes clear that a fast-food chain could make a good profit. I think we should call it McDonalds's"

"You mean if the world were one big country, white people would be a minority?"

"Here, let me show you how to fix this rocket engine. I learned something about rocket engines in a college physics course I took. But let's work quickly. This afternoon I'm due to give a talk on the planet Barbarus on a subject I once covered in a term paper."

In Other → Words

You know and can apply what you are talking about.

You are willing to listen to and think about new viewpoints.

You have several interests/abilities and you can communicate.

- Knowledge, the ability to remember facts related to the course. I know this is the lowest level of competency since it is based only on the ability to recall, not use, information.
- Comprehension, the ability to recognize facts related to course material. It is also the ability to recognize the nature and scope of the course.
- Application, the ability to use what I know and comprehend in new situations, especially situations related to my current or future career.
- Specific skills, developing the ability to function in the career field I have chosen. This course can enhance my ability to function well.
- Evaluation, the ability to read something that's new to me and determine its value. I can get this ability by knowing, comprehending, and applying what I've learned.

- Analysis, the ability to break down course material and analyze its parts.
- Synthesis, the ability to put together different parts of the course material and create something new. Synthesis is considered to be the highest intellectual goal a college student can achieve.

When I take a course I can gain *awareness* by gaining:

- Receptiveness, the ability to focus my attention during study and class by seeing the course's potential worth. Receptiveness also enables me to consider points of view other than my own.
- Responsiveness, developing my willingness to admit there are things I don't know and to share things I do know. I can achieve responsiveness by actively engaging in class discussion and by actively engaging in the completion of homework assignments.
- Attitude, realizing that my opinions can prevent me from learning. For example, I may dislike math. But math can develop my ability to analyze and synthesize, abilities that can be widely used. Therefore, awareness of math's value can help me become more competent. This sort of attitude can help change my view of math or any other subject. Attitude also concerns other people and their ideas. Maybe this course can help me understand the differences in people and come to experience how other people see the world.

When I take a course I can gain *flexibility* by developing:

- General Language skills. By taking this course and engaging in reading, writing, and discussions, I develop these skills to a higher degree, thus enhancing my overall competency. A term paper assignment for this course then becomes more than narrow research. For example, it allows me to demonstrate, to others as well as to myself, my research and writing skills. If they need improvement, then I have learned something about myself and identified an objective to accomplish. Such language skills will always be usable, even if I never apply the specifics of this course after college.
- Specific interests. This course can help by allowing me to pursue special interests in my major. I can also develop new interests and open myself to alternate job possibilities.

That's one way of thinking about the list of educational aims. Of course, since you are an individual, you may read it differently for yourself. What you really should have is a basic list of motivators that you can adopt as your own. Here is such a list. It can be used as a source of basic objectives for any course you take.

Course Motivators or Objectives

Increased Competency

1. I can learn factual information.
2. I can develop my ability to recognize facts related to this course.
3. I can develop my ability to apply this new material to related fields in new situations.
4. I can gain confidence to perform well in my chosen field.
5. I can develop my ability to evaluate the significance of something I read or hear that is related to this course.
6. I can develop my ability to separate out complex ideas and analyze their parts.
7. I can develop my ability to be creative by putting together new ways of looking at things.
8. (Other reasons that I or my teacher feel are important.)

Increased Awareness

1. This course can help me be intellectually and emotionally receptive in all areas if I strive to see what values the course may hold.
2. This course can cultivate my responsiveness to new ideas and information.
3. This course may help me change unproven attitudes I hold about people, places, and things.
4. (Other reasons.)

Increased Flexibility

1. This course can help me improve my reading, writing, discussion, and thinking skills.
2. This course can widen my base of knowledge and thereby make me more valuable and allow me to increase my career options.
3. (Other reasons.)

To obtain the most value from each course, you can establish an individual table for each one. Such a Course Management-By-Motivation Chart is described in the next section. When completed, it can help answer the question, "Why am I taking this course and what can I get from it?"

How to Prepare a Course Management-By-Motivation (MBM) Chart

Figure 5–2 represents the MBM process. The following discussion is keyed to the numbered steps in the figure.

STEP 1. SELECT CURRICULUM

It is clear that you will care for a course if you also care for the associated curriculum. Choosing the right curriculum for yourself may be the single most important motivational factor. For this reason the choice of curriculum is discussed separately and in some detail in the Appendix. However, the rest of this sequence applies even if you have already selected a curriculum or are still to decide. You can apply this sequence to any course including your present ones.

STEP 2. ENTER COURSE NAME AND DESCRIPTION

Prepare a sheet similar to that shown in Figure 5–3 (Course Management-By-Motivation Chart). At the top enter the name and a brief description of one of your courses. You can obtain a brief course description by referring to your college's course catalog.

STEP 3. SELECT MOTIVATORS

Refer to the motivators listed above. Select, from each of the three groups, motivators that you think will apply to this particular course.

Figure 5–2
Steps in the Management-By-Motivation Process

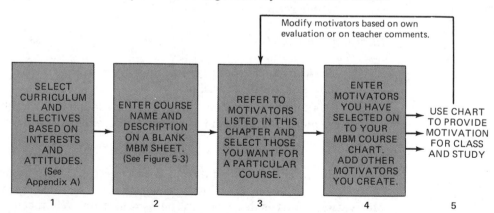

Notes;
1. Numbers are keyed to text description.
2. Process can start at Step 1 or 2.

STEP 4. ENTER MOTIVATORS

Enter onto your MBM Chart the particular motivators you have selected. A completed chart may look like Figure 5–3.

A similar chart may be prepared for each of your courses. You can list as many or as few items in each area as you like. However, each major educational aim should be reasonably represented.

Note that the objectives in Figure 5–3 are based on the list of motivators, but they are not *all* the items in the list. The point is: select or create those motivators you think go well with each of your courses. For example you can relate your choices to academic weaknesses, your part-time job, or your interests/hobbies.

Figure 5–3
Course Management-By-Motivation Chart

Course Name: Social Psychology

Course Description: Psychological principles that influence the social behavior of human beings.

In this course I will try to:

Competency Items

1. Develop my knowledge of related facts.

2. Develop my ability to apply facts to course problems.

3. Identify the major parts that make up this subject.

4. Seek new combinations of facts and ideas.

5.

6.

Awareness Items

1. Identify specific value to my future job.

2. Identify major personalities in field.

3.

4.

Flexibility Items

1. Improve my library research ability.

2. Improve may ability to write clearly.

3. Gain confidence in speaking by asking questions in class.

4.

5.

There may be more specific motivators, sometimes called *instructional objectives,* provided by your teacher. If this is the case, then add these additional items to your list. If you do receive such teacher-prepared objectives, you can consider yourself fortunate, since you will be better able to focus your studies.

The items you list in your chart will depend on the course. If every chart reads the same, you may not have a special reason for keeping up with a particular course. While some items will repeat, your charts should be such that you have varied reasons for studying each course.

How to Use Your Motivation Chart

Did you ever notice those charitable fund drives that measure their progress by a hand-drawn thermometer? The thermometer is always in view and every time some progress is made the red crayon column is extended up. This idea of displaying objectives has long been used by many organizations. Production companies post big charts for workers to see, and sports teams post slogans and sayings. These motivational techniques seem to help, probably because people can see the object of their efforts. The charts, graphs, and slogans are constant reminders of what needs to be accomplished. There is no reason why you can't adopt these ideas to your advantage. On this basis the following is suggested:

- Make two copies of each MBM Chart.
- Hang one near your usual place of study.
- Place the other one into the associated notebook.

Every once in a while look at these charts to remind yourself of the reasons you are taking a specific course.

Unless you have some recurring reason to look at these charts, they may become part of the background and you will tend not to see them anymore. Therefore, you may want to consider their use in the following situations:

- When you have a study assignment to complete and can't seem to get started, look at your motivation chart. Select one or two objectives and study for these objectives.
- When an exam is coming up, look at your chart and select one or two areas in which you may be weak. Study to improve in these areas.
- When determining the subject and emphasis for a term paper, refer to these charts. Select one or two objectives and prepare your paper accordingly.
- If you don't feel like attending class one day but really don't

want to miss it, look at your chart. Select one or two objectives and listen for related information (or ask related questions) while in class.

* If you receive an outside reading assignment, pick an objective or two off your chart and read the assignment with those objectives in mind.

When to Prepare Motivation Charts

The time to prepare an MBM Chart is soon after your first class meeting. Then, with the college catalog in front of you as well as your first class notes and the teacher handouts, you can begin. You may feel a little unsure of yourself the first time you prepare a chart. This is natural and expected and you shouldn't be put off by it. It may take several attempts with your first chart before you are satisfied. Don't get discouraged. Remember you can always change and add to it. After you complete one for each course, you will have taken a giant step in bringing real meaning to the courses you take and to your day-to-day college experience. Your study sessions will be less aimless. You will begin to attain a sense of accomplishment.

Objectives or motivators can be very powerful tools in focusing your energies and in making effective use of your time. However, because they do have this focusing power, they can block out other important areas of interest. For this reason, some people express concern about using objectives. However, there is little danger of this occurring with the course objectives cited in this chapter. Should you create or receive more detailed objectives, just be sure you don't close yourself off from other educational values a course may hold for you.

Exercise 5–1.   Let's Start Now
Prepare an MBM Chart (see Figure 5–3) for the study management course in which you are now enrolled. To get you started, here are some motivators for each of the three main educational aims. You may add others.

COMPETENCY: When I complete this course I will have mastered at least one method of studying a textbook.

AWARENESS: When I complete this course I will have asked or answered at least two questions in class.

FLEXIBILITY: When I complete this course I will have learned to take class notes in outline form.

Exercise 5–2.   Turning It Around
Select a current course which least interests you. Prepare an MBM Chart. Refer to this chart each time you study or attend class for this course.

Exercise 5–3.   Get Involved in All Your Courses
Prepare an MBM Chart for each of your present courses. Use the entries on page

69 as a starting point for selecting motivators. Add motivators that you prepare yourself or that result from completing Exercise 5–4 below.

Exercise 5–4. Identifying Motivators

On the lines below enter the things you wish you had already learned to better prepare yourself for college.

1. _____
2. _____
3. _____
4. _____
5. _____

For each item write a one-sentence statement that describes the improvement you want. For example, assume you identified library use as a weak area. Your statement might read, "I will improve my ability to use the library by locating and reviewing one magazine article related to each of three study assignments." It is important to make your statement in one sentence. This helps focus your objective. For each sentence identify whether it is a competency, awareness, or flexibility item.

Now select a present course that could be used to help you achieve the objective represented by each of your statements. Enter the statement on the appropriate MBM Chart completed in Exercise 5–3.

Exercise 5–5. Looking Ahead

An article in the *Wall Street Journal* of November 12, 1976, reported the results of a survey of college graduates. It read as follows:

> A survey of 4,100 graduates who started college in 1961 shows less than half use their college majors often in work and over half are in careers they didn't plan on. The graduates wish they'd taken more such courses as English, Psychology, and Business Administration and built broad skills such as communications, human relations, and administration, rather than specific occupational training.
>
> The research, sponsored by the College Placement Council and National Institute of Education, showed college was viewed as helpful mainly in gaining general knowledge and getting hired. But it was said to help little in nurturing leadership ability, clear thinking or in choosing goals in life.
>
> The study says the attempt to match majors with future jobs "frequently is too literal" and suggests colleges should stress skills needed for daily "work activities" that cut across occupational lines.

a. What can you conclude about the relative value of the educational aims of specific job competency, awareness, and flexibility?

b. How can you relate this article to the preparation of an MBM Chart?

Exercise 5–6. MBM'ing a Chapter

The next chapter in this book is called "How to Learn at the College Level." To get an idea of its contents, look at the chapter's topic headings, its summary, and its key terms. Now do the following:

  a. Before you read the chapter, prepare an MBM Chart. Enter at least two items each for competency, awareness, and flexibility.
  b. When you read the chapter, read for the motivational objectives in your chart.
  c. When the chapter is completed, check off those MBM items you think you have achieved. Then answer these questions:
      (i) Did having a chart make Chapter 6 more interesting?
      (ii) Did you accomplish your objectives?

Summary

Effective managers have a pretty good idea of how they fit into things. They also have a clear idea of what they want to accomplish. Without these two important ideas, it is very difficult to be effective. Another way to state this is: If you don't know where you are going, how can you tell if you've arrived?

Being effective in college is not only a matter of developing good study habits and techniques. As Adam says in the play, "Getting to be good at something doesn't mean you will like doing it". Being effective is also related to being interested in what you are doing. It is related to achieving motivation.

You are motivated when you do something for a reason. Ideally the reasons will be your own. If they are, your chances of accomplishing something will be much improved.

The Management-By-Motivation system provides a specific motivational method. Establishing reasons for studying courses through the use of the course MBM Chart can be very supportive of your efforts. A completed course MBM Chart provides reasons for taking courses as well as for studying. You (and your teachers) can identify objectives, or motivators. Whatever the specific objectives, the important thing is to have them and to refer to them periodically. They will help you be an effective college student.

The fact that you establish an MBM Chart shouldn't blind you to other rewards a course may hold for you. Don't ignore an area just because it's not on your chart.

KEY TERMS

Change	Flexibility	MBM
Competency	Motivation	MBM Chart
Awareness	Objectives	

1. Describe each of the above key terms.
2. Identify and describe the seven educational aims associated with competency.
3. Identify and describe the three educational aims associated with awareness.
4. Identify and describe the two educational aims associated with flexibility.

1. Let's assume it's a few years after you've graduated college. You're at a party and someone asks what you do. You probably would say, "I'm an engineer" or "I'm a computer programmer" or "I'm an accountant." You would most likely identify your occupation and possibly the company or organization you worked for. Why do you suppose that some college students, when asked what they do, respond by saying, "Nothing." Why do you think some college students hesitate to identify themselves as college students?
2. Which do you think is most important: competency, awareness, or flexibility? Support your selection in a brief paragraph.
3. Studies have shown that boredom with course material is a major reason for dropping out of college.
   a. Identify three reasons why you think students become bored.
   b. What would you recommend doing for each of these "problems"?
4. Two researchers, Barry Jackson and Brenda Van Zoost, conducted an experiment related to the teaching of study skills to college students (*Journal of Counseling Psychology,* 1972, vol. 19, no. 3, pp. 192–195). Their aim was to see which of three groups better learned study skills as measured by answers to a questionnaire and by course grades. All three groups received the same study skills instructions over a six-week period. The only difference was the manner of reward. One group determined themselves whether they should be rewarded, one group was rewarded by a supervisor, and the third group was rewarded for just showing up. In all cases the reward was the chance for the students to earn back the ten dollars they had deposited at the beginning of the course.

   The results were interesting. The researchers reported that the self-rewarded and supervisor-rewarded groups significantly improved their study habits. Of greater interest was what the researchers found out when they followed up on their research. They found that the self-reward group *continued* to show greater study habit improvement than the supervisor-rewarded group.

The researchers had also thought grades would improve as a result of the study skills training. But they found no significant difference in course grades between the two reward groups. They concluded that there is more to good grades than knowledge of study skills. They reasoned that the critical factor in study skills courses may be the other experiences they provide, such as knowledge of motivational techniques, counseling, or career decision making.

   a. Despite an increase in study skills, both the self-reward and supervisor-reward groups showed no significant gain in grades. What conclusions would you make regarding the value of the study skills course?

   b. What factors do you think would improve a student's grade performance?

   c. The self-reward group showed a greater gain in study skills, even when checked four months later. What conclusions can you make regarding the nature of motivation. That is, what factors do you think influence motivation?

5. "The major problem with implementation of such a program is that of inducing (college students) to participate and keeping them motivated to do so. The gravity of this problem is strongly reflected in the (drop-out) data . . . as only 17% of students . . . completed all the lessons."

   Does this sound like student reaction to a course in Microeconomics, Statistics, or Electric Field Potential? It might be, but it isn't. It's related to a program which attempted to teach study skills to college students. The researchers (William M. Beneke and Mary B. Harris, "Teaching Self-Control of Study Behavior," *Behavior Research and Therapy,* 1972, vol. 10, pp. 35–41) concluded that while their study skills program appeared helpful to those students who actually used the suggested study procedures (grade point averages improved), the "program is no panacea for unmotivated students who wish their grades to improve without effort," and it may be added, without reason.

   Only 9 of 53 students (whose ages ranged between 18 and 51 and who *volunteered* to take part) completed the study skills program. The students were to meet roughly twice a week for only five weeks. They received instructions in a specific study method, in taking lecture notes, and in taking exams.

   a. Assume the instructor and the instruction method were adequate and the program materials were easily read and understood (a large but not unreasonable assumption). What would account for only 9 of 53 students completing all eleven lessons?

   b. Do the researchers' own statements quoted above provide any clues?

Note: The list of Educational Aims that appear earlier in this chapter is based in part on several books written basically for teachers. You may find them interesting to look through. They are:

• Bloom, B. S., ed., *Taxonomy of Educational Objectives: Handbook I, Cognitive Domain,* New York: David McKay Co., 1969. *Taxonomy* means the identification and classification of things. *Cognitive* means to get to know. So the book identifies and classifies things that students should know how to do. The book's Foreword, Chapters 1 and 2, and its Appendix should be helpful to you.

• Krathwohl, D. R., B. S. Bloom, and B. B. Masia, *Taxonomy of Educational Objectives: Handbook II, Affective Domain,* New York: David McKay Co., 1969. This book identifies and classifies the actions and feelings that should result from the educational process. Chapter 1 and the book's two Appendices should be helpful to you.

• Harrow, A. J., *A Taxonomy of the Psychomotor Domain,* New York: David McKay Co., 1972. This book will be helpful if you are studying a curriculum that requires both intellectual competency and manual competence.

~II~
Organizing Your Learning: Skills You Need

OBJECTIVES FOR PART II

When you complete this part you should be able to accomplish the following:

1. Identify and describe the essential elements necessary for effective college learning.
2. Apply the concepts of participation, organization, and persistence to your college learning.
3. Determine a word's meaning from its parts, context, or a dictionary.
4. Apply the attributes of a good reader to textbook and nontextbook material.
5. Mark a textbook so it shows what is important to learn.
6. Apply the attributes of a good classroom listener.
7. Use the Term Paper Writing System.
8. Ask and answer class questions, deliver a verbal report, and talk with your teachers.

PREVIEW OF CHAPTERS

Chapter 6, How to Learn at the College Level, discusses the basic methods by which people learn. It shows why some study habits (underlining, memorizing) can be harmful. The chapter presents an approach to college learning that will help ensure that the time you spend studying will result in a significant positive change in your thinking abilities.

Chapter 7, Learning to Think Logically, will help you develop four abilities necessary for college level work: participation, organization, persistence, and cre-

CONTINUED➟

ativity. This is a particularly important chapter. A firm understanding and use of its material are necessary for achieving the maximum benefit from the time spent listening in a classroom and reading and studying a textbook.

Chapter 8, Understanding Words, shows how words are constructed, how a word's meaning can often be figured out from other words that surround it, and how signal words can make you a better reader. You also get a chance to create your own words.

Chapter 9, covers *How to Read a Textbook (Part 1).* Most of your college learning is expected to take place outside the classroom; therefore, skill in textbook reading is absolutely necessary. This chapter will show how to use reading time effectively and how to make yourself an effective textbook chapter reader.

Chapter 10, How to Read a Textbook (Part 2), completes the reading discus-sion started in Chapter 9. It shows how to make friends with your text, how to mark your text, and how to read non-textbook material.

Chapter 11, How to Listen and Take Notes in Class, tells why the classroom is the management center of your college learning. This chapter shows how to make each class meeting interesting, how to become a good classroom listener, how to take notes, and how to use the classroom to cut down on your study time.

Chapter 12, How to Write a Good Term Paper, provides a simple and useful method for writing term papers. It also discusses two techniques for turning a term paper from a chore to an interesting assignment.

Chapter 13, Speaking—In Class and Out, shows how to ask and answer class questions, how to prepare and deliver a verbal report, and how to talk to your teachers.

HOW TO LEARN AT THE COLLEGE LEVEL

BASIC IDEAS
- There is no known easy way to learn college material.
- Memorizing is the lowest form of learning, thinking the highest.
- Your current ideas about learning may not work at the college level.

KEY POINTS
- What is conditioned learning?
- What is learning by thinking?
- What is necessary for effective college learning?

To say you are managing your learning is accurate, but it's not very helpful. What is meant by learning? How does it come about?

Learning is the process of achieving competency, awareness, and flexibility. It requires the use of one or more of the five human senses of sight, sound, touch, taste, and smell. The senses provide information. As a result you learn things in one of three ways: conditioning, thinking, or some combination of the two. Here are definitions of the two basic learning methods.

Conditioning is defined here as learning things with a maximum of physical and emotional reaction and a minimum of thinking. A large portion of conditioned learning is unconscious. You don't think about it. For example, when you first learned that lighted matches are hot and painful to the touch, you didn't say to yourself: "Oh look, the match flame is touching my finger. Match flames are hot. Hot things can hurt so I'd better move my finger away." Rather than going through that thought process, you just moved your finger when you felt pain. From that point on you were conditioned to avoid flames. However, learning by conditioning is not always so obvious. Conditioned learning can take place in a little-noticed fashion over a long period of time.

Examples include your food and entertainment preferences and your present reading and study habits.

Thinking is defined here as learning with a maximum of thought and a minimum of emotional and physical reaction. Thinking can result in attaining understanding. Understanding is the result of taking something, analyzing it, and talking about or describing it in your own fashion. The fact that there is "a minimum of emotional and physical reaction" doesn't mean that these two elements are not present when one thinks. You must be in decent physical and emotional shape to think. You may even emotionally bang the table in joy when you have thought your way through a problem. What it does mean is that you arrive at your understanding primarily by using your brain.

Thinking requires that you observe and understand the order of things (organization), that you actively engage yourself in establishing such organization (participation), and that you stay at it until you achieve a sense of understanding (persistence). Organization, participation, and persistence are key elements in learning by thinking.

So much for definitions. Let's look at the senses and see how they affect the two basic ways we learn—conditioning and thinking.

Learning Through Conditioning and Thinking

Conditioning You may suppose that conditioned learning, because it involves a minimum of thinking, is not very important. That would not be a good assumption on your part. As you will see, conditioned learning can have a large effect on how you learn by thinking.

Sight and Sound. If you always read the same newspaper or magazine or the same parts of any publications, these become familiar and comfortable. If you continually listen to a certain kind of music or listen to a particular disc jockey or radio or television commentator, then what they say and play becomes familiar and comfortable to you. Almost anything that's different will be considered strange. But there is a price you may pay for being comfortable. Such familiar surroundings can prevent you from enlarging your point of view and broadening your understanding of other people and other ideas. It can prevent you from learning.

Touch, Taste, and Smell. The sense of touch accounts for your being conditioned to prefer your own bed because it feels physically more comfortable, or a favorite shirt or blouse because it not only looks good but also feels good. The sense of taste primarily conditions us to prefer certain kinds of food and drink. An Eskimo eating raw fish is doing nothing more unusual than you are by eating a hamburger. You both have been conditioned in part by your sense of taste. If as a very young child (probably up to age 4 or 5) you had changed places with the Eskimo, his or her customs would seem natural to you. The sense of smell can condition us to prefer certain kinds of food, drink, or surroundings. It can have a great impact on our choices.

The senses also provide warning signals which ensure our survival. We will get out of the way when we see a moving train, run when we hear someone yell fire, and reject food that tastes or smells bad. These same senses also determine how we will act under certain conditions. What conditions? Sometimes you are not aware that the ideas you hold and the things you do are more the result of conditioning than thinking. For example:

- How often have you heard, "You must be smart to do well in college"? Do you accept this idea? Is it true? Have you arrived at this conclusion through conscious thought or have you allowed yourself to accept something just because you have heard it so often?

- You are used to learning school material by relying mostly on rote memory, repeating things until you know them. This is how you have always studied (this is how you have conditioned yourself to study), so this is how you will study in college. Is this a valid approach? Will it help you achieve the logical thinking ability college learning requires?

- Sometimes you can be conditioned very quickly. In high school, underlining texts is usually not allowed since texts are used again and again. In college you own your texts. You may, therefore, quickly develop the habit of underlining what you believe are important text passages. Is this a good practice? Have you unknowingly assumed that text underlining is the same as studying? Is it the same?

Do these examples mean that all conditioned ideas and habits you hold regarding learning are not useful? Of course not. But some of them, such as those above, may prevent you from doing well in college.

Thinking

Our senses can also affect the learning we do through thinking.

Touch, Taste, and Smell. A doctor learns through the touch of his or her hands to note unusual lumps during a physical examination. Anything abnormal will cause the doctor to think about the nature and extent of the problem. Taste can assist a chef to ponder the state of a soup as well as help a detective determine the nature of the material found in the trunk of a car. Smell can help a detective determine the cause of a fire. So these senses can be helpful in learning by thinking, but they are really of limited value for most of the courses you will take.

Sight and Sound. The senses of sight and sound are the important ones in learning by thinking. It is obvious that through these senses you are exposed to facts, ideas, and concepts that form the basis of what is studied in college. What is not so obvious is how you may be misusing the sight and sound senses when attempting to learn college course material. Such misuse, along with some poor (conditioned) ideas about how to study in college, may prevent you from experiencing satisfaction for all your time and effort. The following section discusses some of these ideas and methods and considers how they might be preventing you from actually thinking about the material you study in college.

Some Ideas You May Hold About Learning

You probably agree that simply seeing or hearing something doesn't mean you will remember or learn it.

But what about those people who seem to read or listen to something just once and end up knowing the material and doing well on examinations? How do they do it? Are they superintelligent? That brilliant person you know may be a genius, but it is more likely that he or she has developed effective thinking techniques or has been taught such techniques. There is practically nothing in college work that requires anyone to operate at a genius level, so being a genius is of no special value in mastering normal course content. In fact, the whole subject of IQ (intelligence quotient) can cause you a lot of pain. If you know or think your IQ is low, you may feel you will never do well in college no matter how hard you try. You may even be anticipating your failure. If you know or think your IQ is average or above, you may be assuming you will do well in college with little effort. Both assumptions are almost certainly false; both can lead to a short college career. What is IQ anyway?

Intelligence Quotient

Intelligence is the ability to acquire and apply knowledge. A quotient is a number. An intelligence quotient, therefore, is a number that is a measure of your ability to acquire and apply knowledge.

An IQ score is arrived at as follows. A test is administered to groups of people of different ages. The result of this standard test establishes what the average 8-year-old (or 10-year-old, or 12-year-old, etc.) knows. For each age group these normal or average scores are set equal to 100. If your knowledge is above average for your age, you will score higher than 100. If you are below average for your age, you will score less than 100. A score of about 85 is considered slow, 100 is considered average, 120 superior, and 150 or over gifted or possible genius. Most people (about 70 percent) have scores between 84 and 116. That means most people, at least as measured by these tests, are considered neither slow nor superior. Very few people have very high numbers. Less than two people in a thousand achieve scores above 150. But what do these numbers really mean?

IQ tests are usually administered at about age 10, so the score you received then reflects how intelligent you were at that age. It doesn't tell you how smart you are now. And it certainly doesn't tell you how smart you can become. As a matter of fact, your IQ score may not even tell you how smart you were then. Consider these items:

- Your IQ will be lower if you are from a large family and your brothers and/or sisters were born close together. A new child brings zero knowledge to the family. Therefore, the average family smartness is lowered. Children already in the family are now exposed to a lower overall intellectual environment.[1] Thus your IQ may have measured not only how much you knew at age 10, but also the size of your family.

- "It seems that the growth curve of verbal intelligence rises steeply til the age of 20 and . . . continues to rise gently. This growth is not confined to the bright."[2] The older you get (remember the counting starts at about age 10), the smarter you get. And you don't have to be smart to get smart. How much have you learned since you were 10? How much more can you learn?

- "School learning appears to be paced by intelligence prior to 10 but subsequently by skills learned during that period . . .".[3] This says that the ability to learn is not just a function of your IQ. The study attitudes, skills, and habits you develop are more important.

You may not recall, but the IQ test you took when you were 10 years old was timed; that is, you were required to answer the questions within a given time period. So you were tested not only on what you knew, but also on your ability to show what you knew within a certain time. You were being tested on how smart-fast you were. What happened if you were a smart-slow person? Sorry. Your IQ score was penalized. You scored lower. In other words, if you had had more time to answer (maybe 10 minutes, maybe 20) your IQ would most likely be higher. This is one of the factors that make IQ scores suspect and one of

[1]Carol Tavis, "The End of the IQ Slump," *Psychology Today*, April 1976, pp. 69–74.
[2]Miriam E. Hebron, *Motivated Learning* (London: Methuen & Co., 1966), p. 177.
[3]Hebron, p. 37.

the reasons why you should not place emphasis on them. If having one-half hour more time can take you from being classified slow to being classified average or from average to gifted, how valid can we assume IQ scores to be? What's the big hurry? What real intellectual difference is there between someone who takes two minutes to solve a problem and someone who takes four minutes? They both attain the same result. It may even turn out that the time difference is not due to an inability to solve a problem, but to difficulties in understanding the question. This can be so especially if you are imaginative or anxious or are unable to pay attention or concentrate. The notion that because someone is quick he or she is necessarily smarter is a shaky one. Most of the problems you will face in life will afford you more than enough time to think through. This includes your study assignments and most of your college tests and examinations.

For most college students actual IQ scores may mean little or nothing. You may be unhappy because you believe your IQ is low. Then again you may be lulling yourself into a false sense of security because you believe your IQ is high. However you see yourself—top, middle, or bottom—it's important to understand a very basic idea: You have the capacity to do well in college. Regardless of possibly poor marks in high school, despite how you may feel about yourself, despite what others may say or think about you, know this one thing—you have the capacity to learn.[4]

If just taking in information (by reading or listening) or having a high IQ are not the only factors in learning new material, then what else is?

Is It Memorization?

One of the really sad comments you hear on campuses goes like this: "I'm sure glad that test is over; now I can forget all that stuff." Maybe you have said something like that yourself. Consider the foolishness in such a statement. You have gone through years of high school and finally received your diploma. You may have gone through a frustrating college application and selection process. You have spent hundreds if not thousands of dollars to start college; you may even have gone into debt. You may have left home and traveled thousands of miles to get to

[4]"A study of the experience of special risk students at Williams College has provided evidence for the argument that academic records and test scores are not always the best criteria for judging a person's college potential. Over a ten-year period, Williams admitted 358 students who did not meet the college's normal academic standards for acceptance but demonstrated strengths in other ways, such as leadership or nonacademic skills. The students showed a general upward pattern of performance during their time at Williams: 71% of them graduated, compared with the college's norm of about 85%. On the basis of the study, the college plans to continue admitting such 'risk' students. . . ." ("Selecting College Material," *New York Times,* April 4, 1976, Section 4, p. 7.)

your college and gone through the turmoil of registering for courses and purchasing texts, notebooks, pencils, and pens. Finally, you have spent hours attending class and reading texts which contain new ideas and information. And then it turns out—unbelievably—that apparently the only reason you went through all that trouble is so you could now have the presumed luxury of forgetting what you learned. Isn't that kind of wierd? It's sort of like saying, "I can't wait to get that car so I can trade it in" or "I can't wait to go to that party so it will be over" or (if this were possible) "I can't wait to be born so I can die." Why accomplish something if your goal is to deny the accomplishment? If you agree that the main goal of your learning is to become competent, then why would you want to forget your competency? That's what is actually meant when you say, "Now I can forget what I learned." But wait a moment, maybe you really haven't "learned" anything. Maybe that's why you are so willing to give it up. Maybe you have confused learning with memorizing.

Memorizing is the act of storing in the mind ideas and information received through your senses. There are three elements to the memory process. They are *receipt, storage,* and *retrieval.* Information is received through the senses. It is then stored for long or short periods of time in the brain. It is retrieved from the brain, to one degree or another, when the information is to be used. Probably the reason you are so willing to give up information is that your study experiences with receipt and storage have been frustrating, time-consuming, and pointless. In short, the methods you are using may be unattractive and distasteful. They may be inefficient. The methods may not really help you learn in the sense of becoming competent.

ROTE MEMORY

When something is uninteresting or unimportant or when we do not understand it, we sometimes tend to rely on rote memory. Rote memory is substituted for thinking when (1) there is no organization to the material, no way in which it all comes together and makes sense, or (2) we cannot see that there is a way of imposing order or organization to the material, or (3) we don't want to take the time to think about and organize the material. Rote means repetition without thinking, saying things over and over until an impression has been made on the mind. In learning by rote, you acquire a set of words in a mechanical, programmed way, much like a robot. This type of learning fits the definition of conditioning. You will recall that learning by conditioning requires a minimum of thinking. Learning by rote is a way of temporarily conditioning your mind without having to really think.

There are two standard techniques for learning by rote. One, described above, is repetition. The other is called *mnemonics*. Mnemonics is a method of creating or identifying a word, phrase, rhyme, or object that is made to represent other information. For example, the rhyme that begins, "Thirty days hath September, April, June, and November" is a device for remembering the number of days in each month. An invented word such as *roygbiv* is meant to stand for the first letter of the ordered colors in the light spectrum (*r*ed, *o*range, *y*ellow, etc.). There are others. Many commercial memory courses are based on some sort of association device such as a mnemonic; you remember the special mnemonic and, after practice (repetition), you remember the related information. Such devices can be effective memory tools in certain situations, but they are very much limited for the following basic reasons:

- They apply mostly to remembering facts. Therefore their use is limited to the least important of the educational aims— knowledge. They are of little or no help in attaining the aims of comprehension, application, evaluation, analysis, and synthesis. Achieving these aims is, of course, a large reason for your attending college.
- There is a limit to how many such devices you can use successfully. If you incorrectly recall one letter in the made-up word or one line in a rhyme, you will be thrown off because you are responding mechanically.

So the problem with rote memory is that it does not require you to understand. It represents the lowest form of learning. One rote memorization can be mixed up with another. It won't stay with you. It takes away the inherent reward in learning. It is what some students confuse with studying. If you rely solely on such approaches, you will have cause to say, "I'm sure glad that test is over; now I can forget all that stuff."

Is Writing Things Down the Answer?

At this point you might say, "Instead of just relying on my memory, perhaps if I wrote things down, perhaps if I took some notes, maybe that would help." This is a logical next step. Perhaps writing things down will allow you to make sense of things. After all, aren't you more involved with the material when you write it down? Aren't you processing thoughts when you write things out?

It depends. Note taking is usually accepted as a good idea during a class lecture. You take notes when something strikes you as important, when your teacher emphasizes a point, or when he or she writes something on the board. You may take notes because you assume you must be missing something if everybody else is writing and you're not.

It's also possible that your idea of note taking is to turn yourself into a human tape machine and record everything. You may be so intent on this that if the teacher says, "Please stop writing for a moment, I want you to look at this naked gorilla I've brought with me," your notes will reflect, "Please stop writing for a moment, I want you to look at this naked gorilla I've brought with me." Sounds silly? It and sillier things end up in notebooks. It is even possible that you will learn less by taking notes than by just trying to follow what your teacher or the other students have to say.

Consider these items:

- Three groups of college students listened to a 14-minute lecture. One group was instructed to take no notes, another to take detailed notes, and the last to take their normal notes. Retention testing after one week and after five weeks showed no learning difference among the groups.[5]
- Two groups of college students listened to a 30-minute lecture. One group was told to take no notes and the other to take notes after the lecture. A true–false test given very soon after and another given three weeks later showed no learning difference between the groups.[6]
- "Students who listened to a lecture and took no notes at all performed better on recall tests immediately after the lecture and two weeks later than did students who were instructed to take either detailed or outline notes."[7]

At this point you may have concluded that college note taking is the greatest put-on since the circus fat lady sat down. But before you dump your notebooks, maybe you should cast a critical eye at these experiments. Maybe you should question the results. You might start by questioning the skills and abilities of the participants. Were the students who took no notes super-bright students with excellent memories and therefore able to score as well as those who did take notes? If this were so, the results would not be valid. Were those who took notes slow students and therefore able to bring themselves up by taking notes? If this were so, then the value of note taking would have been proven, not apparently disproved. Were the material and the questions so simple that whether or not one took notes didn't matter since the students already knew the material? You could continue questioning the results that showed note taking to be of no apparent

[5]Michael J. A. Howe, *Understanding School Learning* (New York: Harper & Row, 1972), p. 62.

[6]Howe, p. 62.

[7]Howe, p. 63.

value. If you eliminate these possible (but not probable) conditions, you are left without an explanation for a result that appears to go against common sense. But the chances are these students were representative of other students. The chances are that the material was new to them and that the questions were valid. How then can it be possible that taking notes is of no use?

Well, maybe something has been overlooked. Maybe there is a valid explanation. Is it possible that the note-taking methods used were not good ones? Maybe the notes were put down in a nonsystematic way resulting in confusion, not understanding. Is it also possible that the act of note taking itself is not what is important, but that it is only the first step in a more important process? Is it possible the note takers did no better than the others because they didn't *do* anything with the notes after they took them, but just let them sit there on the page, graphite dust trapped in paper fibers? Is it possible that they didn't go back to their notes, didn't take advantage of the fact that they had notes to study, didn't attempt to process the notes in a way that would be meaningful to them? It's not only possible but it is also very probable. It accounts for the seemingly backward results of the experiments.

What About Text Underlining?

Underlining passages in texts is a way of identifying what is important to think about. The act of underlining in itself doesn't help you think. It may even prevent you from thinking. When you underline a text, you are saying: "This looks important. I'd better underline it so I can study it later." But sometimes "later" never comes and you have really wasted your time. Underlining a text is equivalent to taking notes in class. In both instances you are making a record of what you think is important to study. The comments made above about class notes also apply to text underlining. They are both of limited value unless you actively process in an organized fashion the records you have made.

Recognition

What then can you conclude about the items discussed above? It can be summed up this way:

- While some minimum level of intelligence is required for college level work, intelligence by itself is not the most important factor for college learning. It may be the least important.
- While it is obvious that things must be remembered, relying on rote memory is the least useful approach. It is also very time-consuming. It offers no lasting reward for your efforts. You want to forget what you have rote-learned as soon as possible

because the process itself is distasteful and because you have to replace it with other rote-learned material.

- The physical act of note taking or text underlining is in itself of small significance in helping you learn.[8]
- The physical act of note taking or text underlining is just a first step in learning. If notes or underlining are to be of any value, they must be processed by you in a meaningful way that will help you understand, retain, and apply what you are learning.

None of the above methods allows you to organize what you study in your own fashion. They all remove the possibility of creative thought. They inhibit your actively participating in learning the material. They do not create conditions that favor persistence. In other words, misunderstanding and misuse of IQ, rote memorization, note taking, and text underlining can take the enjoyment out of studying by removing the possibility of your achieving a sense of accomplishment.

Implications for College

So far, IQ, rote memorizing, note taking, and text underlining have been discussed as they relate to studying. You have seen they can sometimes be helpful in remembering facts. But they do not help develop the ability to comprehend, apply, evaluate, analyze, or synthesize what you study. These competency factors together with developing awareness and flexibility represent why you are studying at the college level. Therefore, you want to develop methods of thinking and studying that will give you a sense of accomplishment while enabling you to achieve all your educational aims. The question then becomes, "What are those methods and how do I apply them?"

Figure 6–1 contains the basic elements associated with college learning. It shows what it takes to be an effective and efficient learner in college. You can apply these elements to a four-year college program or to one course you take in evening college. All its elements still

[8]The idea that physical note taking is of some value is suggested by the following experiment. Students listened to a passage and were asked to take notes. A week later they were asked to write out what was in the passage. The student-produced passages were then compared with the students' notes. The results showed there was a 34 percent chance of a student's recalling what was put in the notes but only a 5 percent chance of recalling what was not in the notes. In other words, the student was about seven times more likely to remember something he or she had written down than something he or she had only heard but not written down. Another interpretation is that if the student took notes, he or she would remember 34 percent of what was in the notes (not 34 percent of what he or she heard). (Howe, p. 51.)

Figure 6–1
College Learning Requirements

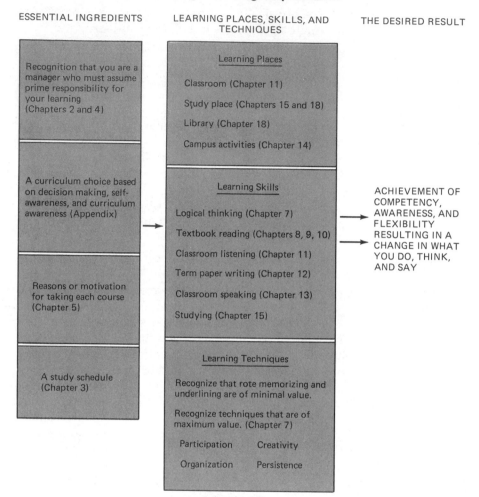

ESSENTIAL INGREDIENTS

LEARNING PLACES, SKILLS, AND TECHNIQUES

THE DESIRED RESULT

Recognition that you are a manager who must assume prime responsibility for your learning (Chapters 2 and 4)

A curriculum choice based on decision making, self-awareness, and curriculum awareness (Appendix)

Reasons or motivation for taking each course (Chapter 5)

A study schedule (Chapter 3)

Learning Places

Classroom (Chapter 11)

Study place (Chapters 15 and 18)

Library (Chapter 18)

Campus activities (Chapter 14)

Learning Skills

Logical thinking (Chapter 7)

Textbook reading (Chapters 8, 9, 10)

Classroom listening (Chapter 11)

Term paper writing (Chapter 12)

Classroom speaking (Chapter 13)

Studying (Chapter 15)

Learning Techniques

Recognize that rote memorizing and underlining are of minimal value.

Recognize techniques that are of maximum value. (Chapter 7)

Participation   Creativity

Organization   Persistence

ACHIEVEMENT OF COMPETENCY, AWARENESS, AND FLEXIBILITY RESULTING IN A CHANGE IN WHAT YOU DO, THINK, AND SAY

apply. Compare and contrast it with conditioned learning. You will see that most conditioned learning does not require the kind of preparations and operations required by organized thinking. Yet you may be approaching your college learning holding old ideas and using study methods that you have conditioned yourself to accept.

To learn is to think in an organized fashion while achieving all your educational aims. This process requires the development of useful learning skills. These skills include classroom listening and questioning and textbook reading and studying. There are certain ideas and approaches that can help you listen in class or read and study a text. These are participation, organization, persistence, and creativity, and they are discussed in the next chapter.

Summary
We learn through conditioning, thinking, or a combination of the two. Conditioned learning requires little thought. Thinking requires little emotion or physical action. Conditioned learning results in our acquiring personal preferences and habits for people, places, things, and ideas. Some of these conditioned responses, as related to college going, may include the belief a high IQ is necessary for college success, that the only way to learn is through rote memorization, that simply taking notes is sufficient for learning, and that underlining passages in texts is equivalent to studying. All these ideas can hurt you in college. But conditioning is an important process in establishing proper study habits (study times, places, and methods). Such habits can free you to learn academic content (facts, ideas, principles) through thinking.

College learning requires that certain thinking skills and techniques be developed and applied. The skills are classroom listening and questioning, textbook reading and studying. The techniques are participation, organization, persistence, and creativity. These elements are discussed in the following chapters.

KEY TERMS

Learning	IQ	Note taking
Human senses	Rote memorizing	Underlining
Conditioning	Repetition	Learning requirements
Thinking	Mnemonics	

REVIEW QUESTIONS

1. Describe each of the key terms above.
2. What is meant by conditioned learning?
3. What is learning by thinking?
4. What is the lowest form of learning? Why?
5. Why can rote memory be considered a form of conditioned learning?
6. Identify and describe those elements necessary for effective college learning.

DISCUSSION AND APPLICATION QUESTIONS

1. Identify three opinions, habits, or perferences that you hold due to conditioned learning: (a) in your family life, and (b) in your school life.
2. Can you identify five factors which describe why someone who is "smart enough" to attend college may nevertheless do poorly in college?

3. Why may learning by rote actually prevent you from learning course material?
4. Describe why just the physical act of taking notes in class or copying or underlining passages from a textbook results in very little learning.
5. With respect to the educational aims discussed in Chapter 5, what is the major drawback of rote memorization, plain note taking, or just text underlining?

CHAPTER 780

LEARNING TO THINK LOGICALLY

BASIC IDEAS
- "In a sense . . . all human thought is a form of play."[1]
- You cannot play unless you participate.
- Organization and persistence lead to participation—and learning.

KEY POINTS
- When related to thinking, what does participation mean?
- What is meant by organization and why is it important?
- What does being persistent have to do with learning?

    Imagine you're watching a motion picture in a movie house. However, the conditions are unusual. You are wearing special glasses that allow you to see and hear only one of the many people in the movie. After about fifteen minutes how interested would you be in continuing to watch the movie? Probably not very. Do you know why? "Of course I do," you might answer. "I can't see or hear anybody else so I can't make sense out of the movie. If I don't have the whole picture, how can I possibly understand what is going on and how can I hope to keep interested?"

    Your present thinking, reading, and study methods may be equivalent to watching a movie under the conditions described above. You start reading a chapter and after about ten to fifteen minutes— since none of it seems to make much sense—you stop. It's just too boring. This chapter will discuss ideas you can bring to any learning/ study situation. These ideas or foundation techniques are participation, organization, persistence, and creativity.

[1] J. Bronowski, *The Ascent of Man* (Boston: Little Brown, 1973), p. 432.

Participation
Have you ever watched someone play tennis, basketball, or volleyball? Do you remember listening to one of your teachers clearly describe how to determine a mathematical quantity through use of a formula? Have you observed someone shape a teapot from a chunk of moist clay? At some point in these experiences you might have said, "I can do that." Well, you are right. You can—but usually not by just observing or listening. You know from your own experience that you learn more easily and fully by actually participating. You didn't learn to ride a bike, drive a car, or find square roots just by listening and/or observing. Whether for a mechanical skill, an intellectual effort, or a combination of both, participation leads to knowledge and understanding. But how does participation apply to college learning?

You participate when you: apply the skills of reading, listening, speaking, and writing; engage the assistance of teachers through class questions and office meetings; and engage the assistance of other students through discussions and study sessions. But most important, you participate when you think in a manner that requires you to organize what you listen to or read about.

Participation is especially important when the subject matter increases in difficulty, as it does at the college level. For example, consider the three circles in Figure 7–1. If asked to arrange them in a logical pattern, you could do so with little effort. Some, but not a lot of participation (thinking), is necessary. You might, for example, choose to arrange them from small circle through large circle or from large through small. But what would happen if you were asked to logically arrange the forms in Figure 7–2? What order would you choose for these figures? Why? Is there only one correct order? There is no way to solve this problem unless you actively participate. You must think

Figure 7–1
How Would You Logically Arrange
These Three Circles?

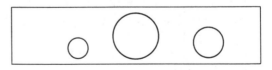

Figure 7–2
How Would You Logically Arrange These Figures?

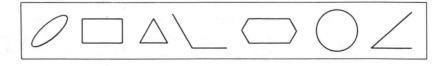

more deeply about the various relationships and then identify some reasonable order. You may even find the need to write things out to assist your thought processes. To say, "I could do it if I wanted to or if I really had to" is not the same as doing it.

The same requirement to participate exists when you attempt to understand and organize ideas. And learning and using ideas is what college is primarily about. If you are to achieve competency, awareness, and flexibility, you cannot be a spectator in your own education. If all human thought is a form of play, then you must be the central player in the game you play with your head.

To play well you must know the rules. The first rule is to participate. A way to participate is to write things down. The second rule is to organize what you study into some pattern that makes sense to you. Using pencil and paper to organize what you study is one way to directly involve yourself. The importance of organization in helping you learn and enjoy yourself at the same time cannot be overemphasized.

Organization Concepts and Practice

Organization is figuring out exactly what needs to be done and how these activities relate to each other—how things should go together.

This need to see how things go together is basic to human nature. It is as powerful as the need to have food, shelter, and love. It is a need that you can take advantage of when studying. When there is order we feel comfortable; we are not upset or threatened. When order is absent we are confused. The need for order is so strong you will go to great lengths to restore or attain it if it is missing. If your attempts at achieving order fail, the result is likely to be frustration and anger, the degree determined by the activity and its importance to you. Consider the following:

One day you look in the mirror and see a fat face. You close in on the mirror, back away from the mirror, try catching yourself in the mirror. None of it works. You finally admit to yourself that you are 20 pounds overweight. At this moment of realization you have caused an imbalance. You may decide that the new you is not all that bad and in fact you feel rather comfortable. As long as your clothes still fit, you may decide to do nothing. If you make this decision, you have brought back to balance a situation first unbalanced by your look in the mirror. Another way of restoring a sense of order in this case is to return to your former weight through dieting. This decision, from a personal organization standpoint, is just as valid as the first. The point is that what you do is not as important as the realization that you will do *something* to restore a sense of organized existence.

Here's another example. Someone enters your room and says, "This place looks like a set for a disaster movie—after the disaster. Why don't you put things in order?" You say, "I can find anything I want; as far as I'm concerned things are in order." People have different views of what order is. What counts is not whether you organize and understand things as someone else does. What counts is that *you* organize and understand things. If the same objective is accomplished (efficiently finding something or understanding something), then the organizational approach used is not important. What is important is that the approach makes sense to you. But notice what is at the center of both points of view: being organized.

Perhaps the most telling example of imposing order involves your college studies. How many times have you been in the following situation? You're studying for an exam. You find the material difficult: you can't see what it's all about, can't relate one part of a chapter to another, and can't afford not to study because an exam is coming up. You decide to start underlining or felt-pen-lining through words, terms, or sentences that seem to be important. After that you may decide to start memorizing some of the things you underlined. Do you know why you employ these techniques in such situations? Consider this. Since the material doesn't seem to have any order, you try doing something that, however ineffective, gives you a feeling of imposing order. You really don't understand the material or have not given yourself time to understand. But your sense of organization tells you that when you study, something should be happening. Since what's happening is not your understanding of the material, you make something else happen. You underline. Your pencil goes for a ride, your textbook looks like someone has studied it, and you somehow feel better about the whole thing. The situation called for some activity to give it a sense of order, and that's what you provided. But the chances are you learned very little, because you could see no sense of order in what you were studying. And it is organization that is at the center of learning by thinking.

You can take advantage of this natural need to organize, and use it to learn to think logically. You can then use your logical thinking skills when reading, listening, writing, speaking, and studying. Learning techniques that assist organized thinking is not difficult. Unfortunately, many students are so busy "studying," they don't realize there are effective and efficient techniques they can easily adopt. If you had to, you yourself could derive techniques for organized thinking. But to save time here are some ideas to consider.

Organizing Objects

The following exercises will allow you to perform some simple organizing tasks.

ORGANIZING YOUR LEARNING: SKILLS YOU NEED

Exercise 7–1. Some Circles

Figure 7–3 shows the three circles presented earlier. They might be arranged as shown in Figure 7–4. Use the empty space in Figure 7–4 to enter the next logical arrangement. Notice that whether shown horizontally or vertically, the objects progress from small to large or large to small circles. Notice also that you really cannot say that one arrangement (answer) is better than another. Each is logical, each is organized. Figure 7–5 shows some other approaches that also qualify as being organized. Did you assume these circles could not be slanted or were solid objects and therefore could not be placed one within the other? False assumptions can prevent you from seeing order where it might otherwise exist.

Figure 7–3
Three Circles

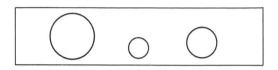

Figure 7–4
Three Circles—Several Arrangements

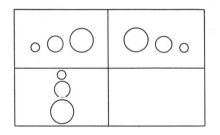

Figure 7–5
Three Circles—Several Other Arrangements

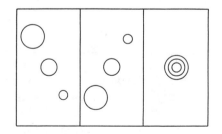

Exercise 7–2. Some Circles and Triangles

Now let's add to this organization game by introducing some more elements, shown in Figure 7–6. These six figures may be logically arranged as in Figure 7–7. Can you draw some other logical arrangements in the space provided? Remember that while there are clearly some incorrect approaches in arrangement, there is no one correct approach (answer). The only question that applies is, "Is there a logical pattern to the arrangement?"

Figure 7–6
Three Circles and Three Triangles

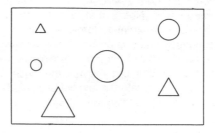

Figure 7–7
Three Circles and Three Triangles—
How Else Can You Logically Arrange Them?

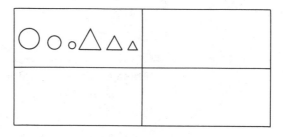

Figure 7–8
Three Circles and Three Triangles—
Another Arrangement

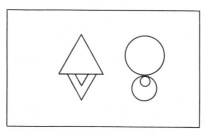

Some patterns may be more complex than others but they may still qualify as organized patterns. For example, see Figure 7–8. Of course, the simpler the pattern, the easier it is to understand. It is most important when arranging organized patterns that you use one or more approaches you understand and personally prefer. If your pattern meets the tests of logical arrangement, then it is acceptable for promoting understanding and remembering. What are the tests of logical arrangement of thought? They are really very simple:

- First you group things or ideas based on their similarities or differences. Sometimes it helps to concentrate more on differences.

- Then you arrange these groupings according to main and subordinate relationships.

In Figure 7–7 the circles, because they are similar to each other and different from the triangles, have been grouped together. The same idea applies to the grouped triangles. The circles were then grouped from large to small (from main to subordinate). The same arrangement was followed for the triangles. The result is not only organized, it is organized in a consistent fashion: large to small circles, then large to small triangles. Consistency is important since it allows systematic analysis. Being consistent really means staying organized as you proceed from the main elements to the subordinate elements.

Exercise 7–3. Can You Organize These Figures?
In your notebook arrange all the items in Figure 7–2 into at least three different organized patterns. Describe why you chose your arrangements. Remember to use the two tests of logical arrangement described above.

Organizing Ideas

You might say now: "Well, the above exercises are okay for organizing pictures of circles and triangles—but what about ideas? I have to learn ideas and related facts in college. And they are not as easy to arrange as pictures." Ah, but they are. The same basic rules that apply to arranging circles and triangles also apply to organizing ideas. The exercises in this section will teach you how to organize ideas.

Exercise 7–4. Rock Music
To start simply, Figure 7–9 contains three figures, but associated with each figure is a corresponding idea. You can see in Figure 7–1 several ways the circles can be arranged. By simply substituting the ideas for the circles, the ideas can be arranged as in Figure 7–10. Notice these are all logical arrangements that follow a pattern. Whether to show ideas horizontally or vertically is a choice you, as the arranger, can make. All the arrangements in Figure 7–10 progress:

Figure 7–9
Three Ideas

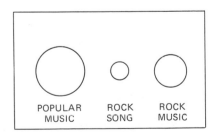

Figure 7–10
Arranging the Three Ideas

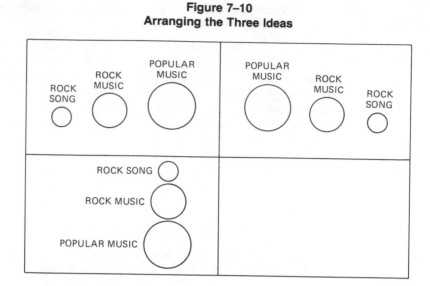

- From a small idea (the *specific* statement, rock song) to a larger idea (a more *general* statement, popular music, which includes the smaller idea of rock song), or
- From a large idea (popular music) to a smaller idea (rock music, which is part of popular music).

Use the empty space in Figure 7–10 to enter the next logical arrangement.

Exercise 7–5.   Popular and Classical Music

Now let's add to this game of organizing some more ideas. Arranging the ideas in Figure 7–11 can follow the same patterns used for the circles and triangles. For example:

Figure 7–11
Six Ideas

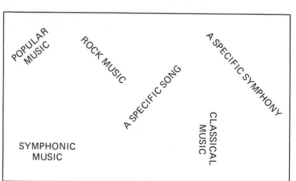

ORGANIZING YOUR LEARNING: SKILLS YOU NEED

Group A	Group B	Group C
Popular Music	Popular Music	_____
Rock Music	Classical Music	_____
A Specific Rock Song	Rock Music	_____
Classical Music	Symphonic Music	_____
Symphonic Music	A Specific Rock Song	_____
A Specific Symphony	A Specific Symphony	_____

In Column C enter a third arrangement.

When discussing or studying ideas, it is usually helpful to start with a main idea and then list the associated subordinate ideas below it, as in Group A above. Group A probably represents a greater sense of organization than Group B. As titles for related ideas, "Group A" and "Group B" are not very descriptive. A more helpful title would be a general term that includes or represents all the listed ideas. In this case the term "music" would be a good substitute.

Notice that the pattern in Group A follows a whole-to-part approach that is repeated halfway through the list when a new major idea (classical music) appears. Many classroom lectures and textbook chapters follow the whole-to-part approach. In some instances the reverse approach is used: first is a discussion of the component or subordinate ideas, leading up to the general main idea.

Organizing Techniques You Can Use

There are several techniques you can use to help organize the thoughts and ideas you hear in class or read in a text. These include:

- Dot/Dash listings
- Topic outlines
- Stick or family tree diagrams
- Block diagrams

This section gives some examples of how these formats can be applied to various groupings.

Dot/Dash Listings

Here is an example of a dot/dash listing:

Types of Music
- Popular Music
  - Rock Music
  - A Specific Rock Song
- Classical Music
  - Symphonic Music
  - A Specific Symphony

The advantages of such an ordered listing are: first, the heading provides an overall idea of what the subject is all about; second, the main ideas (popular music and classical music) stand out visually and are therefore easy to recognize; and third, such an ordered indented arrangement allows you to easily check whether you have correctly grouped related ideas.

Exercise 7–6. Separating Large and Small Ideas
Apply the concepts of organized thinking and prepare a dot/dash listing for each of these groups of terms. Make sure each listing has a heading. You can use the same term within a list more than once.

a. head
   palm
   eyes
   hand
   ears
   fingers

b. adult
   female
   child
   male

c. baseball
   periods
   hockey
   bat
   innings
   puck

Dot/dash listings are useful for class note taking, but they allow only two degrees of division—a dot followed by a string of subordinate dashes. If under popular music you wanted to discuss country and western music, you would be limited to using a dash. You could employ a third symbol such as an asterisk, but after a while this could prove confusing. A more workable approach in such a case is to employ the topic outline.

Topic Outlines

Here is an example of a topic outline:

Types of Music

I. Popular Music
  A. Rock Music
    1. Elec Tricity
    2. Galaxy

B. Country and Western Music
1. Don't Say Goodbye to All Those Hellos
2. A Girl Named Irving

II. Classical Music
A. Symphonic Music
1. Beethoven's Fifth Symphony
2. Respighi's Brazilian Overture
B. Operatic Music
1. La Bohème
2. Madama Butterfly

In a topic outline each idea or topic heading is separately and uniquely identified. As in the dot/dash approach, main ideas are systematically separated from subordinate ideas. Ideas of similar weight carry similar identifiers. For example, the ideas represented by identifiers I and II are of equal logical importance. So are the ideas represented by A and B in each section, and so are 1 and 2 in each section.

A feature of the topic outline which aids organized thinking is that there are always at least two subdivisions. For example:

A			A	
	1			1
	2	Is permitted, but not		2
B				
	1			
	2			

A			A	
	1			1
	2	Is permitted, but not		
B			B	

In other words, where there is a I there must be a II; for an A there must be a B; for a 1, a 2. The absence of a corresponding topic heading usually indicates that the thought is incomplete or that the arrangement is illogical.

The topic outline is wonderfully flexible. You can make it as long or as short as you want. You extend the outline, and emphasize each idea, to the point where you are satisfied that all important items have been covered. You can also approach the arrangement of thoughts or the study of subjects from different points of view. For example, if you wanted to think about music chronologically, you could organize your thoughts as shown on the left below. If you wanted a geographical or space-related approach, the sequence on the right could be used.

Types of Music	*Types of Music*
(Time Arrangement)	*(Space Arrangement)*
I Ancient Music	I Asia
II Early Tunes	II Africa
III Middle Ages	III Europe
IV Seventeenth,	IV The Americas
Eighteenth Centuries	
V Nineteenth,	
Twentieth Centuries	

The approach you select depends upon the nature of the subject matter and your intent. What is fun in all this is that there is no one right way of organizing ideas. As the organizer, you are free to create whatever pattern you wish, provided you observe these simple topic outline rules:

1. Group ideas (topic headings) based on their similarities or differences.
2. Arrange the topic headings according to main and subordinate relationships.
3. Identify each topic heading (using a combination of letters and numbers) in a consistent fashion.

Exercise 7–7. Arranging Ideas
Select one of the three groups of terms in Exercise 7–6 and prepare a topic outline. Before starting the outline, decide on its title. Remember to use the three-step topic outline approach described above.

Exercise 7–8. Outlining Main Ideas
Prepare a topic outline that represents the five basic management functions.

Exercise 7–9. Outlining Main and Subordinate Ideas
Prepare a topic outline that represents the five basic management functions. This time subordinate your outline to show at least two related ideas for each main idea. Make sure your outline has a title.

Exercise 7–10. Starting from Scratch
Each of the following terms represents the title of a topic outline. Create a separate topic outline for each title: (a) The Automobile, (b) Learning to Play the Piano, (c) Dreaming, (d) Love, (e) Getting Dressed to Go Out, (f) Dancing, (g) Studying. Remember to use the three-step topic outline approach described above.

Exercise 7–11. Outlining a Newspaper Article
Read a newspaper or magazine article. (a) Prepare a topic outline based on the article. (b) How many main ideas are there? (c) Which ideas do you think are most important?

Exercise 7–12. Providing Your Personal Touch

Assume you are the reporter who wrote the article in Exercise 7–11. Show how you would outline the story differently to stress a different main idea.

Stick Diagrams

The idea behind the stick diagram is exactly the same as that of the outline. The only real difference is that the diagram starts to resemble a picture rather than just a listing of topic headings. See Figure 7–12.

Figure 7–12
Stick Diagram Examples

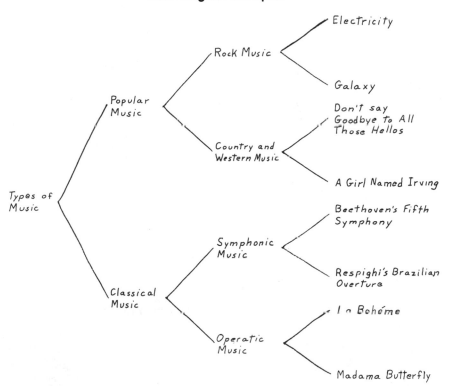

You can describe any subject matter through a series of related sticks. Like topic outlines, stick diagrams have a main theme and associated subordinated ideas. All main ideas are divided in a repeated organized logical pattern.

Exercise 7–13. Changing to a Stick Diagram

Take the outline created in Exercise 7–9 and convert it to a stick diagram.

Exercise 7–14. Diagramming the Government

Prepare a stick diagram that represents the branches of the United States federal government.

Block
Diagrams

Block diagrams are really stick diagrams with boxes around them. For example, Figures 7–13 and 7–14 illustrate horizontal block diagrams.

Figure 7–13
A Horizontal Block Diagram

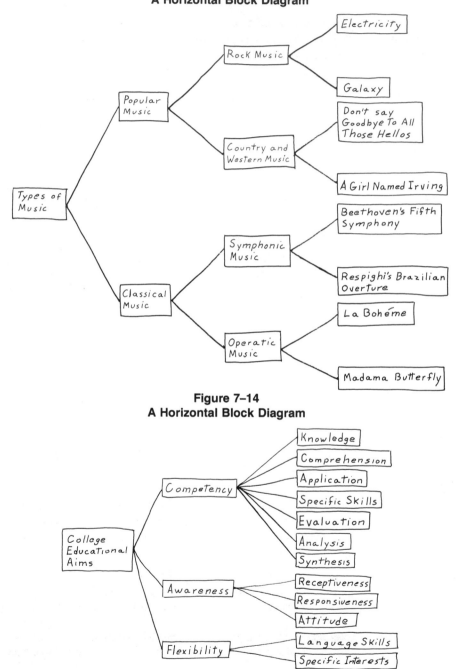

Figure 7–14
A Horizontal Block Diagram

ORGANIZING YOUR LEARNING: SKILLS YOU NEED

Their vertical equivalent can be seen in Figures 7–15 and 7–16.

Figure 7–15
A Vertical Block Diagram

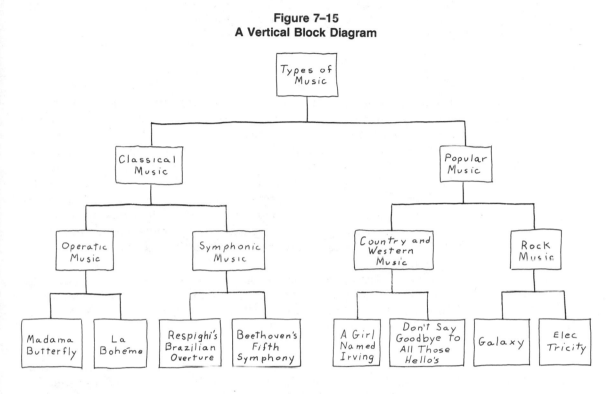

Figure 7–16
A Vertical Block Diagram

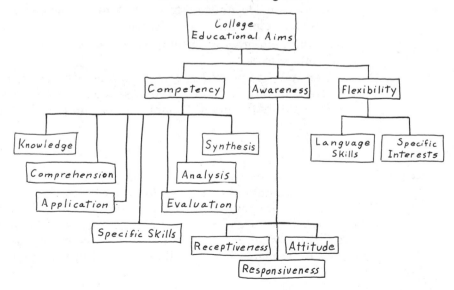

Exercise 7–15. Diagramming the Classroom
Observe your classroom. (a) Prepare a block diagram that represents the furnishings, materials, and equipment in the room. (b) Did you arrange your diagram on the basis of time, space, or quality? (c) Repeat step (a), but this time use a different arrangement.

Using The Organizers

The dot/dash listing, topic outline, stick diagram, and block diagram can help you take notes in class, study those notes, study a text, or arrange your own ideas for special projects such as term papers. Organizers allow you to participate when you study. They enhance your ability to analyze what you are learning. They provide a framework for associating and thus remembering important related facts. Since the ideas progress logically, you rely less on rote memory and more on your natural ability to logically reconstruct a body of knowledge. Once you get the main ideas down, the associated ones often follow. (See the Discussion Questions at the end of this chapter.)

The particular organizing format you choose is not important. What is important is that you do choose. Pick or develop formats with which you feel most comfortable. With consistent application you will accomplish at least these things:

- You will see the overall structure that lies behind all the subjects you study. This awareness promotes interest since it minimizes the feeling you are studying some vague area that does not appear to relate to anything.
- You will provide a mental framework for remembering not only main ideas but their associated facts.
- You will gain practice in thinking at the higher levels required for college work.
- When you get involved in this technique, you may actually find yourself having fun. You will realize then what is meant by the statement, "All human thought is a form of play."

Persistence

When you attend college, you study a portion of mankind's accumulated knowledge. It is to be hoped that you will not only study the best of what has gone before, you will also study what particularly interests you. In this way, you, as an individual, may add to mankind's accumulated knowledge. But it is unreasonable to expect that you will easily absorb difficult concepts that have taken thousands of years to evolve. That is where the idea of persistence comes in.

Persistence means sticking with something until you master it. You have to allow yourself enough time and reflection to think about and understand all that has gone before, all that you are studying. This is why it is necessary that you devote sufficient study time to your subjects. Persistence is not just a matter of devoting enough time, however. It is also a matter of spacing your study sessions and taking advantage of something called the learning curve.

Spaced Repetition

Spaced repetition means repeatedly allowing yourself to think about the material. It means giving yourself enough chances to learn. This could involve studying a chapter twice in one sitting or studying it three times a day for a week. Whatever it may be, if you repeat your spaced efforts at organized thinking often enough, you will find that most material, even difficult material, can be understood.

Learning and studying become more attractive when you take the pressure off yourself. Expecting to learn in one sitting is not realistic. So don't burden yourself with impossible tasks. Use spaced repetition to help you learn more easily and completely.

Learning Curve

When you engage in spaced repetition, the material gets progressively easier to learn. This process is called the *learning curve*. It is a characteristic of how humans learn. Your curve of understanding goes up the more you are exposed to something. You will be relying on what you previously learned to build new learning.

Other than persistently studying in an organized fashion, you don't have to do anything special to take advantage of the learning curve. If this sounds like you are getting something for nothing, you almost are. The only price you pay is being persistent.

Creativity

To create is to produce something new as a result of your own thoughts or actions. Everyone has the potential to be creative; in fact sometimes you can't help being creative. Creativity, in short, is making up things or activities. Sometimes silly things (Totally bandaged patient to doctor: "Why did you become a doctor?" Doctor to patient: "Begauze my mummy wanted me to"). Other times bigger ideas are discovered or created (Newton's law of gravity, Einstein's theory of relativity, the Whopper Burger).

What Has Creativity To Do With College Learning?

Figures 7–14 and 7–16 show the educational aims associated with attaining competency. As related to thinking, these aims can also be shown as in Figure 7–17. Simply learning facts (having knowledge) is the lowest form of learning and requires the least amount of organized thinking. The basic reason for attending college is not to know and comprehend facts; it is to develop the ability to apply, evaluate, and analyze facts and their associated ideas.

Another view of Figure 7–17 is shown in Figure 7–18. What do these figures have to do with college learning? Their implication is clear. They show if you want to be creative you must first work your way up through the intermediate stages of application, evaluation, and analysis. When you engage in these activities, you are thinking at the higher levels, the very levels that most college learning is concerned with. They are the levels in which you will have to become competent if you are to perform well in college and out.

Figure 7–17
Thinking Your Way Up

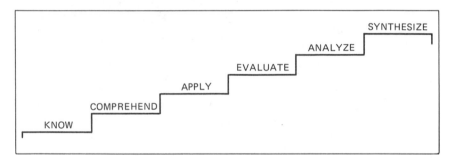

Figure 7–18
Creative Synthesis

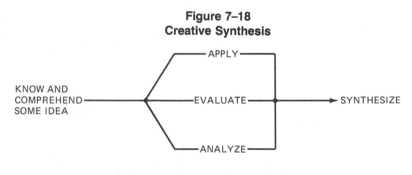

If you know and comprehend some idea, you can then either apply, evaluate, or analyze the idea.
These three activities, individually or in combination, can lead to creative systhesis.

Aids to Creativity

You might be saying to yourself, "Hey, if I have to rely on being creative, I'll never make it through college. The only creative thing I've ever done is grow hair on my head." You do not have to be "smart" to be creative. Most everyone has the ability to create. If you can prepare a topic outline, you can be creative. So the first aid to creativity is to recognize that you actually are capable of creative thought.

A second aid is to develop skills for comprehending, applying, evaluating, and analyzing what you hear in class and read in a text. What are these skills that assist creativity? You are in for a pleasant surprise. They are the same three skills discussed in this chapter—participation, organization, and persistence. You probably agree that these ideas are not difficult to comprehend or apply; therefore it is not difficult to be creative.

A third aid is to work with another person or a group of people. The reason is clear: With more people there are more chances that someone will think his or her way up to the level of synthesis, or help another to do so.

Creativity and Studying

Creativity plays an especially important role in relation to studying. One creative act on your part (for example, organizing the ideas in a text chapter into your own handwritten topic outline or block diagram) may save you hours of mechanical memorizing or of directionless underlining. Most times the structure or organization of what you hear in class or read in a text is clear. All you need do to promote understanding and retention, then, is to:

- First recognize that it is clear.
- Create your own outline or diagram of the material with emphasis on the main ideas and most important facts.
- Test your ability to recall the outlines or diagrams you create.

(Procedures to accomplish these three steps are discussed in Chapter 15.)

Sometimes what you hear in class or read in a text is not clear. Your teacher or the author may have such a special way of looking at things that it's hard for others to follow what he or she has said. If it's your teacher, you can ask questions. If it's an author, you will have to create your own organized view of the material. The study methods described in Chapter 15 will help in such situations.

In any event, the ideas of participation, organization, and persistence will help you be creative. They will also promote understanding and retention of what you are studying.

Summary

Studying can be defined as organized thinking. Thinking, and therefore studying, is enhanced by participation, organization, persistence, and creativity.

Being a spectator at sporting events or at shows is the natural order of things. It isn't the natural order of things when attending college. You cannot be a spectator in your own education. You cannot learn simply by hearing something in a classroom or observing something in a textbook. You must directly involve yourself in the ideas you think about and the people you meet. You must participate. You can participate by learning to be a good classroom listener, by asking questions, by being a good textbook reader, and by studying with other students. You can also participate by learning to organize ideas.

Organization is putting things together in an orderly fashion. If you can organize, you can more readily understand and apply what you are studying. Organization provides a framework for identifying, relating, and retaining factual information. There are many formats used to organize ideas. These include dot/dash listings, topic outlines, stick diagrams, block diagrams, or some combination of these. The format you use is not important. That you do organize is important.

Persistence is a means of ensuring that your efforts at participation and organization are fruitful. If you stick with difficult ideas long enough, the chances are you will come to understand them.

Participation, organization, and persistence form the basics for effective classroom listening, textbook reading, and studying and library use. These aspects of college learning are discussed in the following chapters.

Creativity is the ability to make something new. You have the ability to be creative. Creativity is important to college learning and study because it causes you to apply increasingly advanced levels of thinking.

KEY TERMS

Participation	Creativity	Stick diagram
Organization	Dot/dash listing	Block diagram
Persistence	Topic outline	

REVIEW QUESTIONS

---

1. Describe each key term above.
2. With respect to the four basic techniques that can help you learn: (a) Identify them; (b) Provide two examples of each as related to college learning.
3. Describe organization as it relates to attending college.

4. Identify and describe the two principles of organization.
5. Identify four techniques of organizing ideas.
6. What are the rules for preparing a topic outline?
7. With respect to creativity: (a) What is it? (b) What has it to do with college learning?
8. Describe how persistence relates to college learning.
9. What essential learning elements are missing when someone relies solely on (a) rote memory, and (b) textbook underlining.

DISCUSSION QUESTIONS

1. In 1963 two people named Jensen and Rohwer performed a learning experiment with retarded adults.[2] The learning task was to remember a list of paired words, such as the following:

house–car	foot–ice cream
cookie–stone	mountain–sailboat
tree–hurricane	

The subjects were divided into two groups, A and B. Those in Group A were instructed just to learn the paired words as presented in the list. Those in Group B were instructed to form sentences by using each pair of words in a separate sentence. For example, for the pair *cookie–stone,* a subject could make up a sentence such as, "The boy tossed the cookie in the air and threw a stone at it." The subjects in each group were then tested regarding how much of the paired list they had learned.
   a. Which group do you think performed better?
   b. Why do you think they performed better?
2. Miller, Perry, and Cunningham, three researchers from the Institute for Child Study, Indiana University, conducted an experiment regarding the reading and remembering of textbook-like material.[3] The researchers gave a reading passage to 44 undergraduate college students. They then tested the students to determine if they were more likely to remember the main (superordinate) ideas in the passage or the related minor (subordinate) ideas. The researchers were trying to confirm a theory of researcher David Ausubel, who believes that main ideas are more likely to be remembered than minor ones. They also wanted to confirm the results of other experimenters (Johnson, 1970; Meyer and McConkie, 1973; Meyer, 1975; Kintach, 1975), who had shown that the knowledge a person

[2]Michael J. A. Howe, *Understanding School Learning* (New York: Harper & Row, 1972), p. 62.

[3]Raymond B. Miller, Fred L. Perry, and Donald J. Cunningham, "Differential Forgetting of Superordinate and Subordinate Information," 1976.

gains from reading is related to how the ideas in the material are organized.

Based on the results of the tests, the researchers concluded the following:

- "Immediate and delayed [tests showed that] more subordinate information was forgotten than superordinate. ... It appears that the rate at which information is forgotten is related to the position of that information within the logical structure of the discourse." The lower the idea in the logical structure, the faster the rate of forgetting.
- Although this particular experiment did not show it, it is possible that remembering a main idea increases the probability of remembering an associated minor idea. They cite the work of Meyer (1975) and indicate that she "found that if any particular idea was recalled, there was a high probability that the idea immediately above it in the structure would also be recalled. Put another way . . . these main ideas seemed to serve an anchoring function for lower-level ideas."

To sum up: (1) main ideas are more apt to be remembered than associated minor ones, and (2) remembering an idea in a structure will help in remembering a higher- or lower-level idea.

a. Why may the above two conclusions be valid?
b. Can you identify specifically what you can do as a college student to take advantage of these two conclusions?

UNDERSTANDING WORDS

BASIC IDEAS
- Reading is the best way to learn new words.
- Mastering a course is often a matter of learning its vocabulary.

KEY POINTS
- How are words organized?
- What are signal words?

How Words Are Organized

Many words follow organized patterns. The patterns are based on adding a Greek or Latin prefix and suffix to a root. A *prefix* is the beginning of a word. A *root* is the main part or base of a word. A *suffix* is the end of the word. Here is an example:

- Word: *transportation*
- Parts: trans   port   ation
                    (prefix) (root) (suffix)
- Meaning of Parts: *across   carry   act of*
- Assembled Meaning: *the act of carrying something across*

Here is a list of some common word parts:

Prefixes (the beginning of a word)

Form	Meaning	Form	Meaning
mono-, uni-	one	pro	in favor of
bi-, duo-	two	sym-, syn-	put together
tri-	three	intra-	within
multi-, poly-	many	intro-	inward
micro-	small	anti-, contra-, ob-, op-	against

Prefixes *(the beginning of a word)*

Form	Meaning	Form	Meaning
macro-	large	retro-	backward
equi-	equally	ante-, pre-	before
ambi-	both	extra-, ultra-	beyond
sub-, sum-, sur-,	under	trans-	across
im-, in-	not	inter-	between
co-, com-, con-	with, together		

Roots *(the main part of a word)*

Form	Meaning	Form	Meaning
dic, dict	say	duc, duct	lead
voc, vok	call	ject	throw
vid, vis	see	cept, capt	take
scop, scope	look	ten, tent	hold, have
gram, graph	write, draw	ced, cess	go, yield
scrib, script	write	auto	self
aud, audit	hear	bio	life
tract, trac	draw	nomin	name
biblio	book	ben, bene	good
ambul	walk	philo	love
port	carry	hetero	different
junct	tie	homo	same
		dia	across, part

Suffixes *(the end of a word)*

Form	Meaning	Form	Meaning
-ant, -ent	inclining toward	-able, -ible	fit, capable of being
-y	inclined to	-cy	rank, condition
-al, -ial, -ar, -ary	belonging to or relating to	-acy	quality of being
		-ness	state of being
-ish, -ive	resembling	-cle, -cule	small
-ism	characteristic	-ation, -ment	act or process
-ly	similar	-ee	one who receives
-fy	to make, to cause	-eer	one who produces, manages.
-ise, -ize	to make conform		

Knowledge of word parts can help you figure out a word's meaning. Here are some practice exercises.

Exercise 8–1. Decoding a Word's Meaning

Using the lists shown above, see if you can figure out the meaning of the following words. Note that not all words will have exactly three parts. Some may have two, like the word *bibliophile.* In this case the word starts with the root *biblio* (book) and ends with another root *phile* (love). The word, therefore, means booklover.

a. *Word:* binomial

Meaning of parts: _____   _____   _____

Assembled meaning: _____

b. *Word:* bioscopy

Meaning of parts: _____   _____   _____

Assembled meaning: _____

c. *Word:* antecede

Meaning of parts: _____   _____   _____

Assembled meaning: _____

d. *Word:* intercept

Meaning of parts: _____   _____   _____

Assembled meaning: _____

e. *Word:* autobiography

Meaning of parts: _____   _____   _____

Assembled meaning: _____

Now consult a dictionary. Did you assemble correct meanings?

Exercise 8-2. Create Your Own Words
Create some words of your own by using different word parts. Be imaginative. Don't be afraid to try. The words can be short or long. After you have created a word, look in a dictionary. If your word exists, enter its meaning. If it doesn't exist, find a similar word and enter its meaning. Here is an example to get you started.

Selected prefix, root, suffix: *micro graph ation*

Proposed new word: *Micrographation*

Proposed meaning: *The process of drawing very tiny pictures.*

Dictionary meaning: *Micrography (similar to my word). My definition okay (hey, not bad). Dictionary says it also means the technique of using the microscope.*

a. Selected prefix, root, suffix: _____   _____   _____

Proposed new word: _____

Proposed meaning: _____

Dictionary meaning: _____

_____

b. Selected prefix, root, suffix: _____ _____ _____

Proposed new word: _____

Proposed meaning: _____

Dictionary meaning: _____

_____

c. Selected prefix, root, suffix: _____ _____ _____

Proposed new word: _____

Proposed meaning: _____

Dictionary meaning: _____

_____

As you can see, analyzing words can be fascinating. But you cannot always infer the meaning of a word from its parts. Many words cannot be easily analyzed. Also many English words are based on the German language (English is actually based on German) and the French language. It's also possible that your inference about a word's meaning may be incorrect. Finally, the same word may have different meanings depending upon how it is used in a sentence. When you do infer, make sure your meaning makes sense in light of the rest of the sentence or paragraph. When you are not sure, consult a dictionary. A special effort to memorize the meanings of different affixes and roots is probably not a good use of your time. Try rather to become sensitive to their presence as part of your normal reading. Over a period of time you will build up a store of knowledge about word parts. With what you now know about words, you may find yourself joining a special group of people. They sometimes read a dictionary for pleasure because they believe that each word and its definition is a short story.

How Words Give Themselves Away
A word's meaning can sometimes be figured out by analyzing its parts, by looking it up in a dictionary, or by asking someone. But there is still another way. The other words in the sentence can often be used to figure out the meaning of a new word. You probably already do this, often without realizing it. Here is a sample sentence:

You cannot always *infer* the meaning of a word from its parts.

If you did not already know the meaning of the word *infer,* its position in the sentence (its *context* or the way it is used) would give you a big clue. In this case you could conclude that *infer* meant to figure out or determine. To put it another way, the word *infer* means to say something about the unknown (in this case the word *infer*) based upon the known (in this case the other words in the sample sentence).

Exercise 8–3. Words in Context
Read each of the following sentences. Then infer the meaning of the italicized words by analyzing the context in which they appear.

a. He traced the smoke down the mountainside and saw that it was *emanating* from a riverside camp.

Your inference:_____

Dictionary meaning:_____

b. After making a list of the amount of each loan due, she performed a *quantitative* analysis.

Your Inference:_____

Dictionary meaning:_____

c. Because the lawyer had no facts to back his argument, the judge concluded the lawyer's position was totally *subjective* and dismissed the case.

Your inference:_____

Dictionary meaning:_____

Exercise 8–4. Textbook Words in Context
Gather some of your class textbooks. Open a book to a chapter not yet covered. Read the material until you find a word you don't know. Copy the sentence onto a piece of note paper or a 3 × 5 index card. Underline the unknown word. Now try to infer the meaning of the word from its context. Be sure to make up *some* meaning for the unknown word, even if you are totally unsure of the word's meaning. It might help to analyze the word's parts, as in Exercise 8–1. Now check your meaning with a dictionary. Repeat this exercise for each of the textbooks. Your instructor may ask you to repeat the exercise several times for each book. Use the following format when doing this exercise.

Name of book:_____

Name of author:_____

Selected sentence:_____

_____

Unknown word:_____

My inference:_____

Dictionary meaning:_____

Be aware that overinferring can lead to mistakes since you cannot always correctly infer a word's meaning from its context. Use a dictionary when you are not sure about your inference.

Words That Signal

Sometimes word meanings are important because they provide reading signals. A word that signals tells you what is about to happen. Being aware of signal words helps you understand what you are reading. They keep you in mental contact with the author. Here is a list of some signal words you should learn to recognize and apply.

Situation	*These words signify the new situation:*	
When an *example* is about to be provided	for example (e.g.) for instance therefore	like such as
When an already stated idea is about to be *reinforced* or expanded	again also and because furthermore	in addition likewise moreover similarly
When an idea or example is about to be *contrasted* or a *change* in thought direction is about to take place	alternatively although but despite however nevertheless nonetheless	notwithstanding on the other hand otherwise sometimes true though whereas
when words or ideas are to be *linked*	accordingly consequently thus	therefore finally so
When a *summary* or conclusion is about to be presented	in conclusion to conclude	to sum up in summary

Exercise 8–5. Identifying Signal Words
Try your hand at identifying signal words by underlining all those you can find in the following passage:

> Despite poor conditions, he was able to accomplish his group's goals. His sense of timing was excellent. For example, he knew when to encourage but also when to scold. Furthermore, all members really liked him. Also, they knew he was best prepared. Nevertheless, problems still existed. Consequently, he and they remained determined.

Exercise 8–6. Signal Words in a Textbook

Select one of your textbooks. Open it to any page. As you read the page, enter on the list below all the signal words you see. Next to each signal word enter the situation it represents. Use E for example, R for reinforce, C for change, L for link, or S for summary. Use the list above to help you decide.

Signal Word	Situation	Signal Word	Situation
_____	_____	_____	_____
_____	_____	_____	_____
_____	_____	_____	_____
_____	_____	_____	_____
_____	_____	_____	_____

Punctuation Marks That Signal

A word is a symbol that conveys meaning. When strung together in a sentence, the words convey a complete thought. To help convey a thought, sentences also contain nonword symbols. These are called punctuation marks. Such marks are used to interrupt the flow of thought in order to increase clearness and achieve emphasis. They represent signals that allow you to anticipate (1) what is to come, (2) what is taking place, and (3) what is considered important. Recognize punctuation marks in the material you read. They will help you to understand and identify what is important. Here are some often used nonword symbols.

Symbol	Name	Function
•	Dot	Used to signify or list important or related ideas.
. . .	Ellipsis points	Signifies that a portion of a quotation has been omitted.
:	Colon	Used to indicate that a series of sentence-related statements will follow.
;	Semicolon	Used to join two independent but related thoughts.
,	Comma	Used to separate a parenthetic expression within a sentence. Also used to separate a series of terms.
!	Exclamation point	Used to emphasize a statement.
" "	Quotation marks	Signifies that material from another work is being cited. Also used to attribute a thought or statement to someone or something.

Symbol	Name	Function
( )	Parentheses	Signifies a parenthetic statement that amplifies, qualifies or explains.
[ ]	Brackets	Indicates material has been added
—	Dash	Used to signify or list important or related ideas. Also used to emphasize the importance of a portion of a sentence.
∴	Therefore	Used to link a statement that follows as a consequence of what went before.
————	Underline	Emphasizes that a word, phrase, or sentence is of particular importance.
Slanted Words	Italics	Emphasizes that a word, phrase, or sentence is of particular importance.
1, 2, 3, 4	Numbers	Used to set off a series of related ideas or steps in a process.

Summary

A prefix is the beginning of a word, a root the middle, and a suffix the end. Many words, especially in math and science courses, follow this pattern. As you read and use the dictionary, become sensitive to word parts. Your overall reading ability will grow. A word's meaning can sometimes be inferred, or figured out by using the other words in its sentence. The ability to infer a word's meaning by its context is a skill that can be developed with practice. Sensitivity to signal words and punctuation marks will also increase your reading ability.

Continued awareness of word parts, words in context, signal words, and punctuation marks will save you time, promote understanding and add a measure of enjoyment (if not pride) to your reading. You have already made a start toward such awareness by completing the exercises in this chapter. Now build on this start. Oh, by the way, do you know the meaning of the word *word?* Do you know the meaning of the word *meaning?*

KEY TERMS

Prefix	Inference	Punctuation marks
Root	Context	
Suffix	Signal words	

REVIEW QUESTIONS

1. Write a sentence that describes each key term shown above.
2. Provide an example for each key term.

HOW TO READ A TEXTBOOK (Part 1)

BASIC IDEAS
- Textbook writing is based on organization, and so is textbook reading.
- Your reading rate depends on your understanding rate.
- You must see a word before you can understand its meaning.

KEY POINTS
- Does your reading purpose affect the way you read?
- Is there a difference between reading and studying?
- What is the special significance of a chapter's paragraphs, topic headings, and illustrations?

When reading for enjoyment, you engage in casual reading. But what happens when you read so you can apply what the article discusses, or because you are to be tested on its contents? Your reading purpose changes. The material can still be pleasurable to read but your *attitude* toward reading it will change. You will now assume responsibility for the material. Here are some considerations that affect how you read:

- Degree of comprehension necessary.
- Degree of detail information necessary.
- Responsibility you feel for completing a given portion of reading.
- The amount of time available to complete the reading.
- Responsibility you feel for remembering what you read.
- Responsibility you feel to apply, evaluate, or analyze what you read.

When the last three elements listed are present, you are no longer merely reading. You have begun to study.

The Difference Between Reading and Studying

Assume your text covers what is important to know. Also assume it is clearly written. Does it seem reasonable you will learn, retain, and apply the material, especially if it is hard, from just one reading? Probably not. The question is, then, just how many times should a chapter be read? And will repetition itself ensure subject competency? As you know, mere exposure to material is no guarantee you will learn. It seems clear that other activities, such as participation, organization, and persistence (see Chapter 7), must also occur. It is these other activities that make up studying. Therefore, before important material can be fully studied, it must first be identified through reading. Further, what counts is not the number of times (or how fast) a chapter is read. What counts is (1) how you read a chapter and (2) what you do during and after reading a chapter. This chapter and the next discuss textbook reading skills. Chapter 15 will show how to bring together textbook reading skills into methods of systemized study.

Textbook Reading Basics

A writer of detective stories will attempt to confuse and mislead the reader with false clues, diverting action, and a host of characters. While you may feel some of your textbooks fit this description, most do not. This is because textbooks, almost regardless of the subject, use similar writing elements. Knowledge of these basic elements will help promote understanding. Figure 9–1 identifies and relates the elements associated with reading a textbook chapter.

Some elements, such as words and sentences, are of course common to all writing. Others, such as structured paragraphs, topic headings, and illustrations, find their greatest use in textbook chapters. Knowledge and application of all these elements will greatly enhance your reading effectiveness. Remember that the primary purpose of textbook reading is to identify what is important so it may be studied, remembered, and applied.

A Basic Skill: Finding the Main Idea in a Paragraph

A sentence represents a complete thought. A paragraph is a series of related sentences concerning one main idea. One of these sentences contains the paragraph's main idea. It is called the *main* or *topic sentence*. The other sentences support and develop the main idea. They are called *supporting sentences*. Here is an example:

Figure 9–1
Reading A Textbook Chapter

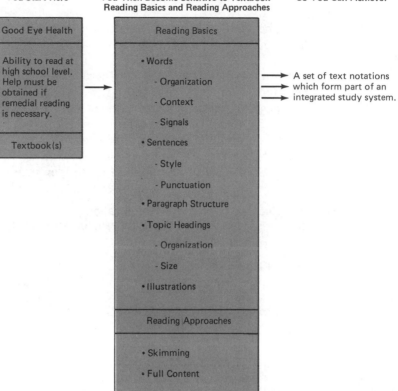

You Start Here

You Then Become Sensitive to Textbook
Reading Basics and Reading Approaches

So You Can Achieve:

Good Eye Health

Ability to read at high school level. Help must be obtained if remedial reading is necessary.

Textbook(s)

Reading Basics

• Words
  - Organization
  - Context
  - Signals
• Sentences
  - Style
  - Punctuation
• Paragraph Structure
• Topic Headings
  - Organization
  - Size
• Illustrations

Reading Approaches

• Skimming
• Full Content

A set of text notations which form part of an integrated study system.

The first manned spaceship to land on another planet was called the Lunar Module. The planet was the Moon. The Lunar Module (LM) was the first true spaceship because it was able both to orbit and to land on another planet. The LM was built by Grumman Aerospace Corporation of Bethpage, New York. It was 25 feet tall and weighed 32,000 pounds. It had a descent engine for landing on the moon and an ascent engine for leaving the moon. Air and water for the astronauts were stored in tanks. Electricity to operate the LM was stored in batteries. These batteries were connected to 15 miles of wires, which ran up, through, and around the inside of the spaceship. One of these wires was connected to a special light bulb. When the long legs of the LM touched the surface of the moon, the light automatically turned on. It read "Lunar Contact."

• Main or topic sentence: *The first manned spaceship to land on another planet was called the Lunar Module.*
• Summary of main idea: *Lunar Module—first manned spaceship on another planet*

- Supporting details: *First true spaceship, built by Grumman, 25 feet tall, 32,000 pounds, carried own oxygen, water, and electricity, 15 miles of wires.*

The main idea or topic sentence usually appears in one of three locations in the paragraph: (1) the first sentence, as in the example above, (2) the last sentence, and (3) a sentence near the middle. Sometimes the main idea is stated in the first sentence and then restated in different words in the last sentence. At other times a paragraph contains two main ideas. But one of them will usually be more important. In some cases a paragraph will serve as an introduction to paragraphs that follow. However, the main thing to remember about textbook paragraphs is that their main idea is *usually* in the first sentence. (But where is the main idea in this paragraph?)

Exercise 9–1. Paragraph Organization
Use the paragraph immediately above to complete the following lines.

Main or topic sentence: _____

_____

Summary of main idea: _____

Supporting details: _____

_____

The ability to locate a main idea is important. But simply underlining main ideas in a college textbook is not an effective way to learn the material. Effective learning requires that you summarize the main idea in your own words. You can use the page margin to write your summary. Use as few words as possible. In the following exercises see if you can first mark off the area of the main idea. Underline only a few key words or use a check mark or a vertical line in the page margin.

As you read, be sensitive to the writing style. Long sentences with frequent punctuation can slow you up and delay understanding. Too many short sentences in a row can tire and distract. You can minimize such problems by recognizing and adapting to the author's style. If the material contains overly long sentences, say something like: "I am going to have to enter the author's framework and carry along the thoughts. I may have to slow down to gain comprehension." If the material mixes long and short sentences, adapt to the resulting pace and rhythm. Do not be quick to put a textbook down because of lack of comprehension. Repeated exposure and adaption to style promote understanding.

Exercise 9–2. Find the Main Idea

Four exercise paragraphs follow. Carefully read each one. Then complete the lines that follow each paragraph. Remember: (1) avoid extensive underlining, and (2) briefly summarize the main idea in your own words.

Paragraph 1

The Gulf Stream's name is misleading, for it is not located in the Gulf of Mexico, and it is not one stream but a combination of many small and large currents. Sometimes these currents reverse themselves, form eddies, or dive to greater depths, but the large mass of water composing the Gulf Stream always moves in the same general direction, speeding boats bound for Europe and bringing with it some of the warmth of the equatorial zone.[1]

Location of main idea: (Beginning, middle, or end of paragraph?)_____

Brief own-word summary of main idea:_____

Paragraph 2

In the relatively calm and quiet equatorial zone, dubbed the "doldrums" by sailors long ago, winds and currents are weak and sometimes nonexistent. Only the soft trade winds remain to stir the waters and generate the motion which again starts the great circular swing of the currents. Below the surface, however, countercurrents and "counter countercurrents" exist which we only now are beginning to chart.[2]

Location of main idea: _____

Brief own-word summary of main idea:_____

Paragraph 3

Many times researchers are curious as to whether populations are similar or different with respect to some characteristic. For example, an instructor may be curious as to whether male professors receive higher salaries than female professors for the same teaching load. Or a psychologist may want to determine objectively whether one group responds differently to an experimental stimulus than another group. In other words, there are many situations which require groups to be compared on the basis of a given trait or characteristic.[3]

Location of main idea: _____

[1]From Vladimar and Nada Kovalik, *The Ocean World* (New York: Holiday House, 1966), p. 90.

[2]From Kovalik, *The Ocean World,* p. 90.

[3]From D. Sanders, A. Murph, and R. Eng, *Statistics: A Fresh Approach* (New York: McGraw-Hill, 1976), p. 277.

Brief own-word summary of main idea:_____

_____

Paragraph 4

The belief that logic will substantially reduce misunderstanding is widely and uncritically held, although, as a matter of common experience, we all know that people who pride themselves on their logic are usually, of all the people we know, the hardest to get along with. Logic can lead to agreement only when, as in mathematics or the sciences, there are pre-existing, hard-and-fast agreements as to what words stand for. In ordinary conversation, therefore, we have to learn people's vocabularies in the course of talking with them—which is what all sensible and tactful people do, without even being aware of the process.[4]

Location of main idea: _____

Brief own-word summary of main idea:_____

_____

A Basic Skill: Analyzing Topic Headings for Their Thought Patterns

Topic headings are bold-type headlines that appear throughout a chapter. They identify the main subject of a group of paragraphs. They are useful for two reasons:

- Their size, form, and arrangement signal their degree of importance.
- They provide information regarding the material's organizational patterns.

Reading awareness of both these factors leads to quicker material coverage and increased comprehension.

The Size, Form, and Arrangement of Topic Headings

A chapter may have four, five, six, or more main ideas. These ideas are represented by the largest, boldest topic headings. They in effect say: "Hey reader, I'm a larger topic heading. That means I'm one of the important subjects in this chapter. Please take note of me." Smaller related ideas are identified with smaller topic headings. Sometimes different colors are used for different level topic headings.

It's important to become sensitive to shifts in topic heading size. Such shifts signal you to adjust your thoughts accordingly. If your eyes become alert to topic heading typography, you will have a much easier

[4]From S. I. Hayakawa, *Language in Thought and Action* (New York: Harcourt, Brace and World, 1964), p. 241.

time recognizing the organizational pattern of the text material. This ability makes reading (and studying) easier since you will not be reading disconnected sentences and paragraphs but organized patterns of thought.

Exercise 9–3. Identifying Topic Headings
Below is a topic outline for the first and second degree topic headings in this chapter. Find the headings and write them in the space below.

Chapter Name: *How to Read a Textbook (Part 1)*

Chapter Outline:

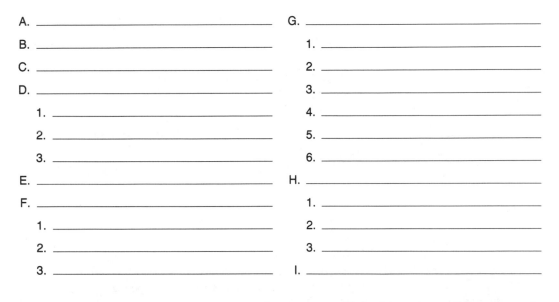

A. _____   G. _____

B. _____   1. _____

C. _____   2. _____

D. _____   3. _____

    1. _____   4. _____

    2. _____   5. _____

    3. _____   6. _____

E. _____   H. _____

F. _____   1. _____

    1. _____   2. _____

    2. _____   3. _____

    3. _____   I. _____

As you have just shown yourself, looking at a chapter's topic heading outline is the same as looking at a chapter's important ideas. And can you think of a better way of getting familiar with a chapter? A better way of reducing your anxiety about identifying and learning the chapter's main ideas?

Common Organizational Patterns

At this point two questions may have occurred to you: (1) Where do a textbook's topic headings come from? (2) Aside from indicating degree of importance, are they of any special significance? The following addresses both questions.

A textbook's ideas and topics are arranged according to a plan. The plan is called the topic outline. (See Chapter 7 for a discussion of topic outlines.) The headings in the topic outline are the origin of a textbook's topic headings.

Topic headings and the material they headline result from organized patterns of thinking. Recognizing the pattern in what you read will help you understand the material. Common approaches for arranging textbooks and textbook chapters are outlined below.

Approaches Used in Arranging Textbook Material

I. Sequential (in order)
   A. Time Related
      1. Recounting (traces events as in a historical accounting)
      2. Process (describes actions that lead to an end result, e.g., the fermentation process, the process of developing photographic film)
      3. Cause and effect (describes relationship between some cause, such as smoking, and an effect, breathing problems)
      4. Problem solving (details the steps necessary to achieve some predetermined result)
   B. Space Related
      1. Vertical/horizontal (relates material based upon up–down, near–far)
      2. Physical whole (relates material based upon sequentially analyzing space relationships)
II. Hierarchical (ranking)
   A. Deductive (thought progresses from whole to part; a generalization is stated and is then supported by logically deduced details)
   B. Inductive (thought progresses from part to whole; a detail is presented which is logically developed into a generalization)

(*Note:* As a textbook reader it is important for you to recognize that *at the paragraph level* all coherent writing uses one or both of these processes. Applying deductive and inductive reasoning is another way of analyzing a paragraph for its main idea.)

   C. Abstraction (a broad statement or term is presented followed by material which clarifies the statement or defines the term)
III. Classification (systematic arrangement of material)
   A. Similarities (material is grouped together because of similarities in type or category; specific arrangements can vary widely)
   B. Relationships (material is grouped together because, al-

though separate and distinct, they all bear on the same subject; specific arrangements can vary widely)

C. Importance (material is arranged by relative importance as viewed by the author)

These arrangements apply to most textbooks and their chapters. An analysis of a text's table of contents or a chapter's topic headings will help you identify the thought pattern. Often main ideas follow one pattern and subordinated ideas another, so it is necessary to be alert to these possibilities. Let's examine the organizational pattern for a typical textbook chapter.

Analyzing Organizational Patterns

Below is a topic outline based on the topic headings in a chapter of a widely used textbook in biology.[5]

CHAPTER 10
NERVOUS CONTROL

I. Evolution of Nervous Systems
   A. Irritability
   B. Simple Nervous Pathways
   C. Nerve Nets and Radial Systems
   D. Evolutionary Trends in Bilateral Nervous Systems

II. Nervous Pathways in Vertebrates
   A. Neurons of Vertebrates
   B. Reflex Arcs
   C. The Autonomic Nervous System
   D. Reflex Control of Breathing and Heartbeat
      1. Control Breathing
      2. Control of Rate of Heartbeat

III. Transmission of Nervous Impulses
   A. Transmission Along Neurons
      1. General Features of the Nerve Impulse
      2. The Nature of the Impulse
      3. The Sodium-Potassium Pump
   B. Transmission Across Synaptic
      1. The Nature of Synaptic Transmission
      2. The Action of Transmitter Substances
   C. Transmission Between the Motor Axon and the Effects

[5] William T. Keeton, *Biological Science* (New York: W. W. Norton & Co., 1967), Chapter 10, pp. 357–425.

IV. Sensory Reception
    A. Sensory Receptors of the Skin, Skeletal Muscles, and Viscera
        1. Types of Receptors
        2. Sensations
        3. Mechanisms of Receptor Functions
    B. The Senses of Taste and Smell
        1. Taste
        2. Smell
    C. The Sense of Vision
        1. Light Receptors of Animals
        2. Structure of the Human Eye
        3. Functions of Rods and Cones
        4. Refraction and Accommodation
    D. The Sense of Hearing
        1. Structure of the Human Ear
        2. Reception of Vibratory Stimuli
        3. The Characteristics of Sounds
    E. The Senses of Static and Dynamic Equilibrium
    F. Lateral-Line Systems
V. The Brain
    A. Evolution of the Vertebrate Brain
    B. The Mammalia Forebrain
        1. The Thalamus
        2. The Hypothalamus
        3. The Cerebral Cortex

The chapter on which the above outline is based is close to 70 pages and contains photos, drawings, tables, and graphs. Now complete the following exercise.

Exercise 9–4. Analysis of Topic Headings
Complete the incomplete sentences.

1. The chapter contains _____ main topics.

2. The main headings are a combination of both the sequential-space and hierarchical-inductive thought patterns. Sequential-space applies since the author progresses from an animal's nervous pathways, to the sense which stimulates the pathways, and finally up to the _____, which collects the pathway information. There is also a very strong hierarchical-inductive pattern since the five ideas progress from pathways all the way up to the collecting brain—from part(s) to whole.

3. Of all the main headings presented the author apparently feels main headings _____ and _____ are most important since the outline emphasizes these points.

4. Main heading IV has _____ subdivisions. These subdivisions follow primarily a _____ pattern which includes the body's skin, taste (mouth), smell (nose), vision (eyes), and hearing (ears), all part of a sequence that results from analyzing the main parts of the head. Whether this was a pattern the author was conscious of is incidental. But recognizing that it is a pattern will help you recall the sensory receptors.

The topic headings in this chapter and in any other textbook chapter can be similarly analyzed. At this point you should be starting to appreciate the difference between just reading a textbook chapter and beginning a study effort which includes participation (preparing the outline) and organization (analyzing the chapter's thought pattern).

Exercise 9–5. Outlining a Chapter
Select one of your textbooks, and open it to any chapter. Prepare a topic outline based on the chapter's topic headings.

Exercise 9–6. Comparing Two Textbooks
Select a library text that covers the same material as one of your existing texts. Find a chapter in your text and one in the library text that cover the same material. Now do the following: (a) Prepare a topic outline for each of the two chapters. Now compare the two outlines. (b) How are they similar? (c) How are they different? (d) Which one do you think is easier to read? Why?

Exercise 9–7. Interpreting Chapter Outlines
Form a group of no more than three people. Select a textbook from one of your courses, particularly one that you feel is difficult. Now select a chapter somewhere near the middle of the book. Working together, analyze the chapter's pattern of organization by doing the following: (a) Analyze first the main ideas and see which pattern(s) you think applies. (b) Next analyze the subordinate headings within each main idea and identify the applicable pattern(s).

A Basic Skill: Reading Illustrations

Writing sentences and paragraphs (called prose writing) is not always the best way to describe something. Sometimes an illustration can be more helpful.

An illustration highlights or emphasizes what is important. Large amounts of information can be presented in a small space. Illustrations can take the form of a cartoon, table, graph, diagram, or photograph.

Exercise 9–8. Interpreting Pictures
Look at the cartoons in Figure 9–2. In the space below briefly summarize the main idea of each cartoon.

Main Idea: _____

Main Idea: _____

Figure 9–2a
Who's Responsible?

Figure 9–2b
The Major Reason for Dropping Out of College

Exercise 9–9. Interpreting Graphs

Carefully review Figure 9–3; and then complete the following sentences.

1. The subject concerns _____.
2. Information is provided for the years _____ and _____.
3. The youngest age group covered is _____.
4. The oldest age group covered is _____.
5. There are more _____ in the age group 75 and over than there are ___.

ORGANIZING YOUR LEARNING: SKILLS YOU NEED

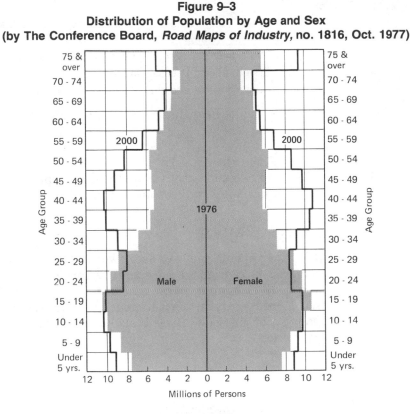

Figure 9–3
Distribution of Population by Age and Sex
(by The Conference Board, *Road Maps of Industry,* no. 1816, Oct. 1977)

6. The age group with the largest population in the year 1976 is _____.

7. Main Idea: _____

Textbook Reading Approaches

There is no doubt that knowledge of words, sentences, paragraphs, topic headings, thought patterns, and illustrations can help make you a better textbook reader. But you eventually must put them all together and it's important that you feel comfortable while doing so. You must develop overall approaches to reading college textbooks, approaches that will save time and increase understanding. To get started in developing reading approaches, complete the following exercise.

Exercise 9–10. Some Reading Considerations
Check the column you think applies.

Agree   *Disagree*

_____   _____   1. It's not necessary to read every word in a sentence to understand its meaning.

———   ———   2. There is something wrong with you if you don't understand something on the first reading.

———   ———   3. The slower you read, the better you understand.

———   ———   4. Speed reading is essential for college survival.

———   ———   5. Reading a text and studying a text are the same thing.

You should have disagreed with all the statements. Here is why.

Must You Read Every Word?

There are two approaches to textbook reading. Either you read every word in a chapter (full reading) or you don't (skimming).

FULL READING

When should you read every word? You read every word when the material is considered important, when it is interesting to you, or when full reading is necessary for understanding. For example, read fully those points the teacher identifies as important, those that match your MBM chart and those that may have been unclear during class discussion.

SKIMMING

In many cases attempting to read every detail is unnecessary, wastes time, and lowers motivation. How can you read a text by not reading every word? Partly by recognizing that textbooks highlight their important points, as we have seen, through a combination of topic headings, paragraph structure, and illustrations. These elements help promote understanding of the material. When used as part of an overall study system (see Chapter 15) they reduce the need to read every word.

Just what is skimming? It doesn't mean wildly jumping from a few words in one sentence to a few in the next. You can't skim a sentence. Each sentence represents a complete thought. Leaving out just about any word in a sentence can destroy its meaning.

Exercise 9–11.   Why You Can't Skim a Sentence

Try leaving out the words (one at a time) in the following sentence: "First of all you can't skim a sentence." What happens to the thought, especially when key words *can't, skim,* and *sentence* are left out?

It's obvious that you can't tell in advance whether a word is a key word until you first read it. Therefore, if you don't read the whole sentence, you don't get the thought. So wildly jumping around is a waste of time. It leads to confusion about the subject matter and promotes anxiety regarding your attempts to learn.

But you can skim a paragraph. The reason is simply that paragraphs are structured. If you are aware of how they are structured (see Exercises 9–1 and 9–2), then you know that large portions of paragraphs can be left unread while you still extract the paragraph's main idea. Developing the ability to skim paragraphs brings with it the following results:

- You identify main ideas.
- You decrease reading time because you decrease the amount of material read.

Is Once Enough?

There is nothing wrong with you if you don't understand something on the first reading. You will put undue pressure on yourself if you approach textbook reading with the attitude that you must do so. The fact that something appears in writing, as in a textbook, doesn't necessarily make it right, and it doesn't mean it's been clearly written.

If you really try and still have trouble understanding, borrow another text from the library. Putting together the viewpoints of several authors is an excellent way to help yourself understand. More than one student has mastered difficult concepts by referring to a second textbook on the same subject. (See thematic studying discussed in Chapter 15.)

The Slower the Better?

If your class teacher sud - den - ly st - art - ed sp - e – ak - in - g v - e - r – y s – l – o – w – l – y, you would probably fall asleep. Reading also involves listening to yourself. So the same thing will happen if you read very slowly. You will bore and tire yourself. See the following section for a discussion on how to increase your reading speed.

Increasing Your Reading Speed

Chances are you now read too slowly. Chances also are you can increase your reading speed if you make a special effort. The special effort involves the use of a few simple techniques faithfully applied. It also requires a commitment on your part to do as much reading of textbooks, magazines, and newspapers as you possibly can.

Before discussing how to increase your speed let's establish what your present reading rate is.

Exercise 9–12. Your Reading Rate
Read the following selection at your normal reading speed. Do not try to speed up or slow down. Just read normally. Time yourself in minutes and seconds. (Your instructor may want to time you; if so follow the instructor's directions carefully.)

Out in the Cold

Lucinda was very young and she was crying. As she left the building the cold New England air seemed to freeze the tears on her cheeks. She thought about the just completed meeting. The president of the college and his advisors had found her more than qualified. Her appearance, her manner, her speech, her religiousness, her intellectual ability—all were excellent. She was just the kind of college student they were seeking. She was fine in every way except one; she was of the wrong sex. That final phrase kept echoing in her head, "Sorry Miss Foote, but we just cannot admit you to the freshman class of Yale University."

Now back in 1783 when Lucinda Foote was denied college entrance to Yale, it created a problem not easily fixed. Back then (about the time of the American Revolution) there were only nine colleges in all the United States. The first of these was Harvard, founded in 1636 by English immigrants. So there were not many places where Lucinda could apply. (There weren't many students attending these nine colleges; probably less than one thousand.) And she couldn't commute as many students now do. George Washington rode a horse and then rowed a boat to get to school. That's not exactly a method in much use today.

If there were only nine colleges in 1783, there were even fewer fields of study. A student had little to choose from in terms of selecting a major or a curriculum. A person who played a large part in developing colonial colleges was King George III of England. In 1762 (before the American Revolution of 1776) King George wrote a letter to wealthy people in England. He asked that they send money to support the colleges in America. Among the reasons he cited for such college support were to instill just principles of religion, to instill loyalty to England, and to instruct in branches of useful knowledge. As it turned out, these activities were the basic curricula that then existed. You could major in one of three fields. The choice was basically to study religion and become a minister, or study general knowledge and become a gentleman, or study both and become a teacher. Since there was relatively little to know then, most everybody studied the same thing.

So Lucinda was confronted with a system that featured little choice. It was a system organized and run by men whose furthest thought was that women belonged in college. What if Lucinda were somehow able to apply to college today? What kind of choices would she have? By about 1860 the nine colonial colleges with about 1,000 students had grown to 250 colleges with about 50,000 students. Today there are about 3,000 colleges attended by over 11 million students. So Lucinda wouldn't have much trouble finding a college she liked and one that liked her.

If the number of colleges has grown, so have the number of available curricula. Fields of study are no longer limited to the ministry, general study, and teaching. Today's colleges offer many areas from which a student might choose. The choices include advertising art and design, automotive technology, business administration, dental hygiene, data processing, nursing, fine and applied arts, law, engineering, medicine, and many more. Some colleges offer as many as 35 different fields of study. Lucinda would be sure to find something that matched her interests and aptitudes. If today she were to find herself out in the cold, it would be because she was studying forestry, civil engineering, or construction technology. A woman today can choose any field. She is limited only by her imagination.

Record your reading time here: _____ minutes _____ seconds. Now answer these questions about the article:

ORGANIZING YOUR LEARNING: SKILLS YOU NEED

1. The name of the article is _____ .

2. The first name of the young girl is _____ .

3. The college that denied admission to the young girl was _____ .

4. In what year was she denied admission to college? _____ .

5. Why was she denied admission? _____ .

6. Who helped establish the early colleges in America? _____ .

7. The first college in America was _____ .

8. About how many colleges existed in 1783? _____ .

9. About how many colleges exist today? _____ .

10. A curriculum should be selected based upon a student's _____ .

Number of correct answers (refer back to article) _____ .

The article has 600 words. Figure your reading speed by dividing your time in decimal format (for example, 3 minutes and 30 seconds is written as 3.5 minutes) into the number 600. The result is your normal reading speed in words per minute Now look at your reading rate and the percent of correct answers given above (5 right is equal to 50%, 6 right 60%, 7 right 70%, and so on). These two numbers provide you with a rough idea of your ability to read and comprehend material of average difficulty.

Following are some simple techniques that will help you increase your speed. When you first use them, your comprehension may drop. This will happen because you will be worrying more about learning to read faster than about what you are reading. However, with practice, your comprehension, and your speed, will grow.

• *Avoid Vocalizing.* If you vocalize or move your lips, you are almost certainly limiting yourself to a maximum reading rate of around 200 words per minute. If you break the vocalizing habit, you will automatically achieve a speed increase. This is because it takes time to move your lips, tongue, and teeth. Do not feel you are dumb or slow if you vocalize; it is a *habit* that can be changed, especially if you have access to a reading instructor and reading laboratory.

• *Avoid Subvocalizing.* If you are successful at not vocalizing, you will then be subvocalizing (silently saying the words to yourself without involving the speech mechanism). This may be happening right now, or hadn't you noticed? Subvocalizing cannot be totally eliminated. But reducing subvocalization will allow you to achieve large increases (50 to 100 percent or more) in reading speed. You can minimize subvocalization if you increase your visual bite, avoid going back to reread, and use your hand as a pacer. These three practices are discussed next.

• *Increase Your Visual Bite*. When your eyes move across a page they move in a series of stops called fixations. (You can prove this to yourself by watching someone read.) When fixating, many people just read one word. This amount can be increased. You are capable of fixating on or biting off two, three, or more words at a time. The way to achieve this is to use your peripheral vision (the ability to use your side vision to see more than what is directly in front of you). The way to use peripheral vision is simply to concentrate on reading more than one word at a time when you read. Don't worry about your brain's ability to process words at a faster rate. It can process more than you can ever consciously give it.

• *Avoid Going Back*. When you are proving to yourself that people's eyes move in a series of stops, also notice that every once in a while they also retrace what they have already read. This is called *regressing*. If you avoid going backward, you can use the time saved to go forward. Regressing can be minimized by using your hand as a pacer.

• *Use Hand as Pacer*. There are reading machines that expose several words at a time and always move forward. These machines help increase your visual bite and eliminate regression. They help develop your overall reading ability. But you can't carry one around with you. A good substitute is the middle finger on your hand. Use it to gently underline each line as your eyes move across the page. Do not rub your finger along the page. With practice you will develop a smooth technique. Moving your hand at a slightly faster pace than your normal reading rate will force you to increase your visual bite and avoid regressing. With practice you will reduce subvocalization. The result will be increased reading speed and comprehension.

• *Make a Conscious Effort*. It may sound unlikely, but you can increase your speed by at least 10 percent simply by telling yourself to speed up. It helps, therefore, if you make a definite commitment to increase your reading speed.

Exercise 9–13. Increasing Your Reading Speed

What is subvocalization?_____.

What is a fixation?_____.

Identify six ways to increase your reading speed_____

_____

_____

It may surprise you to learn that speed-reading courses counsel their students to slow down to about 100 wpm or less for difficult material. One such course spends about one-fourth the time teaching how to study—at a reduced reading rate. It is important to recognize that we have been discussing how to increase your reading rate, not how to speed-read a textbook. The hurricane of page turning you sometimes see advertised on television for speed-reading courses is misleading. You cannot read that way and learn. You cannot read that way and comprehend, recall, and apply the material. Speed reading is popularly understood has little if anything in common with textbook reading and studying. Save the hundreds of dollars some speed-reading courses charge and practice the techniques described above. Above all, read as much as you can. And remember what Woody Allen had to say about speed reading:

"I took a speed-reading course, learning to read straight down the middle of the page, and I was able to go through War and Peace in 20 minutes. It's about Russia."[6]

Here is a summary of ideas on reading:

- Some students can't read because they can't see properly. Make sure you are aware of your eye health. Your eyes are as subject to change as is the rest of your body. Check them at least once a year or whenever you feel discomfort.
- If you have access to a reading laboratory at your college, be sure to take advantage. Your reading ability will be appraised and help provided—including avoiding vocalization.
- You cannot understand a thought unless you first read and understand the words that describe the thought.
- No matter how quickly you can read, you will have to slow down when you encounter difficult material, often to far below your "easy reading" rate of 200 or more wpm. With practice you will know when to speed up or slow down. You have a built-in guide to tell you when to do which—your sense of whether or not you understand the material as you read.
- Read as much as you can. Familiarity with more words and ideas has its own way of increasing your confidence and willingness to read.
- Understand and apply the organizational ideas associated with topic headings, paragraphs, and illustrations.
- Apply skimming intelligently.
- Last, recognize that your goal as a college student is not to turn pages quickly but to turn them at a rate consistent with achieving competency, awareness, and flexibility. For this you need a systematic study approach. Such approaches are dis-

[6]Carver, Ronald P., "Speed Readers Don't Read; They Skim," *Psychology Today,* August, 1972.

cussed in Chapter 15. Your instructor may wish (or you may wish) to go directly to Chapter 15 after you have completed this and the next chapter.

Exercise 9–14. Practice in Increasing Your Reading Speed

Select one of your textbooks and mark off five 1,000-word passages. (Note: Your instructor may provide or direct you to other reading material.) Read and time each passage. Then determine your reading rate in words per minutes. Be sure to apply the speed-increasing techniques discussed above. Do not worry about your comprehension; this exercise is aimed at increasing your reading speed. Repeat this exercise at least two or three times a week for four weeks to gain confidence.

Exercise 9–15. Speed and Comprehension

Repeat Exercise 9–14 with five other 1,000-word passages. This time, after reading each passage, jot down its main ideas. Your reading rate may fall off initially. With repeated practice your rate and your comprehension will increase.

Learning to Read Critically

A critical reader is one who, *while reading,* thinks his or her way up the thought ladder shown in Figure 7–17. The critical reader is most concerned with analysis, evaluation, and synthesis. As applied to critical reading, analysis means recognizing supporting details. Evaluation means using the details to either recognize or make a conclusion or draw an inference[7]. Synthesis means accepting, as new information within yourself, the conclusions reached or inferences drawn.

Assume you had never read paragraph one in Exercise 9–2. Suppose you read the paragraph, not just to identify its main idea, but to critically determine if the main idea is valid.

- *Analysis Step* (Supporting details, both facts and ideas, are identified.) Gulf Stream not in Gulf of Mexico, not one stream but many.
- *Evaluation Step* (Details are used to come to a conclusion or draw an inference.) Based on the details presented, the writer has concluded that the Gulf Stream name is misleading. I think the conclusion is valid.
- *Synthesize Step* (New knowledge and understanding is gained.) Based on analysis and evaluation, I now understand why the Gulf Stream's name is misleading.

[7]As discussed earlier an inference is something said about the unknown based upon the known. If you know a friend who likes raw apples (the known) you might reasonably infer that he or she also likes apple pie (the unknown). To infer that your friend would not like apple pie would ordinarily be a poor inference.

As you can see, critical reading requires you to recognize when a writer has come to a conclusion or when an inference has been drawn. *It also requires that you determine whether such conclusions and inferences are valid.* Note that in addition to the inferences the writer may draw *in* the material there are also inferences a reader may draw *from* the material. For example, from the second paragraph in Exercise 9–2 you might infer that long ago sailors did not like being in the equatorial zone.

Exercise 9–16.   Critical Reading Practice 1
Reread the first two paragraphs in Exercise 9–12 and answer the following questions.

Analysis (Identifying supporting detail) Mark each statement either true or false in the space provided.

_____1. The story takes place in Florida.

_____2. The college advisors found Lucinda academically qualified to attend college.

_____3. In 1783 there were 100 colleges in America.

_____4. The first American college was Yale.

_____5. Harvard refused to admit Lucinda.

Evaluation (Validity of conclusions and inferences) The following statements represent information that does not directly appear in the material. You decide if each statement represents a good or a poor inference. Mark good or poor in the space provided.

_____1. It is wintertime.

_____2. Lucinda is a teenager.

_____3. The president of the college is a woman.

_____4. There were no women in college at that time.

_____5. Lucinda left the building by herself.

_____6. Lucinda eventually went to college.

Synthesis (New understanding or knowledge gained) In the space below write in your overall conclusion based upon the analysis and evaluation performed above.

_____

_____

_____

_____

Exercise 9–17. Critical Reading Practice 2

Read this excerpt from the autobiography of Ben Franklin[8] and answer the following questions.

About this time (while working in a printing shop) I met with an odd volume of the *Spectator.* It was the third. I had never seen any of them. I bought it, read it over and over, and was much delighted with it. I thought the writing excellent, and wished, if possible, to imitate it. With this view I took some of the papers, and, making short hints of the sentiments in each sentence, laid them by a few days. (Then) without looking at the book, (I) tried to complete the papers again, by expressing each hinted sentiment at length, and as fully as it had been expressed before, in any suitable words that came to hand. Then I compared my *Spectator* with the original, discovered some of my faults, and corrected them . . .I also jumbled my collection of hints into confusion, and after some weeks endeavored to reduce them into the best order, before I began to form full sentences and complete the paper. This was to teach me method in the arrangement of thoughts. By comparing my word afterwards with the original I discovered many faults and amended them; but I sometimes had the pleasure of fancying that, in certain particulars of small import, I had been lucky enough to improve the method or the language. (This) encouraged me to think I might possibly in time come to be a tolerable English writer, of which I was extremely ambitious.

Analysis (Identifying supporting detail) Mark true or false.

_____1. Franklin borrowed a book called the *Spectator.*

_____2. He did not like the book.

_____3. He made notes relating to the material he read.

_____4. He showed his sentences to someone for correction.

_____5. He sometimes felt his writing was better than the *Spectator's.*

Evaluation (Validity of conclusions and inferences) Mark each statement good or poor in the space provided.

_____1. Franklin knew many words.

_____2. He had clear handwriting.

_____3. He used one word to represent each sentence.

_____4. He was attending school during the time he describes.

_____5. He obtained additional copies of the *Spectator.*

_____6. The *Spectator* was not generally available.

_____7. He became a fairly good writer.

[8]*The Autobiography of Benjamin Franklin.* Pocket Books, Inc. New York (Undated)

Synthesis (New understanding or knowledge gained) Check your answers. Now write your conclusion below.

_____

_____

_____

_____

Exercise 9–18.   Critical Reading Practice 3
Read the following material[9] and answer the questions that follow.

Birth Order As Related To Popularity

For one reason or another—possibly related to the way they have exercised responsibility or to their level of anxiety—firstborn are apparently not the most popular with their peers. In one study, more than 1,000 children in grades 3, 4, 5 and 6 chose which classmates they liked most and which they liked least. The most popular turned out to be, in order, youngest children, only children, and the second of two children. Then came the second of more than two children, firstborn children, and, as the least popular, middle children.

Norman Miller and Geoffrey Maruyama, of the University of Southern California, recently studied 1,750 grade school children in Riverside, California, to test the idea that last-born children should be the most popular—and firstborn children the least. The children were asked individually:

- Suppose you were picking teams to play ball during recess.
- Who in your class would you most like to have on your team?
- Pretend your teacher is going to let all of the children in your class sit next to his/her best friend. If you had your choice, who would you like to sit next to?
- Suppose your teacher told you that you could pick a work partner from anyone in your class. Who would you pick to be your work partner doing school work?

The results confirmed the investigators' hunch. Most often chosen to be teammates and seatmates were last-born children. Then came the middle-born. *Last were the firstborn.* There were no significant differences among the three groups, though, in the choice of job-mates, probably because in that case the children were looking primarily for achievers.

Analysis (Identifying supporting details)—Mark true or false.

_____1. In the first study the children were 3, 4, 5 and 6 years old.

_____2. The first study involved more than 1,000 children.

_____3. Two people conducted the second study.

[9]Yahraes, Herbert, *Science Reports,* National Institute of Mental Health. United States Department of Health, Education and Welfare. Publication No. (ADM)78-638, 1978.

_____4. The second study concerned students in Connecticut.

_____5. The second study concerned college-age students.

Evaluation (Validity of conclusions and inferences)–Mark each statement good or poor in the space provided.

_____1. The children in the first study were all on the honor roll.

_____2. In the first study about half the children were girls.

_____3. The people who conducted the second study were teachers.

_____4. Firstborn children, even when they become adults, will most often be least popular.

_____5. Last-born children usually achieve more.

Synthesis (New understanding or knowledge gained)–Check your answers. Now write your conclusions below.

_____

_____

_____

_____

Summary

You read textbooks for two reasons. One is to identify what is important to know, the other is to learn what is important to know. The first is called straight reading. The second is called studying. This and the next chapter cover straight reading. Textbook studying is covered in Chapter 15.

Reading a college textbook requires good eye health and the ability to read at the high school level. If these conditions do not exist, then obtain help.

Textbook reading requires knowledge of reading basics and reading approaches. Reading basics include knowledge of words, sentences, paragraph structure, topic headings, and illustrations. Analyze words by looking at their parts. Read sentences by adapting to the author's style. Locate the main idea in paragraphs. Use topic headings to identify the material's pattern of organization. Find the main point in illustrations. Reading approaches include full content reading and skim reading. A paragraph, but not a sentence, can be skimmed.

You can increase your reading speed by avoiding vocalization and subvocalization, by taking a bigger visual bite, by avoiding regression, and by using your hand as a pacer. It is necessary, however, that you make a commitment to yourself to speed up. It is also necessary that you practice as much as possible.

Mark text pages as you read to identify what is important. How to mark textbooks is discussed in the next chapter.

KEY TERMS

Paragraph	Full reading	Illustration
Main idea	Skim reading	Vocalization
Topic sentence	Reading rate	Subvocalization
Supporting details	Reading comprehension	Fixation
Topic headings	Organizational patterns	Regression
Reading approaches	Pattern analysis	Critical reading

REVIEW QUESTIONS

1. Write a sentence that describes each key term shown above.
2. What is the difference between textbook reading and textbook studying?
3. What five elements comprise textbook reading?
4. What is the difference between skimming and full reading?
5. What conditions can cause you to change your reading rate?
6. What can you do to improve your reading speed?

HOW TO READ A TEXTBOOK (Part 2)

BASIC IDEAS
- Recognizing a book's organizational pattern promotes understanding.
- The main purpose of textbook reading is to take notes.
- Textbook reading skills also apply to nontextbook material.

KEY POINTS
- How do you say hello to a textbook?
- What are the several methods of textbook marking and note taking?
- What if your textbook is four or five paperbacks?

Making Friends With Your Text

Chapters are easier to understand if you first place them in context. If you spend fifteen or twenty minutes getting familiar with your text, you can: (1) help overcome the fear some texts may hold for you, (2) see the chapters' organizational pattern, and (3) reduce anxiety about picking up your text in the first place. The whole point is: Learn to adjust to your texts by making friends with them. Here is a method for doing so.

Read the preface. The author will usually tell you the purpose of the book, give his or her point of view, and explain the organization of the book. The preface allows you to understand the reason for and the placement of each chapter. Since there are many ways of arranging ideas and studying a subject, the author may also suggest alternate ways of proceeding through the book. (This is one of the reasons your teacher may jump from one text part to another during the term and why outside reading is often assigned.) Reading the preface helps humanize the book as well as providing a very broad idea of the subject matter. Sometimes the book's introduction or first chapter covers these points.

Review the table of contents. Topic outlines are discussed in Chapter 7. You will recall how important they are to organized thinking and how they help promote understanding. A table of contents is usually a very good topic outline of the text's main ideas.

Look through the index. The index will allow you to recognize names, places, and ideas you already know. You can familiarize yourself with the subject's vocabulary. Reviewing the index will help make the book less awesome and distant.

Leaf through the book. Just casually turn the pages. Occasionally read a paragraph. Nothing heavy. Just try and attain a sense of the author's writing style and illustrations.

Randomly select two or three chapters and read the summaries that may appear after each. Also read the topic headings in another chapter or two.

Most of all, relax. You will be with your text for three or four months. You are starting on a trip and, as the manager of your learning, you have the power to make it very interesting. So relax and just try to make the book familiar to you. Pick a time and place that will allow you to be alone. Then follow the steps described above.

Exercise 10–1.   Analyzing Overall Organizational Patterns

A major reason for making friends with your book is to establish its organizational pattern. You are more or less asking the question, "How has the author arranged the chapters; what thought sequence has been employed?"

Evaluate your ability to understand a text's organizational pattern by doing the following:

a. Select one of your course textbooks and complete the first two columns below.

b. Establish the book's thought pattern by referring only to its table of contents.

c. Enter the pattern name you think applies in the third column below. (Use the organization pattern terminology outlined on page 132. Remember: more than one pattern can apply.)

d. Repeat this procedure for all your current textbooks.

Subject	*Textbook Name*	*Overall Text Pattern*

Why Textbook Marking Is Important

You listen in class and you read a textbook for the same purpose: to attain a set of notes to study. In class you write in your notebook the important things said. But with textbooks the important things have already been written down. Your textbook reading aim therefore is to identify and mark what is important to know. Marking a textbook is equivalent to classroom note taking.

A reasonable question at this point is, "If it has been written down, I already have the notes, so why bother marking at all?" The answer is basic. There is no way you can remember *all* you read. Therefore, you mark what is *essential* so it may be studied. You also mark a text for another important reason. Reading a textbook can be compared to watching some social, political, or sporting event. The chances are you would find such events more understandable, interesting, and rewarding if you participated rather than simply watched. The same applies to textbook reading. Too often you probably find yourself "watching" a text rather than really getting involved in the material. Textbook marking or note taking allows you to participate more directly in what you read. And, as you already know, participation is an aid to learning.

In summary, textbook marking promotes understanding, provokes interest, provides a tangible record for your efforts, and assists learning.

How to Mark a Textbook

Marking a textbook requires first a recognition of what is important to mark and then application of clear, simple, systematic marking methods. Here are some helpful approaches to both recognition and marking.

Recognizing What Is Important

There are three sources that help establish what is important: your author, your teacher, and yourself.

An author provides three main clues to important material. These are paragraph structure, topic headings, and illustrations. See the discussion in the previous chapter on how to identify main ideas using these three elements.

A teacher provides at least three main clues. These are (1) a course outline (syllabus) or a list of objectives at the first class meeting, (2) classroom comments which indicate where emphasis should be placed in a given chapter, and (3) responses to your direct questions on what is considered most important.

You decide what is important by (1) being sensitive to author and teacher clues, (2) referring to your self-derived and/or teacher-based Management-By-Motivation Chart (see Chapter 5), and, if you lack the first two clues, (3) by emphasizing material that happens to interest you.

Marking What is Important

There are two approaches to textbook marking or note taking. One uses identifiers, the other the white space on a text page. When you underline, highlight, number, bracket, or place a check mark to identify important material, you are using *identifiers*. This paragraph has been marked to illustrate some of these techniques. You can also use available space on a page to summarize or restate text material. An example of this is shown in Figure 10–1. Marking a text page helps you participate in what you read. It involves you directly with the material. Marking results in study notes and promotes understanding and retention.

One last point. Some students don't mark their books because they plan to sell them. College costs represent a real problem for many students. But not marking texts is a poor way to meet expenses. With the few extra resale dollars you might receive, you could never purchase the lost learning that results from leaving your books unmarked. (Remember, you can always use a pencil and later remove the marks.)

Things to Do When Marking

A text page full of identifiers with most every line underlined can confuse rather than promote understanding. Therefore:

- Use identifiers sparingly.
- Stick to marking main ideas.
- *Do not underline long passages* of text material. The chances are you will confuse this act with studying. You will deprive yourself of the use of the study systems described in Chapter 15. It's better to use a vertical line in the margin or a simple check mark.
- When using white space, keep your comments simple and direct. Your ability to create simple and direct comments is a signal that you have achieved adequate comprehension.

Figure 10–1 shows a reasonably marked textbook page. Note how the few underlines and comments adequately mark what is important

Figure 10–1
Using Identifiers and Available Page Space to Mark a Text[1]
(Note use of margin comments, vertical brackets, and limited use of underlining)

tain, they do not refer to reality." Therefore, even in an area such as chemistry, in which the vocabulary is quite strictly "policed," statements logically deduced *still have to be checked* against extensional observation. This is another reason why the rule for extensional orientation—cat_1 is not cat_2—is extremely important. No matter how carefully we have defined the word "cat," and no matter how logically we have reasoned, extensional cats still have to be examined.

[margin: STEREO-TYPING IS DANGEROUS]

The belief that logic will substantially reduce misunderstanding is widely and uncritically held, although, as a matter of common experience, we all know that people who pride themselves on their logic are usually, of all the people we know, the hardest to get along with. Logic can lead to agreement only when, as in mathematics or the sciences, there are *pre-existing,* hard-and-fast agreements as to what words stand for. But among our friends, business associates, and casual acquaintances—some of them Catholic and some Protestant, some of them no-nonsense scientists and some mystics, some sports fans and some interested in nothing but money—only the vaguest of linguistic agreements exist. In ordinary conversation, therefore, we have to learn people's vocabularies in the course of talking with them—which is what all sensible and tactful people do, without even being aware of the process.

[margin: LOGIC HAS ITS LIMITATIONS]

On the whole, therefore, except in mathematics and other areas where clear-cut linguistic agreements either exist or can be brought into existence, the assiduous study and practice of traditional, two-valued logic is not recommended.[5] The habitual reliance on two-valued logic *in everyday life* quickly leads to a two-valued orientation—and we have already seen what *that* leads to.

[margin: NON-MATH THINGS CAN BE LOOKED AT FROM MORE THAN 2 WAYS]

Korzybski was rarely concerned with the specific *content* of people's beliefs—whether people were religious or unreligious, liberal or conservative. He was concerned, rather, with how people held their beliefs and convictions: whether with a two-valued orientation ("I am right and everybody else is wrong") or a multi-valued orientation ("I don't know—let's see"). Korzybski saw the two-valued orientation as an *internalization* of the laws of Aristotelian logic, which say that:

[5]It is interesting to note that even in mathematics, stress is laid today on the fact that two-valued logic is only one of many possible systems of logic. The logic of probability, on the basis of which insurance companies quote premiums, bookmakers quote odds, and physicists predict the behavior of neutrons, may be regarded as an infinite-valued logic.

[1]Excerpted from S. I. Hayakawa, *Language in Thought and Action,* 2nd ed. Copyright © 1964 by Harcourt Brace Jovanovich, Inc., New York, and reprinted with their permission.

to know. Remember the basic aim of marking is to assemble such marks (notes) into a systematic method of study.

Exercise 10–3. Marking a Text Page
For each chapter used in Exercise 10–2 select a page at random. Then read and mark each page as illustrated in Figure 10–1, using identifiers and page space.

Reading Nontextbook Written Material

Teachers will often assign supplemental reading in order to:

- Allow you the opportunity to consider alternative viewpoints.
- Update material that appears in the text.
- Supplement the text for selected topic areas.
- Expose you to advanced concepts concerning the subject matter.

If the supplemental material is another textbook, you can read it as you would any other. But often the supplemental reading is drawn from paperbacks, magazines, and newspapers. These may not have the highly organized structure common to textbooks. The usual clues found in topic headings and illustrations may be missing. Also you are usually not in a position (unless you erase) to mark the material as you would a textbook you own. How do you read such material?

In textbook reading you rely on topic headings to provide an understandable framework. Then you read. In supplemental reading you are more or less forced to do the reverse. As you read the material you must be sensitive to the main ideas so you can construct a thought pattern in which to place the material. Here is a procedure for doing so:

1. Read the first and last paragraphs in the article.
2. Go back to the beginning and, as you *completely* read each subsequent sentence or paragraph, write down a key word or phrase.
3. When you've completed the reading, construct an outline based on your markings. Reread the article and revise and add to the outline as necessary to achieve understanding.

Figure 10–2 illustrates how to apply this system to an article which contains minimal content clues. The first set of notes is a result of an initial reading. Depending upon your reading purpose these notes may be sufficient. The second set of notes represents the result of an attempt to organize the material in your own fashion. These notes may not follow the pattern of the original article; but your pattern will be more meaningful to you simply because it's your own version of what you've read.

Figure 10–2
Reading Non-Textbook Material

Typical key words or phases resulting from an initial review of the newspaper article.

Survey of College Graduates (WSJ 12/12/76)
- *College graduate survey*
- *Half in different field than major*
- *Should study other subjects*
- *College helpful for jobs*
- *Should broaden studies*

Typical resultant outline based on above notes and a second reading. The outline represents your reading notes.

Survey of College Graduates (WSJ 12/12/76)
I   *College graduate survey (1961, 4100 students)*
II *Survey Results*
- *One half in different field than major*
- *Students said they should have taken broader subjects. i.e:*
  - *English, psychology, business administration*
  - *Communications, human relations,*
III *Conclusion, (by College Placement Council)*
- *College helpful for*
  - *broad knowledge*
  - *job finding*
- *But not helpful for*
  - *leadership ability*
  - *clear thinking*
  - *choosing life goals*
- *College should stress courses that promote job flexibility, not just preparation for a specific occupation because of 50% factor*

With practice you will be able to produce notes for nontextbook material which will be equivalent to a set of class or text notes.

Exercise 10–4.   Reading Nontextbook Material
Select a short article in a magazine. Create an outline for the article using the three-step procedure described above.

Attributes of a Good College Reader

Here is a summary of the reading skills discussed in this and the previous chapter. Apply them and you will be a good textbook reader.

Portion of Text	Action to Take
Total text	• Review for general familiarity. • Identify organizational pattern.
Chapters and topic headings	• Review for general familiarity. • Identify organizational pattern.
Paragraphs	• Recognize that most paragraphs follow inductive or deductive pattern. • Look for main idea.
Sentences	• Become sensitive to author's writing style. • Look for words and punctuation that signal changes in thought direction.
Words	• Promote interest and understanding by analyzing affixes and roots. • Look up words in dictionary. • Enhance vocabulary through increased general reading.

Condition	Recognition to Make
Speed reading	Is of little or no use for most college level material.
Skimming	Cannot skim sentence but can skim paragraph.
Eye health	Check periodically.

Activity	Recognition to Make
Reading	Reading approaches and techniques depend upon your purpose. Skill in textbook reading is cumulative. Your skill increases every time you read.
Studying	Is more than reading. Studying requires a systematic effort employing participation, organization, and persistence.
Marking	Text marking is equivalent to class note taking. Use identifiers and white space on page.
Nontextbook material	Create own outline.

Summary

Making friends with your texts is an important step in the learning process. Help yourself understand and retain what you read by becoming familiar with the author's intent. Then determine the book's overall thought pattern. Both these are accomplished by reading the book's preface, looking at its table of contents and index, and sampling a few chapters.

You mark a textbook to identify what is important to know. Marking techniques include the use of identifiers and restatements. Text markings should be used sparingly. The aim is to identify main ideas.

Supplemental reading is assigned to promote wider appreciation for a subject. Such readings may not have neatly structured paragraphs, topic headings, and illustrations. This chapter provides a method for reading such material.

The end result of classroom listening and text and nontext reading is to identify what is important to know. Chapter 15 provides several methods of study that allow assembly of all your notes into systemized methods of study. The systems of study will promote interest in and retention of the material you study. You or your instructor may now wish to go directly from this chapter to Chapter 15.

KEY TERMS

Preface	Identifiers
Table of contents	White space
Index	Restatement
Organizational pattern	Nontextbook outline
Course outline (syllabus)	Reader attributes
Course objectives	

REVIEW QUESTIONS

1. Write a sentence that describes each key term above.
2. Describe three methods of marking a page through use of identifiers.
3. Describe how to use the white space on a text page.
4. Describe the three-step process for reading nontextbook material.
5. Why should you avoid underlining?
6. Select and describe three reader attributes you think most important.

HOW TO LISTEN AND TAKE NOTES IN CLASS

BASIC IDEAS
- The classroom is the center of your college education.
- Class meetings result in learning and a record for study.
- Listening is voluntary.

KEY POINTS
- Can the classroom help you manage your studies?
- What is the difference between hearing and listening?
- What are the attributes of a good classroom listener?

Maybe you were up late the night before. Perhaps you rushed from work to make a 6 P.M. evening class. In any event you enter class and find a seat near the back. The teacher starts talking. You open your notebook and start writing. Before too long your eyes glaze over and your pencil falls to the page. You then fall asleep sitting straight up—with your eyes open.

What can you do to promote more learning and avoid boredom and indifference in the classroom? "Wait," you might say, "isn't that the teacher's job—isn't he or she supposed to keep me interested?" To a degree the answer is yes. The things to expect from a teacher are: an interest in the course; an indication, spoken or written, of what you are expected to learn; an ability to explain things; preparation for each meeting; homework and project assignments; clear answers to all questions; counsel and advice when asked; and timely return of exams and assignments with written comments as necessary. To expect teachers also to hold up your end of the classroom bargain is not fair or possible. What is your end of the bargain?

The first test you take in class is not four or five weeks into the term. The first test occurs at the first class meeting. And the same test is repeated at each subsequent meeting. It's a test of your ability to manage your education. Your end of the bargain, therefore, is to develop the ability to keep yourself interested in your own education. How can you do this?

Applied to the classroom, this question can be rephrased: "What is the classroom all about and how can I get the most from it?" This chapter will help provide an answer.

Educational Aims and the Classroom

It's true that little time is spent in class. Does this mean class is not important? "If the material is already in the text and I know how to study a text, why should I bother with classes in the first place?" The answer is that texts are limited. They cannot provide answers to the questions shown below. These questions relate to the educational aims of competency, awareness, and flexibility.

Competency

- What is important to know in this course?
- Is all the course material in the text?
- What can I do if I don't understand the text?
- What are the assignments and special projects?
- What should I emphasize when I study the text?
- Does the text cover all that is important to know?
- Where can I find out the latest developments regarding this subject?
- Will the exams be weighted more toward the class work, the text, or about even?
- Can I find someone who is specially trained and qualified to discuss this subject matter—someone who will explain the ideas and answer my questions?
- Where can I get answers to my questions?
- What will exams be like?
- Where can I determine the underlying ideas that tie together all the course material?

Awareness

- Where can I find a group of people who are interested in this same subject; people with whom I can talk and study?

- What options are open to me if I need help?
- Where can I learn about this subject other than the text?
- Where can I gauge my level of achievement?
- Where can I get to know what others different from myself are like?

Flexibility

- Where can I develop my ability to work with others in a constructive fashion?
- Where can I test my understanding and display what I know?
- Where can I learn to socialize with people?
- Is there a friendly environment where I can develop speaking confidence?

You can, of course, find answers to some of these questions without ever attending class. You can achieve a measure of college credit through correspondence schools or through programs such as "College Without Walls." For some people at certain points in life these may be entirely appropriate choices. But you have chosen to register for classes. And your college, although it provides many outside-the-classroom learning experiences, is geared to answer most of these questions in the classroom. Therefore, the time spent in and around class, though small, becomes all the more precious.

Necessary Classroom Skills

Figure 11–1 shows what you need to do well in class. It also shows that the prime reason for attending class is to achieve increased competency, awareness, and flexibility plus—and it's a big plus—notes for later study.

Aside from an ability to think in an organized fashion, the college classroom requires that you arrive prepared. It also requires that you achieve at least a minimum capability in classroom listening, note taking, and sociability. These points are discussed in the following sections.

Listening

How Much Do You Listen?

Suppose you were asked to identify which occupation involved the most amount of listening. Would it surprise you that students—despite the rather small amount of time spent in classrooms—lead the way? Students spend 20 percent of all waking hours just listening. If

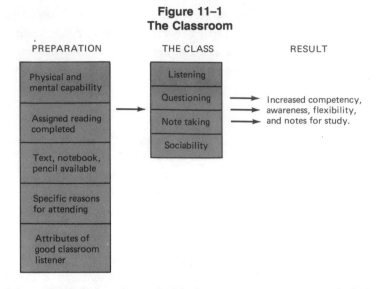

Figure 11–1
The Classroom

PREPARATION

- Physical and mental capability
- Assigned reading completed
- Text, notebook, pencil available
- Specific reasons for attending
- Attributes of good classroom listener

THE CLASS

- Listening
- Questioning
- Note taking
- Sociability

RESULT

Increased competency, awareness, flexibility, and notes for study.

television watching and one-half of conversations are included, students spend approximately 50 percent of their waking hours listening.[1] For those waking hours spent in class, the amount of listening time can approach 100 percent. Think of your own communicating activities, especially those related to college. Aren't most of your actions and reactions gained through listening, especially when in the classroom?

A clear conclusion can be drawn. As a student you obtain a good portion of your information through listening. The quality of the decisions you make, the understanding you achieve, and the notes you take is directly related to how well you listen.

You do a great deal of listening for very important reasons. It's obviously something at which you want to be good.

Just What Is Listening?

If you ask a group of people to give a one-word description of *listening,* some would say *hearing.* And that can be a problem, because the word hearing is not an adequate substitute. It doesn't describe the process of listening. Hearing is physical. If your ears are not impaired, you can hear. You make no special effort to hear sound. But you do make a special mental effort if you want to follow and understand the sound (determining whether steps are approaching or receding, the nature of a baby's cry, someone speaking). The special effort is what distinguishes listening from hearing. Hearing is simply receiving sound. Listening is following and understanding the sound. It is hearing with a purpose.

[1]Drawn from L. Samovar, R. Brooks, and R. Porter, "A Survey of Adult Communication Activities," in James W. Gibson, *A Reader in Speech Communications* (New York: McGraw-Hill, 1971).

Are you attaching to the word *listening* a meaning it doesn't deserve? For example, a topic heading in this chapter is "How Much Do You Listen?" Did this heading make you think you were in for a lecture on why you should be a good person and always listen to others? Remember the last time somebody said to you, "You never listen" or "You're not listening" or "You always misunderstand me—why don't you listen?" It's possible such experiences have biased you against the word *listening*. When there are discussions dealing with listening (such as this one) you may react unfavorably because you think you are in for another sermon. This discussion is not aimed in that direction. The kind of listening that will really help you in the classroom is related to keeping an open mind so you can change and develop. It is through such openness that you will achieve your educational aims. Listening well in class is not easy, but it is a major factor in college learning. And listening is your main classroom activity.

Managing Classroom Listening

There is a basic question you must answer when you step into a classroom: "Do I want to listen?" No one can force you to listen. Listening is voluntary. Furthermore, it's not enough to say: "Okay, I'm committed, I'm willing to focus my divided interests in one direction. I want to listen in class." Your *desire* to listen must match an ability to listen. The following discusses techniques you can use to become a good classroom listener.

Exercise 11–1. Listening Situations and Remedies

Form a group of at least three for the five listening situations in this section. Have one member read Situation 1 and its remedy while the others record the main ideas. These ideas should be recorded in your notebook in two columns, one labeled "Situations" and the other labeled "Remedy." Members take turns reading a situation and remedy.

Your instructor may decide to read the material to you or have you read it by yourself. If so, follow the directions given.

Situation 1. Mind Wandering: Experiments show that most people prefer to receive spoken words at an average of about 175 words per minute. While this may be comfortable, it also allows time for your mind to wander. This occurs because your mind can process words faster than someone's physical ability to say them. That you prefer to listen to someone who speaks at 175 words per minute only means you can clearly make out the spoken words. It doesn't mean you understand the meaning of the words or the ideas they represent. Therefore, a teacher has to speak slowly enough to promote understanding. This may require rates below 100 words per minute supported by chalkboard diagrams. Of course, if the teacher slows down, there is still more opportunity for your mind to wander.

The Remedy: To minimize mind wandering use these five techniques:

1. Select one or more items from your self-derived and/or teacher-based Management-By-Motivation Chart or create some just prior to or even while you are in class. This helps focus attention. The more specific your reasons, the more you will listen for and recognize related material.
2. Read assigned material and identify questions before you go to class. Then listen for the answers or ask for clarifications.
3. Review assigned problems even if they are due at a later date. Then listen for the answers in class. This can keep you interested in class and cut down homework time. This is an example of using class time as study time.
4. Recognize that you will soon forget most of what you listen to. Therefore, you will have to keep a record of the important things said. You can promote interest by keeping good notes. These notes will improve the effectiveness of study sessions.
5. Look directly at the teacher. This helps focus attention and allows you to observe visual clues that add meaning to what is said.

Situation 2. Critical Listening: Your personal evaluation of a teacher can prevent new learning. If you like a teacher, you are apt to accept what he or she says. While this may be comfortable, it may not be intellectually correct. A special critical effort is necessary when listening to teachers you like. Conversely, a teacher you don't like will nevertheless have valid and important things to say.

The Remedy. Make a special effort not to prejudge what a teacher can contribute to your learning. Regardless of the source, you should question words or ideas that don't fit your existing views and understandings. You can, of course, mindlessly accept or simply dismiss words or ideas that you don't understand or that don't match your own point of view. But if you do, aren't you also dismissing the very reason why you are sitting in class?

Situation 3. Distractions: Here are some methods that will absolutely ensure your distraction in class: (1) Sit in the very back of the class. This makes it difficult to hear and will allow distraction by the movements, side conversations, and quirks of those in front of you. (2) Sit by a window. (3) Wear a watch twice the width of your wrist. Look at it every 4.2 seconds. Make sure the watch has stop-second hands with a two-way laser beam TV/CB weather vane radio combination.

The Remedy: You get the idea. Why encourage divided attention by subjecting yourself to unnecessary distractions? Where should you sit? You might try somewhere in the front half of the class around the middle.

Situation 4. Organization: The presence of organization promotes understanding. Most lectures will be organized; they will usually follow a topic outline format. However, this organization may not be obvious unless you recognize clues provided by the teacher.

The Remedy: Observe, understand, and adapt to the speaking and teaching style of each of your instructors. Develop the ability to identify spoken and visual clues. The teacher may write the topics on the chalkboard. If so, you have the main lecture ideas. The teacher may verbally describe what is to be covered by saying, "Now let's talk about . . ." or "There are four items of interest; these are . . . ." If no verbal clues are provided, look for a shift in tone of voice or body position. Some clues are obvious, some not. If you practice recognizing them, the lecture's sense of organization will be more apparent to you.

Situation 5. Unasked Questions: Classroom listening is not a one-way communication. An unasked question is a lost opportunity. When you ask a question you gain at least two things: understanding and reduced study time.

The Remedy: To learn to ask questions in class, see the first part of Chapter 13.

Exercise Exercise 11–2.   The Effect of Culture, Education, and Experience:

You (and all other people) have arrived at your present life stage with a particular way of functioning in and looking at the world around you. Culture, education, and experience have all combined to shape your view of people, places, things, and ideas. But since it's your unique view, it cannot coincide exactly with those of other people. (See Figure 11–2.)

Even people whose backgrounds are essentially similar (i.e., brothers and sisters) can and do have different viewpoints. This special view is an image you carry of yourself. Psychologist Carl Rogers calls this image the *self-concept.* You tend to reject ideas or thoughts and their associated words because they are not consistent with your self-concept. To accept them requires a self-concept change, a difficult task because of years of thinking and acting in established patterns.

What has all this to do with listening? Reacting as above means you will put your own special meaning on words, especially abstract words such as *love, democracy, management, education,* and *listening.* Such views, since they represent your personal biases, can prevent you from acquiring new learning.

Giving personal meanings to words is a way of showing that all people hold

Figure 11–2
The Effect of Culture, Education, and Experience
on Classroom Listening

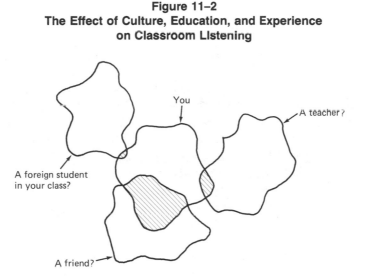

- Shaded portions represent areas of mutual understanding.
- The closer the three factors of culture, education, and experience, the better the chance of understanding.
- Clear areas represent potential to exhibit biases toward people and ideas, but they also represent great potential for increased learning. Which it will be depends upon your desire to give yourself a chance to comprehend and reflect when you meet new people and new ideas.

biases with respect to things, ideas, and people. You can be biased for or against something. Whichever it is, the ability to recognize that you do hold biases is necessary. Such recognition will help promote new learning. This exercise game shows that the meanings of even common words depend on the individual.

Form a group of four or more people. Across a piece of paper each member writes the words *love, food, democracy,* and *pencil.* Now beneath the word *love* list at least two other words that you believe describe the word *love.* Repeat for the remaining three words. Have one of the group members make a consolidated listing of all entries.

    a. What do you think accounts for any differences that show up?

    b. Which words had the most differences? Explain why.

Exercise 11–3. Listening Clues

Make a two-column table. Head one column "Teacher Name" and the other "Speaking or Teaching Characteristic That Indicates a Main Point." Then, for your next series of classes, complete the table by making a special effort to identify each instructor's "Teaching Code." Try to make a game of it. You will engage in an interesting exercise and learn something about human nature as well.

Taking Notes

Even if it were possible to listen to everything in class, you would soon forget most of it within 24 hours. You need to study class material until you are reasonably sure of it. To study you need a record of what was said. Notes provide that record.

The Notebook

Consider these points when purchasing a notebook:

- Loose-leaf books have more flexibility than bound books and can be divided to accommodate the notes taken in each course.
- If you are taking a math or science course, cross-section paper will help in drawing diagrams and graphs.
- Generally speaking, an 8½ x 11 page size is better than smaller sizes simply because you can record more related ideas on one page.
- Make sure you always have something to write with.

What to Record

Note taking is a compromise between just listening to everything and trying to record everything. You cannot do both. But you do have to make a record of what is considered important. How do you know what is important?

- First, review the pointers discussed in Situation 4 above.
- Second, the teacher may have provided course objectives at the first class meeting; record material related to these objectives.

ORGANIZING YOUR LEARNING: SKILLS YOU NEED

- Third, record items that are interesting or important to you.
- Last, the teacher will actually tell you what is important. He or she will:
    - Write on the blackboard.
    - Emphasize points in his or her speech by saying, "Now this is important" or "The three main ideas are . . ." or "This is a point to remember."
    - Ask questions.
    - Change the tone and rate of speaking or change his or her body position.

How to Record

Follow this approach when taking notes:

Format the page: Divide the page into two sections. Label one section "Key Words" and the other "Notes" (see Figure 11–3).

Use thought organizers: Record notes in outline format. You can use a modified topic outline, dot/dashes, stick diagram, or a combination of the three. See Chapter 7 for a discussion of these thought-organizing techniques. Use a symbol (e.g.,*) to highlight definitions or points that are repeated or stressed during the lecture.

Write clearly: Since notes are for later study, they must be clearly written. If your script handwriting is less than desirable, then print your notes. Print writing or a combination of script and print can be faster than plain script since many connecting lines and loops are eliminated. For example, instead of *k, d, f, p* and *y*, write k, d, f, P and y .

Abbreviate: Note-taking speed is often important. One basic rule is to avoid completely writing out a term that is likely to occur frequently during a lecture. For example, if the term *computer* keeps recurring, write $c = computer$ and then use c in the remainder of your notes for that lecture. Do the same with names, places, and ideas that are likely to occur often. After a few class meetings you should be able to develop your own shorthand for each course.

Here are some abbreviations you can use:

std = standard	bus = business	e.g. = for example
def = definition	gvt = government	∴ = therefore
info = information	eco = economics	+ = and
eng = English	psy = psychology	w/ = with

Key your notes: Soon after the lecture (or during the lecture, if possible) write in key words that summarize main points. Use the "Key Words" column. This serves two purposes: (1) it helps fix in your mind important points covered and (2) it makes your class notes more useful when you employ the study systems described in Chapter 15.

Figure 11-3
A Sample Page of Class Notes
(note use of thought organizers—see Chapt. 7)

March 7	*PSY 202*
Key Words	Notes
Behavior therapy ↓ Control excesses	Behavior Therapy (BT) 1. Idea behind self-control method is: person doing too much of one thing or not enough of another.
Poor habits	eg: — eating too much — sleeping too much — not studying enough — smoking too much — watching too much TV
Self-Mgt.	2. BT is method that allows person to manage self to achieve change (also called Behavior Modification–BM) • Some problems require therapist • Others can do by self
Practical uses	eg: — Ben Franklin monitored own actions to improve self. — Japanese students write on walls to keep goals in mind * — Students can use BM to increase study time, lose weight, etc. (Check this out-get reference)
Behav./ thought	3. Basic Techniques • Influence behav. directly • Influence thoughts which in turn infl. behav.

Figure 11–3 illustrates the points discussed above.

Exercise 11–4.   What Do You Know About Listening and Note Taking?
Fill in the blank lines in the following table.

Factor	What to Do
Preparation	• Listening is enhanced if you are familiar with the words and ideas to be discussed. Therefore, prior to class:

	• _____
	• _____
	• _____
Mind Wandering	• Establish specific listening purposes. _____
	• _____
	• _____
	• _____
Biases	• Recognize you have them. _____
	• _____
	• _____
Distractions	• _____
	• _____
Organization and Questions	• Look for written and spoken evidence of lecture's main points. _____
	• _____
	• _____
	• _____
Note Taking	• Use thought organizers. _____
	• _____
	• _____
	• _____
	• _____
	• _____
Teacher	• Don't confuse like/dislike for subject with like/dislike for teacher. _____
	• Represents one part of listening bargain; you represent the other. _____
	• _____

Exercise 11–5. Listening in Class
Have someone read three pages from a textbook to you. Ask questions during the

reading. (Your instructor may want to give you or read you special material.) Be sure to apply the listening and note-taking techniques discussed in this chapter.

Exercise 11–6.   Listening in the Library
Listen to an audio tape in the college library. Apply the listening and note-taking techniques described in this chapter. Write a one-page summary of the tape based on your notes.

Exercise 11–7.   Listening at Home
Repeat Exercise 11–6 but this time use a one-half hour television news program.

Sociability

Sociability is the quality of being with people in an agreeable manner. The first person you are always with is yourself. Not feeling well physically or mentally reduces your ability to function in a classroom. A good diet and a reasonable amount of physical activity will help maintain your physical condition. You can try handling emotional problems by seeking help or trying to help yourself. You can also use the classroom for temporary change or relief from the tensions and problems that may be bothering you.

The next person of concern is your teacher. You have seen how difficult it can be to listen well, even if the speaker is good and the subject interesting. Teachers also know that listening is difficult. Therefore they are concerned with providing clear explanations and keeping the attention and interest of those in class. When someone comes in late, drops books, scrapes chairs, falls asleep, or continually engages in side conversations . . . well you can see the distracting effect this has on both the teacher and students. The last thing most teachers want to do is reprimand someone for poor class behavior. Having to do so wastes time and is demoralizing.

It is important to relate positively to your classmates. The classroom is an excellent place to find friends and study partners. There you can be and work with people different from yourself. You will meet life's challenges in the company of others for the rest of your life. The classroom is a positive mutually supportive place to learn to meet such challenges.

Summary

The classroom is the center of your college learning. From class you determine what is important to learn and how you will be evaluated. The class allows direct access to a knowledgeable teacher as well as students to study with.

The basic classroom skills are listening, questioning, note taking, and sociability. Listening is hearing with a purpose. To listen requires effort because your mind wanders, you tend to exhibit your biases, and you are subject to distractions. You can minimize mind wandering by establishing reasons to attend class and by note taking. Handle your biases by first recognizing that you do hold them; then act to minimize their influence, perhaps by asking questions. Minimize distractions by sitting center-forward in the class.

Questioning can promote understanding and save study time. The ability to question is the mark of a good manager, one concerned with being both efficient and effective.

The purpose of notes is to provide a record of what you should study. Notes taken in an organized fashion will be usable for later study.

Sociability means getting along with those around you. The classroom offers an opportunity to meet and work with people different from yourself. In class you can build competency in a particular subject, develop your sense of awareness of new ideas and people, and gain flexibility by sharpening your ability to speak and listen.

KEY TERMS

Educational aims	Critical listening	Note taking
Hearing	Distractions	Printing
Listening	Thought organizers	Abbreviations
Mind wandering	Questions	Key words
Preparation	Teaching code	Sociability
Word meanings		

REVIEW QUESTIONS

1. Describe each key term above.
2. Which educational aims are associated with the classroom?
3. Describe why the classroom is the center of your college learning.
4. What skills are necessary to achieve capability in the classroom?
5. Describe the difference between hearing and listening.
6. List and briefly describe the major factors that concern listening.
7. What purpose is served by class notes?
8. Prepare a topic outline based on Figure 11–1.
9. Prepare a stick diagram that describes why listening in class requires a special effort.
10. Prepare a block diagram that shows how you can become a better class listener.

HOW TO WRITE A GOOD TERM PAPER

BASIC IDEAS
- Your main job as a writer is to promote understanding.
- The most important person is always the reader.
- Always tell the reader what you plan to say.

KEY POINTS
- Why are term papers assigned?
- How can you pick an interesting topic?
- Can you manage a term paper project?

Why Term Papers?

There are valuable learning experiences associated with writing a term paper. Some of these, which may surprise you, are as follows:

- Term papers tell whether you can put your ideas in order. They tell if you can promote understanding in others. The ability to write a clear term paper will help you speak clearly in class and answer essay questions.
- A term paper allows a mistake to be made in a friendly environment. You gain insight into the things you do well and those needing improvement. The result is improved overall performance.
- One of the reasons for attending college is to assume greater job-related responsibilities. On-the-job assignments require you to work efficiently, correctly, and independently. So do term papers. Employers prize the ability to work by oneself with a minimum of direction. Preparing a term paper simulates job conditions. It allows you to show initiative, exercise judgment, and use your problem-solving abilities. Doing these successfully provides you with the self-confidence to perform similarly when on the job.

- Term papers provide a learning experience outside the classroom. They allow you to apply and interpret classroom learning in a new setting. How well you transfer such knowledge will show you how much you have learned.
- No one can know everything about anything. This applies to the authors of your texts, to your instructors, and to yourself. The world outside the classroom contains many resources, which provide you with new sources of information, new ideas, and alternate viewpoints. Getting a student into this setting is a responsibility your instructors feel—and one you should accept. After all, it's the setting we actually live in.

The Term Paper Writing System

Here are the steps in this simple writing system. Follow them and you will write good term papers.

1. Determine the purpose of your paper.
2. Prepare an outline.
3. Gather facts.
4. Write your paper.
5. Review your paper.
6. Prepare and assemble your paper.
7. Submit your paper on time.

This system will allow you to plan, organize, and control your term paper efforts. The following discusses each step.

STEP 1. DETERMINE THE PURPOSE (TOPIC)
OF YOUR PAPER

Before you can hope to promote understanding in others, you must first promote it in yourself. If your intent is not clear in your mind, it won't be clear in your instructor's when he or she reads the finished paper. Your paper will be downgraded.

If your instructor provides a general topic, then work that topic into a one-sentence statement of purpose. The statement must be (1) narrow in scope, (2) interesting to you, and (3) clearly stated in writing. Here is an exercise that shows how to achieve all three.

Exercise 12–1. Creating a Narrow Topic
Assume your instructor has asked you to "Write a five-page paper on outer space exploration in the last 25 years." Here is how to narrow the topic using the Question-Then-Narrow Technique.

General Topic: Outer Space Exploration—Last 25 Years

Questions

1. Should I discuss balloons, rockets, unmanned spaceships, or manned spaceships?
2. Should I discuss their design or their mission?
3. Those that orbited the earth or those that visited other planets?

Narrowings

1. I think I will choose unmanned spaceships.
2 Their mission (why they were sent) sounds more interesting.
3. Other planets.

You could continue to question and narrow, but let's stop here. Notice that the topic has not only been narrowed. Since you are asking the questions and making the choices, you are also guiding the topic to reflect your interests.

The next step is to prepare a one-sentence statement of purpose. The information for this sentence comes from all your entries in the "Narrowings" column. Here is an example: "The purpose of this paper is to discuss the missions of unmanned space flights to other planets during the last 25 years." This topic sentence (statement of purpose) is a long distance from the instructor's original statement. At this point show your sentence to your instructor for approval. When you write the paper, be sure to include the statement either in your paper's title or somewhere in the paper's first paragraph.

Exercise 12–2. Practice in Narrowing a Topic
For each general topic below prepare and complete "Questions-Narrowings" columns in your notebook. Then create a statement of purpose for each topic. Narrow the topic as much as you want, but use at least three steps.

1. The Family
2. Sports in America
3. Protecting the Environment

Sometimes instead of supplying a topic, your instructor may ask that you originate one. In such cases, proceed as follows.

Exercise 12–3. The Self-Interest Method of Creating a Term Paper Topic
If you are stuck for an idea, take a piece of paper and prepare at least four columns as shown below. In the first column copy the chapter titles that interest you (or copy the title of every other chapter) from the course textbook. This will ensure that you select a topic associated with the course material. In the second column enter *your* hobbies or special interests. If you run out of entries, just repeat what you already have as shown. In the third column enter various numbered years. In the fourth column enter various countries (or states in the United States). The result might look like this:

Chapter Title	*Hobbies/Interests*	*Years*	*Countries*
1. Capitalism	1. Stamp collecting	1. 1850	1. Brazil
2. A Typical Business	2. Coin collecting	2. 1870	2. Germany
3. Management	3. Needlepoint	3. 1890	3. England
4. Finance	4. Sailing	4. 1910	4. Zanzibar
5. Production	5. Fixing cars	5. 1930	5. Nigeria

Chapter Title	Hobbies/Interests	Years	Countries
6. Marketing	6. Stamp collecting	6. 1950	6. India
7. Personnel	7. Coin collecting	7. 1970	7. China
8. Social Responsibility	8. Needlepoint	8. 1990	8. Russia
9. Business and Governmnent	9. Sailing	9. 2010	9. France

Now randomly select a series of four numbers from 1 through 9. You can do this by opening your textbook to four different pages and (in this case) copying down the last digit in the page number. Say you obtained the sequence 4-9-3-8. This corresponds to the entries Finance-Sailing-1890-Russia. You now have an idea for a term paper. For example, you might say, "The purpose of this paper is to show how Russian boat owners financed the building of their sailing vessels in the period around 1890." You can repeat the process with four more numbers. Do this until you hit upon a combination that holds special appeal for you. If the topic needs narrowing, use the procedure described in Exercise 12–1. Students using this system report they have turned their term paper assignments from boring tasks into exciting adventures. It is clear why. The nature of the process assures the selection of a topic that is inherently interesting to you.

Exercise 12–4. Practice in Using the Self-Interest Method
Select a course in which a term paper has been assigned, and obtain the course text. Apply the Self-Interest Method and create at least three statements of purpose that can serve as candidates for a term paper topic.

STEP 2. PREPARE AN OUTLINE

Lack of a suitable outline will result in a poor sequence of ideas, in repetition, and in misplaced emphasis. Your reader (your instructor) will be confused. Instructors are quick to notice when papers lack a logical sequence of thought. *See Chapter 7 for information on how to prepare a topic outline.* When the outline is prepared, show it to your instructor and ask for comments.

STEP 3. GATHER FACTS

Instructors are not interested just in your opinion. They want informed opinion, and informed opinion requires facts.

There are four ways to gather facts: (1) by reading books, magazines, and newspapers (called bibliographical research), (2) by asking people questions, (3) by visual observation, and (4) by experiment. Your fact gathering will primarily involve Methods 1 and 2.

Bibliographic research is discussed in Chapter 18. When interviewing people, write your questions down in advance of the interview. This will ensure that you obtain the information you want while not wasting the other person's time.

When researching, be sure you can tell the difference between a fact, an inference, and a judgment. A *fact* is something that can be proven to be true. An *inference* is something said about the unknown (it will rain this afternoon) based upon the known (it is raining now). A *judgment* is an expression of good or bad. (See *Learning to Read Critically* in Chapter 9 for additional discussion.)

Facts can be arranged to represent special interests. So to minimize biased sources make sure: (1) you gather information from various sources, (2) your information is up to date, and (3) you accurately show what you found. To help accomplish this, refer to the thematic studying discussion in Chapter 15.

STEP 4. WRITE YOUR PAPER

Notice that this step comes only after you have stated a purpose, prepared an outline, and at least started to gather facts. Students who write poor term papers start with this step. From all of the above discussion you can see why their efforts are almost sure to be poor ones.

Your biggest responsibility at this point is to write clear sentences. The techniques associated with paragraphs, topic headings, and illustrations, all discussed in Chapter 9, should be used.

One note of caution. If you are going to copy material word for word from one of your sources, make sure you surround the copied material with quotation marks. It is all right to copy, but you must inform the reader through the use of quotation marks and you must cite your source. Limit such copying to no more than 20 percent of your paper. The rest should be your own words. Some instructors will give the paper a failing grade if material has been copied without quotation marks. Some will fail the student for the whole course. How can an instructor tell? After reading thousands of term papers, instructors develop the ability to distinguish original work from copied material. They are almost always right.

STEP 5. REVIEW YOUR PAPER

Before typing, or after you have typed a first draft, put your paper away for at least a day. Then review the paper for writing clearness, misspellings, and misstatements of fact. An even better idea is to show your draft to someone else. Ask the person to mark the areas that are not clear or that contain errors.

STEP 6. PREPARE AND ASSEMBLE

After making corrections, carefully type your paper. Be sure to follow the format required by your instructor. Follow standard procedures regarding footnotes and list of sources. See page 264 for footnote examples.

STEP 7. SUBMIT YOUR PAPER ON TIME

A thorough review of many term papers represents a demanding task. Therefore, most instructors set aside a special time and place to evaluate the papers. Papers that miss this special time represent extra effort and concern on the part of the instructor. Avoid having your paper considered a problem by submitting it on time. A procedure for accomplishing this follows.

Managing the Total Effort

Establishing a program plan such as that shown below will help you follow the writing system and help you submit the paper on time.

Program Schedule for Preparing a Term Paper

Receive assignment	Prepare and submit outline for review	Research and write paper using outline as guide	Review paper	Review paper with teacher

Weeks Into Semester

1 2 3 4 5 6 10 11 12 13 14 15

Decide topic

Receive outline approval, revise as necessary

Submit paper

It takes about ten minutes to prepare such a program plan. The steps then become part of your normal college activities. Term paper assignments can then be performed in a deliberate scholarly fashion that will yield the most benefit from the assignment.

Exercise 12–5. Establishing Term Paper Schedules
The information shown above can also be shown in table form. Complete the table below for each current course that requires a term paper. Then make sure you meet the established dates.

Activity	Course:_____ Expected Completion Date	Course:_____ Expected Completion Date
1. Receive assignment		
2. Decide topic		
3. Prepare and submit outline for review		

Activity	Course:_____ Expected Completion Date	Course:_____ Expected Completion Date
4. Receive outline approval, revise as necessary	_____	_____
5. Research and write paper	_____	_____
6. Review paper	_____	_____
7. Submit paper	_____	_____
8. Review paper with teacher	_____	_____

Exercise 12–6. Practice in Developing Term Paper Outlines

Here are some general term paper topics:

The Family	The Home of the Future
Equal Opportunity in America	The Automobile of the Future
Selecting a College Curriculum	The Person of the Future
How to Be a Good Listener	The Future of Space Travel
Protecting the Environment	Television Watching
Computers and Medicine	Energy Alternatives

1. Select any three topics and develop a statement of purpose for each using the Question-Then-Narrow technique.
2. Prepare a topic outline for each statement of purpose you developed in question 1. Develop at least four main ideas and carry the outline to at least the second degree of division (see Chapter 7 discussion on preparing outlines).
3. Exchange outlines with another person. Evaluate each other's statements and outlines for logical flow of thought.

Summary

A term paper assignment is a chance to show yourself (and others) how good a college student you really are.

Writing a term paper allows practice in expressing yourself clearly, working independently, and solving a series of problems. Such skills are highly prized in the job market.

Selecting a narrow, interesting topic is the key to term paper writing. This chapter describes two methods for selecting interesting topics. It also presents and describes the Term Paper Writing System, a simple system that leads to good term papers.

The chapter closes by presenting a method to ensure the completion and timely submittal of term papers.

Narrowing	Outline	Judgment
Statement of purpose	Fact	Quotation marks
Self-interest method	Inference	Program plan

REVIEW QUESTIONS

1. Describe each key term above.
2. List the steps in the Term Paper Writing System.
3. In any communication who is the most important person? Why?
4. Describe the Question-Then-Narrow Method of determining a term paper topic.
5. Describe the Self-Interest-Method of creating a term paper topic.

SPEAKING—IN CLASS AND OUT

BASIC IDEAS
- Class time can also be study time.
- Delivering a talk in class is an opportunity for self-development.
- Teachers can help in and out of class.

KEY POINTS
- Can you overcome the fear of speaking in class?
- How should a verbal report be prepared and delivered?
- Why and when should you talk to teachers?

In college learning there are three main situations that require speaking. These are (1) when asking or responding to a question in class, (2) when delivering a verbal report, and (3) when talking privately with your teacher. This chapter covers each of these areas.

Asking and Answering Class Questions   Here is what class questions can do for you:

- Answering questions is a means of showing yourself whether or not you actually understand the material.
- Asking a question allows you to expand your knowledge.
- Asking a question can save you study time.

Whether in class, in a teacher's office, or in discussion with friends, asking and answering questions allows you to obtain valuable information about yourself, information that can be used to control your future study efforts. You can then spend time on those subjects in which your answers are not accurate. When questions and answers are looked at as management tools that allow control of your studies, they lose some of the fear they may hold for you.

A suggestion that you ask questions is apt to be met with, "If I ask a question, the teacher will think I'm a dummy" or "I hate to ask questions in class; I may appear foolish or silly" or "What happens if the teacher puts me down or the other students laugh?" These are natural fears shared by others in class. But there are two good reasons why it's possible but not likely that you will be embarrassed.

One is that most teachers like questions. When questions are asked, teachers obtain knowledge about how well they explain material. It also helps them to know that people are actually listening. The second reason is that if you have a question, the chances are, other students do also. Asking or responding to a question is an excellent way of both learning the material and helping those around you. Ask the question when it first occurs to you. If you delay, you may forget the question and the answer you receive will not be in the original organizational context. It takes courage to break through and ask questions. But doing so will allow you to achieve the understanding you came to class to obtain.

(Some of your classes may be so large that it is either not practical or possible to ask questions. In that event you can ask before or after class or during the teacher's office hours.)

Exercise 13–1. Afraid to Ask?

The purpose of this exercise is to compare your fear of speaking or asking questions in class with that of others. Use the scale to register your degree of agreement or disagreement with the statements below. Here is the scale:

    0 Strongly disagree with statement
    1 Disagree with statement
    2 Am neutral about statement
    3 Agree with statement
    4 Strongly agree with statement

In regard to speaking in class, I am concerned with:

_____Freezing up and stopping in midsentence.

_____Revealing I don't know something.

_____Being ridiculed by the teacher.

_____Being ridiculed by students.

_____Being asked to repeat the question.

_____Being told that I should already know the answer.

_____Not being able to think clearly.

_____My voice trembling or breaking.

_____Appearing foolish.

_____Expressing my opinions.

_____TOTAL

Each person should complete the survey individually. Then form groups of at least five people. Compare your responses with those of the other group members. Identify three items that all or most group members have rated 3 or 4. For these items have the group draw up a list of suggestions to help overcome the anxiety.

Exercise 13–2. Becoming Unafraid

Consider establishing a self-management program aimed at reducing your fear of asking questions. Your *initial* goal should be something like, "The next time a question is asked in class, instead of worrying about whether or not I'll be called upon, I'll try to answer the question silently to myself." When you can do this, then try whispering the answer under your breath. The next step can then be, "I will attend ten class meetings next week; I resolve that before the week is out I will ask or answer at least one question."

Be sure to use a self-monitoring chart of the type shown in Chapter 4 Figure 4–2. Label the Y (vertical) axis "Number of times I participate in class." Label the X (horizontal) axis with the dates for fifteen consecutive classroom days. Across the top of the graph write, "I want to participate in class." Pin this graph on a wall in your room. For each class day enter on the chart the number of times you participated in class by either asking or answering a question. If you need help getting started, your first class question could be to ask the instructor to repeat his or her last point.

This exercise, which only you have to know about but the results of which you may want to share with others, should help you ask questions. It works because once you have made a commitment to change and have developed a method for evaluating your progress, you will hesitate to let yourself down. You will want to see the graph reflect your progress.

Preparing and Delivering Verbal Term Reports

Preparing Here is a system for preparing a verbal report.

1. Determine the purpose
2. Prepare an outline
3. Gather facts
4. Prepare speaking notes
5. Prepare visual aids
6. Practice your talk
7. Deliver your talk

Steps 1, 2, and 3 are the same as the first three steps in the Term Paper Writing System discussed in the last chapter. Use the rest of the system as follows:

• *Prepare speaking notes.* Transfer portions of your outline onto separate cards. These notes are best written on 3 by 5 or 5 by 7 index cards. Enter only key words and phrases. They will serve as reminders of what to say. Anticipate likely audience questions, and build the answers directly into your talk. The quantity of your notes should reflect the amount of speaking time available.

• *Prepare visual aids.* Visual aids help promote understanding. Make your selection based upon your outline, your research, and your speaking notes. Illustrations should serve a specific purpose. Select and use them carefully. Make sure the room is equipped to handle any visual aids that require electricity (such as motion picture projectors, overhead projectors, and others). Make sure they can be seen from the back of the room; otherwise pass several copies through the audience.

• *Practice your talk.* Do this by having a friend(s) sit for you, by talking out loud to yourself, or by talking into a tape recorder. There are at least three benefits from practicing. First you will see how the talk might be rearranged to make it clearer; second, you will become familiar with how to show and use the visual aids; and third, you will gain confidence in yourself as a speaker. Time yourself to make sure you finish on time.

Delivering   There are two main concerns when talking to an audience. One is physical, the other mental.

Physical considerations include your appearance and how you use your body, voice, eyes, and head. Audiences will initially react to your appearance and your outward attitude. Dress neatly and have a positive manner. Avoid body stiffness. Don't stand motionless in one spot; move around. Avoid unnatural gestures and excessive mannerisms. You must speak clearly and you must be heard. Use a moderate speaking rate (100–150 words per minute) and speak so those in the back can hear you. Avoid speaking in one tone of voice. Use simple words and short sentences, and clearly indicate when you are going on to a new topic. Avoid constantly looking at the ceiling, floor, or only one person. Periodically make eye contact with audience members for a few seconds. Keep your head up, to allow voice projection and eye contact. Remember you are delivering a talk to an audience and not solely to your instructor.

Mental considerations include fear, the audience, handling of questions, and defensiveness. The chances are you will experience fear. It is not likely you will be attacked by the audience or that the building will collapse on you. Therefore, fear will spring from your concern over doing poorly. The best way to minimize such fear is through proper preparation (see section above) and practice. But remember that even the best of speakers suffer some fear. The last thing the audience wants is to be bored. It is therefore up to you to prepare an interesting and lively talk. Think of the audience as friends and not judges. You will find this makes a difference in your attitude, manner, and degree of fear. Audience questions show they are interested and are listening. Treat each question at face value. Give the best answers you can. If you really don't know the answer to a question, then say you don't know. Avoid being defensive. Defensiveness arises when you treat each question as a personal attack on you or when someone seems not to be paying attention. Don't expect to hold the undivided attention of everyone (see Chapter 11 for reasons why this is so). Remember the most important person is not you the speaker but those in the audience. If you respect them by preparing well and being honest, they will forgive mistakes on your part.

Talking With Your Teacher

There is nothing wrong in seeking assistance. It is not an indication of weakness. The President of the United States has many advisors, as do the presidents of private corporations. If you look at your college catalog, you will find that your own college president has many advisory boards. Your own teachers seek the advice of other teachers and students. Good managers want and seek the assistance of others. There is no reason why you shouldn't do the same.

Teachers, as well as counselors and librarians, expect to be asked for help. It is part of the reason they became teachers in the first place. They expect all types of questions and are usually willing to go out of their way. Because they come in contact with many people, teachers usually know a lot about college students and related problems. They can be a very good source of counsel and advice. They are obviously a source of expert help on the subject they teach.

When do you ask a teacher for outside-the-classroom help? The answer is, when you want to discuss a situation of a general nature or when you are having trouble with course material or assignments. For personal problems (finances, friends, family, your future) select a teacher with whom you feel comfortable and one you think can help. Sometimes just talking with someone eases a problem. Most teachers will be glad to listen. For course-related problems don't adopt the attitude that completing assignments and taking tests is a matter of the teacher's trying to catch you on what you don't know. Don't feel the teacher should not help you with assignments. This kind of logic leads to a situation where a student says to him or herself, "I can't ask about how to answer this homework question or how to complete this term paper assignment because that would mean the teacher is giving me the answer." If you have tried and are stuck, there is absolutely nothing wrong with a teacher's providing you with or guiding you toward an answer. It's part of a teacher's job and a part he or she welcomes. Most teachers want to catch you on what you do know, not what you don't know. A teacher can work with a student who says, "I just don't know what's going on." But it helps if you first narrow down, preferably in writing, what is troubling you. In this way you can get specific help and you avoid wasting your time and the teacher's.

When is a good time to seek individual help? The answer is, any time you need it. If it's a small problem, then before or after class may be all that's necessary. Otherwise take full advantage of your teacher's office hours. These hours are scheduled especially for you. If your schedule conflicts with the available office hours, then make a special appointment.

Exercise 13–3. Teacher's Office Hours
Complete the following table. Then use the information whenever you want help.

Course Name and Number	Teacher's Name	Office Location	Phone Number	Hours
_____	_____	_____	_____	_____
_____	_____	_____	_____	_____
_____	_____	_____	_____	_____
_____	_____	_____	_____	_____
_____	_____	_____	_____	_____

Exercise 13–4. Visit a Teacher
Select two teachers from the list in Exercise 13–3. Pick those subjects you find most difficult. Show each teacher the results of Exercise 13–2, and ask the teacher to comment. Prepare a one-page summary of your meeting.

Summary

This chapter discusses asking and answering class questions. It also presents information on preparing and delivering verbal reports and how and when to use teacher office hours. These activities can save you study time. They allow you practice in job-related skills such as expressing yourself clearly, working independently, and solving problems.

KEY TERMS

Self-management program   Practice   Seeking assistance

| Speaking notes | Physical concerns | Counsel and advice |
| Visual aids | Mental concerns | Office hours |

REVIEW QUESTIONS

1. Describe each of the key terms above.
2. List the steps for preparing a verbal report.
3. What is meant by defensiveness when speaking?
4. Identify three methods of practicing a verbal report.
5. Describe three physical concerns when speaking. What should be done about them?
6. Describe three mental concerns when speaking. What should be done about them?
7. What can you do to make effective use of teacher office hours?

·ᵴ III ᵴ·
Your Learning
Staff

OBJECTIVES FOR PART III

When you complete this part you should be able to know how, when, and where to enlist the aid of others to help achieve your educational aims.

PREVIEW OF CHAPTER

Chapter 14, You Are Not Alone—People Who Can Help, will show that while you are in charge of your actions and decisions, you should not expect that all the subjects you study should be mastered without help from other people. This chapter will discuss methods of enlisting the help of others, especially teachers and librarians, in attaining what all of you are after, your increased competency, awareness, and flexibility. This chapter also includes a discussion of what teachers will expect of you and what you can expect of teachers. Also included are results of a national survey of college presidents on the qualities a student should posses to achieve success in college. You may be surprised by what they have to say.

CHAPTER 14

YOU ARE NOT ALONE—PEOPLE WHO CAN HELP

BASIC IDEAS
- Nobody knows everything about anything.
- A good manager knows how to accept the help of others.

KEY POINTS
- How can college people help me?
- What will teachers expect of me?
- What can I expect of teachers?

From previous chapters do you now feel that even if your texts are unclear, your teachers vague, and conditions poor, you are nevertheless primarily responsible for your learning? If you do feel so, you have taken a big step toward becoming a good manager. But does all this self-reliance mean that you have to do everything by yourself? The answer is no. There are other people who can help you become an efficient and effective college student. And that is what this chapter is all about.

The Orientation

You weren't sure whether to attend, but the college made a point of stressing the importance of this session. So you now enter the auditorium with your friend. You find seats toward the back and settle down. In the mail you received a copy of the college student handbook and have brought it along. At the auditorium doors you were given a copy of the agenda for this meeting. It shows the following:

AGENDA
ORIENTATION MEETING—NEW COLLEGE STUDENTS

- Initial Comments—The Academic Dean
- Welcome to College—The President
- The Director of Student Services
- The College Librarian
- Closing Comments

Attached to the agenda is a chart. A note indicates that the chart will help explain how a college is organized and where you can find help. You turn to the chart, which is reproduced in Figure 14–1. The note continues:

> The word college means a group of people gathered together for a common purpose. The common major purpose of a college is to instruct students in a field the student selects. Early European colleges and universities were simply groups of scholars and students who worked very closely with each other. American colleges have grown to the point where many more people help a student accomplish his or her education. These include administrators, counselors, librarians, and teachers.
>
> Private colleges are considered nonprofit corporations, and state or community colleges are considered public corporations. The college is run by a board of trustees. The ultimate responsibility for success in achieving the college's purpose rests with them. They set policy, select the college president, approve the selection of teachers, and, although it is nonprofit, make sure the college is financially sound.
>
> The president is the chief executive of the college. He or she is directly responsible for running the college and reports directly to the trustees. The president must work very closely with and gain the confidence and trust of the members of the college, in particular the faculty and students. The president must possess educational and managerial leadership. He or she must possess knowledge, wisdom, and insight and must be capable of expressing such qualities in a persuasive manner.
>
> The president operates the college through an organization which includes these four major elements:
>
> Academic Administration   Business Administration
>
> Student Personnel Services   Community and Public Relations
>
> The business administration area is concerned basically with receiving money in the form of tuition, grants, endowments, and scholarships and spending it on college salaries, facilities, maintenance, and student aid. The public relations area is concerned with representing the college to and working with the community, alumni, and others in providing services and raising funds. However, it is the academic and student personnel areas that will be of prime interest to you. Most of today's orientation meeting will be given over to discussing these two.

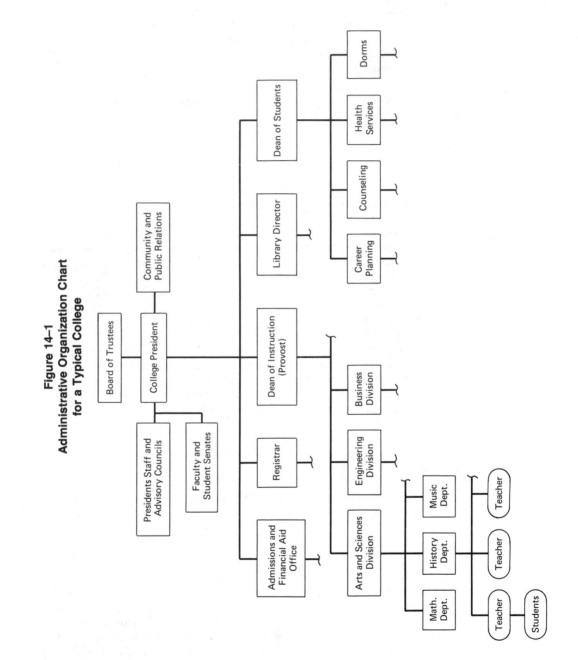

Figure 14–1
Administrative Organization Chart
for a Typical College

You might find it a bit surprising to notice yourself way down at the bottom of the administrative chart. Don't be misled by this conventional approach to drawing an organizational chart. This approach to chart drawing is something we have borrowed from the business world. But it really doesn't fit the purposes of a nonprofit educational organization such as a college. The chart is meant to show how all college services are delivered to the student, in other words, how the college supports the student in his or her pursuit of educational goals. It's an administrative chart, not a functional chart. If you held the chart upside down, you might get a better idea of how the college is organized to support your activities.

Following this chart is another, which is shown in Figure 14–2.

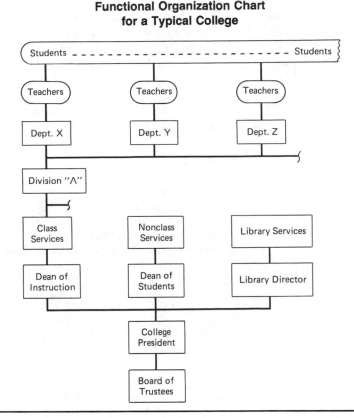

Figure 14–2
Functional Organization Chart
for a Typical College

This is a functional chart so it doesn't mean that you are in charge of anyone—except, of course, yourself. But what it does mean is that the whole of the college and the people in it are there for one basic purpose. That purpose is to instruct you in a field you have selected and to help you as an individual. The purpose of this orientation is to help get this point across.

When you finish reading, you are a little surprised at all that surrounds you, the classroom, and the teacher. Are all those functions really necessary? You begin to realize that while you, the classroom, and the teacher are the main points, your college experience is really meant to be a whole lot more. Of course, some of the functions shown are strictly to allow the college to operate as an organization. But you also notice that most of the functions shown are for your use.

The Academic Dean

Just as you finish reading and thinking about the above charts, the academic dean steps to the podium and introduces himself. You have read your handbook and reviewed the college catalog, so you know the academic dean's basic concern is instruction. Sometimes called *provost* (a person in charge), a dean has the responsibility to recruit, hire, and retain good faculty memebers. New and effective curriculums, programs, and teaching methods are other areas of concern. A dean's desire is to help students achieve the best possible learning. Now the dean briefly describes his responsibilities and then introduces the college president.

The College President

The president of your college then delivers a welcoming address. It stresses the central role that you, the student, must play. As it comes to a close you lean forward a little to make sure you catch her last words:

> . . . and so as your college experiences begin here today, remember that no matter how much you may learn you will always need help in some fashion. All the people on this campus are here because they have an interest in helping you. There is no sense in needing help and not seeking it. There is great waste in having help and not using it. Thank you and good luck.

The Director of Student Services

The director of student services takes the podium and describes the area of student services by saying:

> Last week I had a meeting with all the groups whose work is concerned with student relations. Present at the meeting were the:
>
> - *University Registrar,* who is concerned with admitting students and keeping college records.
> - *Director of Dormitories,* who is responsible for all on-campus student housing and who may also help in locating off-campus housing.

- *Director of Student Activities,* who is concerned with the awareness and flexibility aspects of your education. This includes college clubs, recreation, and other extracurricular activities.
- *The Director of Placement,* who helps secure part- and full-time jobs for students.
- *The Director of Financial Aid,* who provides available assistance for tuition, dormitory fees, books, and other expenses associated with attending college. These aids include:

Scholarships	Grants	Part-time Jobs
Fellowships	Loans	Deferred Payments
Assistantships		

- *The Director of Health Services,* who can provide treatment ranging from dealing with simple ailments like colds and headaches through handling cases requiring emergency services.
- *The Director of Counseling,* whose services include help with personal emotional problems as well as help on curriculum and course selection and college transfer.

Now in some colleges some of these services are provided by fewer people; at some colleges, more. But whatever the number, those who assist students are professionally trained individuals, many of whom have advanced degrees. They get great satisfaction from helping others. At our meeting we discussed this orientation and what I should say to you this morning. The director of counseling, a psychologist, said, "I think we should tell the students that no one has all the answers to problems; that it is unreasonable to expect they should be able to solve all their new problems and make all decisions without help from informed, thoughtful, interested people; that we can help save them hours of time and headfuls of frustration by providing counsel, advice, and support. But also tell them that we really can't help unless asked. We—including librarians and teachers—have no way of telling what may be troubling someone or what assistance is needed unless we are told. Tell them that a sign of maturity is the ability to ask for and accept help." The others at the meeting all agreed with the counselor's comments. They also agreed that whatever I said I should keep it short. So I will. Thank you, and think of us when you think of yourself.

The Librarian

The chief librarian steps to the podium, delivers some welcoming remarks, and then says:

As you all may know, there is to be a separate meeting on how to use the library, so I won't say anything on that now. However, I have just received a report from our college president and she suggested I tell you about it. She feels it effectively summarizes some of the points she made earlier.

The librarian then describes the report. It seems that a national survey was made of college presidents. They were asked to identify those qualities a student should possess to allow him or her to be successful in college. The librarian says:

I am going to project on the screen behind me a tabulation which summarizes the results of the survey. The summary reflects responses from 41 colleges representing 22 states and the District of Columbia. Those taking part in the survey responded to the following question, "Could you provide a short list that represents those qualities a student should possess to allow him or her to be successful in college." You should note that although responding as officers of the college, the writers, as a group, are also speaking from their own experiences as students and teachers. Therefore, their comments, although obviously representing their own individual judgments, reflect a view of almost the total college experience.

The librarian then shows the summary and it looks like this:

Student Learning Qualities for Success in College
Results of Survey of College Presidents

General Category	% of Time an Item Associated With General Category Was Mentioned	Examples of Terms Used That Are Descriptive of General Category
Motivation	20%	Motivation for academic program, interest in learning, sense of purpose, desire to succeed, important personal goals, interests in self-development and integration
Self-Reliance	20%	Self-discipline, ability to plan and direct activities, self-confidence, maturity, responsibility, self-awareness, self-worth
Thinking Skills	20%	Curiosity, tools of language and expression, humility regarding existing ideas (keep open mind), questioning, study methods, tolerance for ambiguity
Willingness to Work	14%	Industry, perseverance, willingness to devote time, hard work, tenacity

Social Consciousness	9%	Moral concern for society, awareness of others, desire to help others, religious values
Native Ability	8%	Intelligence, intellectual resources
Recognition/ Use of College Services	4%	Recognition of faculty as resource, ability to seek out those who can help
Previous Academic Success	3%	Past achievement, demonstrated ability in secondary school[1]
General	2%	—

At this point the orientation is about complete. The college business director comes on and reminds you that while the theme of this orientation has been how the college can help you, the college also needs your help. The director then reminds you to pay your bills on time. The academic dean then closes the meeting by wishing you good luck and inviting you to call on him when you need help. You now feel you have gained a better understanding of the total college.

Teachers

The relationship between student and teacher is really one of expectations. For the most part these expectations come together in the classroom. The following describes what teachers will expect of you and what you can expect of teachers.

What Teachers Will Expect of You

The word *educate* is derived from the Latin and it means, "to lead forth." A teacher, then, is one who helps another person become educated by leading them toward their educational aims. Many teachers will feel their subjects are the most important and interesting ones. Their expectations of you will be high. They will expect that:

1. You possess basic reading, writing and study skills.
2. You attend college because you want to and are interested in learning.
3. You can and will accept the challenge associated with intellectual pursuits. These include:

[1]The survey information is based on research conducted by the author. Great appreciation is expressed to all who took time to express their views. Their names and colleges appear at the end of this chapter.

a. A willingness to spend time outside the classroom on assigned reading, research, and problem solving.

b. A knowledge of basic learning skills, including organized thinking, classroom listening, questioning, and textbook reading.

c. An ability to study.

4. You will be active outside of class by utilizing campus facilities such as the library and by taking advantage of your teacher's office hours.

The expectations of interest, control, and homework are especially important to a teacher.

INTEREST

Some students adopt attitudes such as, "Teach me," "Let's see how good you are," "Entertain me," "It's up to you to make this stuff interesting," and similar sentiments. They expect a teacher to do all the work while they passively sit in the classroom. If you have come this far in this book, you realize what a misguided view of college this represents. Put quite simply: If a student is not somewhat interested in college or in a particular course, how can a teacher who is seen from a distance a few hours a week in a classroom provide such interest? It is true that some teachers are capable of inspiring students, even in a lecture hall holding 500 students. However, it is not likely that you will always have teachers whose inspiration you can borrow to help you make it through college. You must really make your own inspiration and motivation.

CONTROL

Teachers expect that there will be some small amount of talking between students during the course of a lecture period. A few words of comment is natural. It becomes a problem, though, when there is a prolonged discussion. Even a whispered discussion is distracting to the teacher and other students. Under such conditions neither the teacher nor the student can accomplish much. Most teachers dislike having to discipline a presumably mature college student. Teachers will expect that college students will be able to exert reasonable control over their actions in class.

HOMEWORK

Teachers expect you to do a considerable amount of outside study. It will be up to you to establish a study schedule to meet these expectations. While teachers may sympathize with other demands on your time, they cannot be expected to lower what they and the college consider to be acceptable standards. Expect to work hard. That's part of college.

What You Can Expect of Teachers

A teacher is supposed to lead you in a course of study. You should expect him or her to provide you with direction and assistance. Here are some things you can expect from a teacher:

- An interest in the course being taught.
- An indication, spoken or written, of what you are expected to know and learn.
- The ability and patience to explain.
- Preparation for each class meeting.
- Homework and project assignments.
- Clear answers to all questions.
- Counsel and advice when asked.
- Timely return of exams and assignments with written comments as necessary.

In general you can expect your teacher to be a good explainer, a fair evaluator, and a willing helper.

A GOOD EXPLAINER

The minimum you should expect from a teacher is that he or she have a reasonable grasp of the subject being taught, be prepared for class, and above all, be a good and patient explainer. Teachers will vary in their ability to clearly explain subject matter. If you do not understand something, that may not be a teacher's fault. If most of the class understands, then you have to assume that either you did not ask enough questions, you were not prepared, or you simply need more personal detailed instructions. That's the time to seek help outside the class. Your teacher, a classmate, or special tutors can be of assistance.

A FAIR EVALUATOR

The grades you receive represent your performance. You must be willing to accept responsibility for your work. However, you can expect the following from your teacher:

- That exam questions reflect assignments. The fact that something wasn't mentioned in class doesn't mean you won't be asked about it.

- That a consistent method be used in evaluating each student's work.
- That a marking error not involving opinion will be fixed.

A WILLING HELPER

You can make college much more rewarding if you recognize that most teachers actually like talking to students in class and out. (See Chapter 13 for information on how to talk with your teachers.) Perhaps the following will help. What will a teacher be to you when no longer your teacher? If anything, a teacher will eventually be your friend. Therefore, why not move up the timetable? Why not make the teacher your friend now?

All of the above and more is what you can expect of teachers. You may not always get it: in every profession you will find some who either shouldn't be there or have temporarily lost their direction. Sometimes it's a matter of attitude. Some faculty members believe they are not teachers at all. They believe that their job is simply to profess and that students must either sink or swim on their own. If that's the case, however distasteful it may be, you will have to learn to swim. But then again that's what this book is all about.

There is really no question that a good teacher can help you learn and at the same time make it a rewarding and enjoyable experience. But if you are in actual control of your own learning, if you have adopted a management approach to college, there is no way a poor teacher can prevent you from learning. There is just too much other help available. This includes yourself, your fellow students, counselors, librarians, and not least of all—other teachers.

How You Can Help the College

You might well say, "I see how those on campus can help me, but how can I possibly help them?" A college is helped most when:

- Its people, facilities, and activity programs are used to the maximum extent by the students.
- You offer your point of view regarding operations.
- You attain your educational aims and graduate.

People, Facilities, and Activities

Not all colleges will have the elements listed on the following page. Some may be combined with others. But all colleges will have some of them.

People	*Facilities*
Academic advisors	Library
Counselors	Student Union
Financial aid officers	Gymnasium
Librarians	Cafeteria
Medical staff	
Job placement officers	
Teachers	
Tutors	

Activities	
Student government	Social clubs
College senate	Special interest clubs
Campus newspapers	Athletic programs
Campus broadcast station	

Your college catalog and student handbook will contain additional information regarding names, telephone numbers, and locations for the above listings.

How does your involvement in the above help your college? Colleges are concerned with two aspects of your education: in class and out. The Management-by-Motivation system described in Chapter 5 is not dependent on just the classroom for its effectiveness. A large part of your education should take place outside the classroom. Colleges realize that it is difficult to gain a reasonable measure of competency, awareness, and flexibility by just sitting in classrooms twelve or fewer hours a week. It is for this reason that the kinds of people, facilities, and activities described above are made available. When you use them, you help the college attain its goal of providing a rounded, rewarding educational experience for each of its students. Don't hold back—you may one day regret never having taken advantage of the out-of-class opportunities available on campus.

Join a club, use the gym, run for office, join the campus newspaper, talk to your teachers, counselors, and librarians. Perhaps, like Adam in Chapter 5, you will discover what a truly fantastic experience college can be.

Offering Your Point of View

Colleges, like any organization or any person, can be helped by those they serve. You can help your college by candid criticism of their people and operations. To ensure maximum effectiveness in establishing your point of view, you should criticize what is done and not the doer. Criticizing people directly may be both unfair and a waste of time. It's unfair because the person may be unaware that a problem exists; it's a waste of time because people tend to get defensive and thereby reject what may be valid criticism.

What might you be asked to criticize and how should you go about it? The following discusses some of these areas and provides suggestions for handling them.

AREAS OF CRITICISM

On a college-wide basis you may be asked to evaluate the college policies and procedures regarding almost any element appearing in Figure 14–1. In some instances you and other students may initiate a review of college operations on your own. In both instances you have the student government representatives to advance your points of view. In some cases you may be asked directly through a questionaire. Some of the areas students are asked about are curriculums, courses, textbooks, and teachers.

EVALUATION APPROACHES

When asked to make evaluations you will usually be given a list of topics or questions. Sometimes you may just answer yes or no, other times you may simply make check marks. On what basis will you answer? Here are some suggestions for use when evaluating teachers.

You don't have to personally like the doctor who treats you, the driver who operates your bus, or the waiter or waitress who serves you. Yet there is no doubt that a more personal relationship can enhance the quality of an experience. Such relationships with teachers can add a great deal to your college education. It may not be realistic, though, to expect such a relationship with all your teachers. All you can reasonably expect is that a person will provide you with professional help. Don't confuse personality and sociability with the ability to teach.

What criteria should you use? Certainly not dress, looks, or manner of speaking. Assuming a teacher has a reasonable amount of subject matter competence, evaluation narrows down to three things:

1. Has the teacher stated what is to be accomplished and what is considered important?
2. Has the teacher helped you in attaining these ends by clear explanations and by responding to requests for help?
3. Has the teacher made a fair evaluation of your accomplishments?

Teachers who provide these should be considered good teachers regardless of how you may otherwise evaluate their personality, personal mannerisms, or other characteristics.

A teacher will evaluate you on how well you can demonstrate achievement of essential course material. Why not evaluate a teacher on how well he or she has helped you achieve such essential course material? Your comments will then serve their intended purpose: to help teachers improve so they can do a better job of helping students.

Attaining Your Educational Aims

Colleges exist to help you achieve personal satisfaction. They also exist to help you preserve and protect a society based on personal freedom and personal initiative. The most important thing you can do for a college is to apply what you have learned. You can then help yourself, those around you, and the society in which you live. If you do, the college and its people will not have served in vain.

Exercise 14–1. Get Involved
Prepare and complete the following table in your notebook.

Name of College Club You May Be Interested In Joining	Meeting Location	Meeting Time	Order of Interest, Ranked by Number 1, 2, 3 etc.

a. Select the clubs you have numbered 1 and 2. Attend their meetings.
b. Prepare a one-page report on how you and the club would mutually benefit should you decide to join.

Exercise 14–2. Loan Yourself Out
Loan yourself to one or more of the following campus activities for a period of three weeks: the college newspaper, the student activities office, the student government office, other college services or activities. Just experience the result of involving yourself on campus outside the classroom. Write a one-page summary of your experiences.

Exercise 14–3. Put These People on Your List
By referring to your college catalog and student handbook, and by talking with people, complete the following table:

Position	Name	Location	Phone Number
College President	_____	_____	_____
Academic Dean	_____	_____	_____
Curriculum Department Head	_____	_____	_____
Academic Advisor	_____	_____	_____
Chief Librarian	_____	_____	_____
Director of Student Activities	_____	_____	_____
Career Counselor	_____	_____	_____

Position	Name	Location	Phone Number
Psychological Counselor	_____	_____	_____
Financial Aid Officer	_____	_____	_____

Exercise 14–4. Visit Your Counselor

Make an appointment to visit the career or guidance counselor or the person who performs that function at your college. Ask whether the college has available an interest or aptitude test they can administer to you. If so, take the test. Discuss the significance of the test results with your counselor.

Exercise 14–5. Visit Your Department Head

Make an appointment to visit the head of the department in which you are majoring. Ask him or her to discuss part-time job opportunities in your area of interest. Write a one-page summary of what you find out.

Exercise 14–6. Talk With Your Teachers

If you haven't already done so, complete Exercises 13–3 and 13–4 in Chapter 13.

Summary

Figure 14–1 shows how a typical college is organized. The board of trustees is responsible for setting policy and for selecting a president to operate the college. A national survey of college presidents shows they believe the qualities that best serve college students are motivation, self-reliance, thinking skills, willingness to work, and social consciousness. It is not necessary to have all these qualities when you start college. Many students do not. But there are people, facilities, and activities on campus that can help you achieve these qualities.

On a college level, education is not confined to the classroom. A college provides many nonclassroom opportunities that will help you achieve your educational aims of competency, awareness, and flexibility. Those who work at colleges are there for the most part because they like helping others. While it's healthy to have confidence, it's just plain silly not to admit a need for help. A good manager recognizes his or her limitations and seeks help as appropriate.

Teachers expect students to possess basic learning skills, to be interested in class work, and to do a considerable amount of homework. On the other hand, you can expect teachers to indicate what is to be learned, to clearly explain material, to respond to requests for help, and to fairly evaluate your efforts.

The greatest reward a college can have is for its students to apply what they have learned in the service of themselves, their community, and society.

Administrative organization chart   Student expectations

Functional organization chart   College facilities

College personnel   College activities

Teacher expectations

REVIEW QUESTIONS

1. Describe each key term above.
2. Identify and describe the main functions performed by a college.
3. Identify and describe the basic responsibilities of a college student.
4. Identify and describe the basic responsibilities of a college teacher.

DISCUSSION QUESTION

The following table can be completed by yourself or in groups of two or three.

List outside-the-classroom activities you can engage in

Check off one or more of the educational aims you will experience by participation in the activity

Competency   Awareness   Flexibility

Prepare a table as above. Have handy your student handbook or college catalog. When your table is completed, exchange it with another person or group. Add additional items to the other's table and return.

The following is a list of the names of those who took part in the survey described in this chapter.

Colleges Responding to National Survey
Concerning Student Qualities for Success in College

College	Person Responding*	State
Adelphi University	Timothy W. Costello	New York
Alma College	Daniel W. Behring, Dir. Counseling	Michigan
University of Alaska	Maurice P. Arth, Executive V.P.	Alaska
Amherst College	John W. Ward	Massachusetts
Bob Jones University	Bob Jones III	South Carolina

College	Person Responding*	State
University of California	David S. Saxon	California
Carnegie-Mellon University	Richard M. Cyert	Pennsylvania
Case Western Reserve University	Louis A. Toepfer	Ohio
University of Cincinnati	Warren Bennis	Ohio
The Citadel	Lt. Gen. George M. Seignious, II Ret.	South Carolina
Colby-Sawyer College	Louis C. Vaccaro	New Hampshire
Colgate University	Thomas A. Bartlett	New York
Cooper Union	John F. White	New York
Dowling College	Allyn P. Robinson	New York
Hampden-Sydney College	W. Taylor Reveley	Virginia
Hampshire College	Charles R. Longworth	Massachusetts
Haskell Indian Junior College	Wallace E. Galluzzi	Kansas
Howard University	James E. Cheek	Washington, D.C.
Humphreys College	John Humphreys	California
Lewis and Clark College	John R. Howard	Oregon
Miami-Dade Community College	Suzanne B. Skidmore, Admin. Ass't.	Florida
University of Nebraska	Ronald W. Roskens	Nebraska
New York Institute of Technology	Alexander Schure	New York
New York University	John C. Sawhill	New York
Pace University	Edward J. Mortola	New York
University of Pennsylvania	Martin Meyerson	Pennsylvania
University of Pittsburgh	Wesley W. Posvar	Pennsylvania
Radcliffe College	Matina S. Horner	Massachusetts
Ricks College	Henry B. Eyring	Idaho
St. John's College	Richard D. Weigle	Maryland
Scripps College	Robin Trozpek, Ass't to the Pres.	California
South Oklahoma Junior College	Gary E. Rankin, V.P. of Stud. Develop.	Oklahoma
U.S. Air Force Academy	Lt. Gen. James R. Allen	Colorado
U.S. Coast Guard Academy	Capt. R. M. White, Dean of Academics	Connecticut
U.S. Military Academy	Brig. Gen. F. A. Smith, Jr., Dean of Academics	New York
U.S. Naval Academy	Rear Adm. Kinnaird R. McKee	Maryland
Vassar College	Colton Johnson, Dean of Studies	New York
Weber State College	Joseph L. Bishop	Utah
Westbrook College	Richard F. Bond, Dean of the College	Maine
College of William & Mary	Thomas A. Graves	Virginia
Yavapai College	Joseph F. Russo	Arizona

*All respondents are the college presidents, chancellors, or superintendents unless otherwise indicated.

~IV~
Directing Your Learning

OBJECTIVES FOR PART IV

When you complete this part you should be able to accomplish the following:
1. Describe and apply SCORE and other study systems.
2. Know what to emphasize when studying math and science subjects.
3. Describe and apply the Creative Study Method.
4. Know and apply the four methods of using a college library.

PREVIEW OF CHAPTERS

Chapter 15, How to Study a Textbook, features the SCORE study system. Do you bore easily when studying? Do you spend too much time and get little learning in return? SCORE will help make your study time interesting and rewarding. Chapter 15 also covers studying nontextbook material and studying with another person. It also shows how to deal with troublesome subjects through thematic studying.

Chapter 16, How to Study Math and Science, presents some helpful ideas and approaches for studying these subjects. This chapter includes a brief arithmetic review and a standard problem-solving method.

Chapter 17, How to Study Creatively, presents a totally new way to study. Simply trying to memorize things not only is boring, it takes the fun out of studying. The study methods described in Chapter 15 go a long way in reducing study boredom. The Creative Study Method goes still further. But before attempting CSM, be sure you can apply either the SCORE or SQ3R systems.

Chapter 18, The Study Palace: How to Use the Library, shows what today's college library has to offer. Do you know how to break through the curtain of catalog cards a library appears to put between you and its resources? Do you know how to find materials that relate directly to your curriculum? Chapter 18 answers these and other questions.

CHAPTER 15 ❧

HOW TO STUDY
A TEXTBOOK

BASIC IDEAS
- Studying means bringing together the skills and techniques of learning.
- Effective study systems involve thinking at the higher levels.
- Efficient study systems are easy to use.

KEY POINTS
- Can you personalize studying?
- Can you actually be a manager while studying?
- How do you study nontextbook material?

Each day, all over the world, college students sit down for what is called, but may not actually be, studying. Over 11 million students attend college in the United States. If each one studies a modest ten hours per week for thirty college-year weeks, then over 3 billion hours per year are spent studying, over 14 million hours per day. What an incredible investment in time! Is it time well spent? Is your study time well spent?

Study systems must be both effective and efficient. *Effectiveness* means actually accomplishing your intent. *Efficiency* means accomplishing your intent in the least amount of time. Learning a chapter in three hours when one is needed is being effective but not efficient. But covering a chapter in one hour may give the appearance of efficiency but could also result in learning and retaining very little. This chapter will present study systems that are both effective and efficient.

What makes a study system productive? Certainly not disorganized skimming, speed reading, underlining, and rote memory. Rather, you should use methods that allow you to bring together your listening and reading efforts in a way that promotes participation, organization, and persistence. Figure 15–1 summarizes the qualities

Figure 15–1
Studying A Textbook Chapter

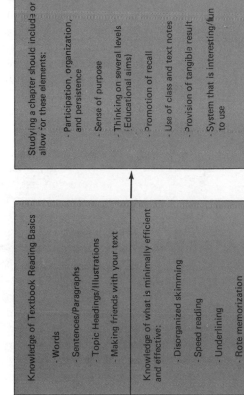

Start Here

Knowledge of Textbook Reading Basics

  - Words

  - Sentences/Paragraphs

  - Topic Headings/Illustrations

  - Making friends with your text

Knowledge of what is minimally efficient and effective:

  - Disorganized skimming

  - Speed reading

  - Underlining

  - Rote memorization

Study Here

Studying a chapter should include or allow for these elements:

  - Participation, organization, and persistence

  - Sense of purpose

  - Thinking on several levels (Educational aims)

  - Promotion of recall

  - Use of class and text notes

  - Provision of tangible result

  - System that is interesting/fun to use

To Achieve

  • Increased competency, awareness and flexibility.

  • A sense of accomplishment.

  • Exam preparation.

that you, the studier, and the study system should possess if studying is to be productive.

Why Is It Important to Study?

Many students already know the necessity of studying outside of class. Others, especially if carrying a full credit load, holding a part-time job, and dealing with other responsibilities, may not be willing to accept its necessity. Here are some reasons for studying:

- Taking notes in class or underlining sentences in texts provides little assurance of learning and retaining course material.
- The nature of most classroom lectures (teacher talking, student listening) provides little opportunity for participation, organization, and persistence.
- The ultimate aim for each course is to work your way up the thought competency ladder (see Figures 7–17 and 17–4). The small amount of class time is not enough to make the climb.

It seems clear. The only sensible approach is to spend time in organized thinking applied in a systematic manner over a period of time—in other words, to study. The major question then becomes: "All right, I see the need for studying, but how do I go about it?"

Can You Concentrate?

Being ready to study is just as important as any study system you use. Here is how to help prepare yourself:

Sleep is important. You can't play with your head if it's resting on one ear.

Eat in reasonable quantity and sufficient variety. But be careful. There was a student who came to associate studying with eating. In his first college year he gained one pound per credit earned. His body was growing faster than his mind.

Associate getting high with climbing the ladder in Figure 17–4, not with chemically reorienting your body's natural balances.

Get help if distraught. It can be a tough world. Find someone who you trust and try talking it away. It can really help.

Avoid tension by scheduling sufficient pressure-free study time.

Face your desk anywhere but at a bed. (Remember the student cited in Chapter 4 who came to associate studying with sleeping.) Keep your desk reasonably clear of items not related to studying.

Minimize distractions by not using a record player or radio. A few students are able to concentrate with background sounds, but if you are easily distracted, then you will have to operate accordingly.

Display visual cues that promote studying. Your study schedule, previous exams, and list of course motivators are good starting points. Hang pop posters and look out the window if you like, but remember that your place is primarily a space for study.

Avoid lying down while studying. Research shows that lying down helps promote creativity but the chances are it really promotes sleeping.

Give your eyes a bath with sufficient light. A fixture with two 15- or 20-watt "cool" fluorescent lamps is best. You could also use a shaded nonglare 100-watt incandescent lamp. Have your eyes checked at least once a year.

Find a place in the library for those times when staying in your room proves too distracting. Because its environment promotes studying, many students make the library their study headquarters.

The SCORE Textbook Study System

The SCORE System

SCORE stands for *S*atisfy, *C*opy, *O*bjectives, *R*ead, and *E*valuate. Students who use this system typically react as follows:

> I have always had difficulty studying for any subject. . . . After [finding out about] the SCORE System for studying, I tried it. In fact, I became so involved in studying . . . I went back and restudied all the preceding chapters. I'm sure I know more than I did before I tried SCORE. . . . I'm happy that I feel like I'm learning and I thought I'd let you know . . . . "

Here is how SCORE works.

SATISFY

The first step is to satisfy yourself that you have a rough idea of the chapter's content. Therefore:

1. Read the chapter title and the first few chapter paragraphs.
2. Leaf through the pages, reading *only* the topic headings. Mentally note their size and placement. They represent and show the relative importance of the chapter ideas.
3. Read the chapter summary if one is provided.
4. Go back and again read all the topic headings. This time also note the illustrations and their basic content.

This step is performed at a comfortable but not dawdling rate. Total time will depend upon chapter length and complexity, but about five minutes is usually sufficient. The prime purpose of this step is to demystify the chapter by promoting familiarity with its ideas. It's easier to build confidence in your ability to master a chapter if you are first familiar with its contents.

COPY

Proceed as follows, trying to write as little as possible.

1. Take a clear sheet of paper and at the top write the chapter title.
2. Now proceed through the chapter, copying the topic headings into a topic outline format. Leave space between headings.
3. As you copy, turn the headings into questions. If they are already stated as questions, compose your own version of the question. For example, the topic heading, "Why Is It Important to Study?" can be shortened and rephrased to "Why Study?" Other questions can be created by starting with the words who, what, when, where, and how.
4, If there are illustrations, note their page numbers on your sheet as you evolve the topic outline.

The purpose of this step is to pull you directly into dealing with the chapter by promoting your active participation. The result of this step is a condensed version of the chapter which highlights the nature and number of main and subordinate ideas.

OBJECTIVES

You now apply a bit of management theory. You plan which chapter sections to read first. You then study these areas and then, if time or desire permit, you go to the remaining chapter sections. Students using SCORE especially like this step. It provides a feeling that you are in charge of your studying since you are making decisions and controlling what you study.

How will you decide your chapter objectives? Here are several approaches. Use those that seem to fit the subject and the situation.

- Your teacher may have given you a list of chapter objectives. If so, mark your outline accordingly and study such items first.
- Your teacher may have said, "Make sure you concentrate on points X and Y when you study the assigned chapter."
- Something in class may not have been clear. Make this a priority.
- Consult your MBM Chart and study accordingly.

- Lacking all of the above, you can look at your topic outline and decide which chapter part at that moment sounds most interesting to you, and which next most interesting. Perhaps you can relate the topics to your job or hobbies. In this fashion identify the order in which you will study the chapter.

Note that this Objective step has its greatest application in social science courses (anthropology, business, economics, geography, history, sociology, and political science) and in some science courses (psychology, biology). For courses such as physics, chemistry, and math it is advisable not to jump around. For these textbooks the discussions rely heavily on what has gone before. Therefore, read the material in the order in which it appears. With practice you will develop the ability to know when topics can be taken out of their given order.

READ

Now read to identify and mark the chapter's main ideas. If you have not already read Chapters 9 and 10 on textbook reading and marking, it is suggested you do so. Knowledge and application of the reading techniques described in those chapters will allow you to complete this step in a minimum of time with a maximum of effectiveness.

As you read, be sure to mark the text, make comments in the margins, ask questions, and restate ideas in your own words. Such markings represent your reading notes. As you finish reading each main chapter section, summarize and transfer your text markings to the appropriate portion of your topic outline. To this material add the important portions of your class notes not covered in your text. You may want to consider transferring a chapter outline section to a separate sheet to facilitate adding your class and text notes. It is important to write as few words as possible. This helps you to reduce ideas to essentials and prevents you from ending up with long notes that obscure important facts and ideas. Underline key words in your outline. A key word is one that represents a main idea.

When you complete the Read step, you will have in front of you, in your own hand and in your own words, a concise summary of all that is important to know regarding a particular portion of a course.

EVALUATE

When your SCORE notes are completed, evaluate your learning by engaging in one or more of the activities described later in the "Remembering Techniques" section.

Figure 15-2
An Illustration of the SCORE Study System

Using S. I. Hayakawa, *Language in Thought and Action*, 2nd ed. (New York: Harcourt Brace Jovanovich, 1964), Chapter 10 as an example.

(a)
Topic headings as they
appear in the chapter

(b)
After *satisfying* yourself about the chapter,
the *copy* and *objective* steps are performed
with the following results:

(Note: Headings
have been turned
into questions)

How We Know What We Know
(Chapter title)

Bessie, the cow

The process of abstracting

Why we must abstract

On definitions

"Let's define our terms"

Operational definitions

Chasing oneself in verbal circles

The distrust of abstractions

"Dead-level abstracting"

How Do We Know What We Know?

① I. What is the significance of Bessie the cow?

II. What is the process of abstracting?

III. Why is abstracting necessary?

② IV. What is a definition?

③ V. How should terms be defined?

VI. What is an operational definition?

④ VII. What is a verbal circle?

VIII. Should abstractions be distrusted?

IX. What is dead-level abstracting?

Numbered reading order

(c)

Here is a chapter section marked as a result of the *read* step.

"Let's Define Our Terms"

An extremely widespread instance of an unrealistic (and ultimately superstitious) attitude toward definitions is found in the common academic prescription, "Let's define our terms so that we shall all know what we are talking about." As we have already seen in Chapter 4, the fact that a golfer, for example, cannot define golfing terms is no indication that he cannot understand and use them. Conversely, the fact that a man can define a large number of words is no guarantee that he knows what objects or operations they stand for in concrete situations. Having defined a word, people often believe that some kind of understanding has been established, ignoring the fact that the words in the definition often conceal even more serious confusions and ambiguities than the word defined. If we happen to discover this fact and try to remedy matters by defining the defining words, and then, finding ourselves still confused, we go on to define the words in the definitions of the defining words, and so on, we quickly find ourselves in a hopeless snarl. The only way to avoid this snarl is to keep definitions to a minimum and to point to extensional levels wherever necessary; in writing and speaking, this means giving specific examples of what we are talking about.[1]

(d)

Here, also as a result of the *read* step, is a portion of the topic outline with the most important text markings transferred.

③ I. How should terms be defined?

- inability to define doesn't mean can't use.

- ability to define terms doesn't mean understanding or ability to apply.

- Words are defined with others words. ∴ word definitions are not always clear.

- Better to *show* what is meant. When speaking/writing give a specific example.

[1]From S. I. Hayakawa, Language in Thought and Action, 2nd ed. Copyright © 1964 by Harcourt Brace Jovanovich, Inc., New York, and reprinted with their permission.

214

Below are results of two recall efforts performed as part of the *evaluate* step

(e)

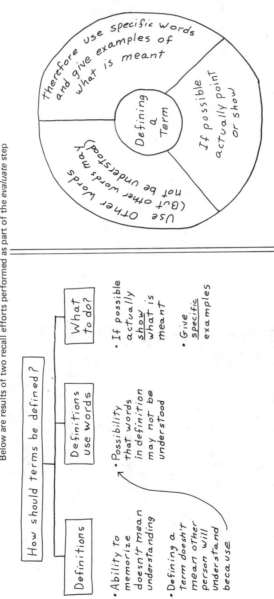

Defining a Term

Use Other Words
(But other words may not be understood)

Therefore use specific words and give examples of what is meant

If possible actually point or show

How should terms be defined?

| Definitions | Definitions use words | What to do? |

Definitions
- Ability to memorize doesn't mean understanding
- Defining a term doesn't mean other person will understand because use

Definitions use words
- Possibility that words in definition may not be understood

What to do?
- If possible actually <u>show</u> what is meant
- Give <u>specific</u> examples

Note the following regarding Figure 15–2:

- All nine major chapter topic headings appear on the SCORE study sheet.
- Each heading has been turned into a question [compare parts (a) and (b)].
- Space should be left between each main topic heading to enter appropriate class and reading notes. With practice you will become adept at judging the space to allow.
- Subordinate or smaller topic headings do not appear since none appears in the sample chapter. In such cases create your own headings after reading a chapter section.
- Part (c) represents the first part of the Read step. When reading, read to answer the topic heading question. Notice how the marking techniques described in Chapter 10 are used.
- Part (d) represents the second part of the Read step. The text markings have been summarized and transferred to the space provided under the fifth heading in the SCORE sheet. Avoid straight copying of the text. Such copying has little learning value. You will also have too many study sheets.
- Part (e) is the result of the Evaluate step. Your SCORE study sheets now represent a summary of what is important to know. When you are preparing for exams these are the sheets to periodically review and recall. Note the topic headings have been rearranged into diagrams, in order to promote recall. The next section discusses additional recall techniques.

Here is a summary of the SCORE system:

SCORE is a study system that actively involves you in learning in an organized fashion leading to a tangible reward for your efforts.

S–Satisfy   C–Copy   O–Objectives   R–Read   E–Evaluate

Satisfy yourself that you are aware of the total chapter:

- Read initial paragraphs and all topic headings.
- Read summary.
- Read topic headings again, this time noting illustrations as well.

Copy the chapter topic headings (turn them into questions) onto a separate sheet in topic outline form.

Objectives are determined by looking at the topic outline and determining which topics you will study and in what order.

Read and mark important ideas directly on the text page. Transfer the most important of these markings to your topic outline.

Evaluate your learning by engaging in specific remembering techniques.

Remembering Techniques

You may have noticed that built into SCORE are the learning and remembering techniques discussed in Chapters 6 and 7, namely: thinking, participation, organization, and persistence. Here is a summary of techniques that will promote further learning and recall.

Intend to remember. Don't fight the material. Many ideas you will study are relatively simple. Therefore, promote confidence in yourself by adopting a positive attitude. If you intend to learn, you will learn.

Use prime study time. Prime time is just after class (when ideas are still fresh and easily related) and the time set aside in your study schedule (see Chapter 3).

Recite. When you have completed assembling your class and text notes (as described in the Read step above), put your class notebook and your textbook aside. Turn your SCORE notes over and verbally attempt to recall them in order. If stuck, refer briefly to key words and the notes, and continue. It is important that within each chapter section you attempt to recall the ideas in their ordered organizational relationships. Another approach is to have someone give you key words and have them check what you say against your notes. You can also try reciting the answers to chapter-end questions.

Use spaced repetition. You won't learn everything in one sitting. So periodically recite your notes or recall them in memory or writing. This will help take the pressure off and promote understanding and retention. When exams come you will be prepared. Review your notes daily the week before an exam.

At the center of remembering lies the ability to organize material in a personal way so you can understand it. Such organization is built into the SCORE system. Here are some additional organizational schemes that will promote understanding and retention. Use them in the Evaluate step.

Use key words. Identify key words in your SCORE notes. With repetition you will associate such key words with the larger body of material they represent.

Create a trigger word. A trigger word aids recall of key words, which in turn enable you to associate related ideas and facts. For example, assume you were studying business and had identified economy, production, marketing, and government as key words. To help you remember these key words (and thus trigger your store of associated knowledge), you could make up the term MPGE (pronounced mipgee). This term (or "word") is based on the first letter in each key word. Such words can be used to recall lists of names and places as well as related ideas.

Draw diagrams or pictures. Cast your notes into a special framework such as a block/stick diagram or an original picture, such as those in Figure 15–2, part (e). You might use a spoked wheel with the hub representing the main idea and each spoke a subordinate idea, or a house with rooms, or a chest with open drawers. The more directly related to the subject matter your picture is (and the more imaginative—even silly), the better your chances of recall. When you attempt recall, always recall the material in the special framework you have chosen. Drawing pictures can be a particularly useful recall aid.

The SCORE system is a powerful study tool. It is easy to master and is adaptable to a variety of subjects and situations. SCORE is also very useful when cramming is unavoidable. It provides a very quick, meaningful exposure to material.

Exercise 15–1. The SCORE Study System
Describe in writing what each letter in the word SCORE represents.

Exercise 15–2. A Partial SCORE
Apply the S, C, and O steps to Chapter 13 in this text. Repeat for Chapter 18.

Exercise 15–3. A Full SCORE
Apply SCORE to Chapter 16 in this text.

Exercise 15–4. SCORE Another Textbook
Apply the S, C, and O steps to three chapters you select from another textbook. (Your instructor may wish to specify certain books and chapters.) Then select one of these chapters and perform the R and E steps.

Exercise 15–5. Create Trigger Words
Use your notes from the three chapters used in Exercise 15–4 and create several trigger words.

Other Textbook Study Techniques

The OORE System
OORE stands for Overview, Objectives, Read, and Evaluate. It is useful for those situations when you find yourself with the time and desire to study but when separate writing may be awkward (as in a car, bus, or train, or sitting under a tree).

OVERVIEW

This is just another way of referring to the Satisfy step in SCORE. The same procedure is followed.

OBJECTIVES

Use the same approach as before, but this time you emphasize what happens to interest you in the chapter at the moment.

READ

This is the same as in the SCORE system. The emphasis is on marking the text rather than on marking and then rewriting onto separate notes.

EVALUATE

When you apply the evaluation techniques, choose verbal recall methods rather than written.

Remember this system does not have as much learning and recall value as SCORE; it is meant for use only in those instances where writing is awkward.

The SQ3R System

SQ3R translates to Survey, Question, Read, Recite, and Review. This is probably the first widely practiced study system. It was developed by Francis P. Robinson of Ohio State University some years ago and practically every study system developed since is based in part on Professor Robinson's work. The steps in the Survey Q3R method are as follows:

SURVEY 1. Glance over the headings in the chapter to see the few big points which will be developed. Also read the final summary paragraph if the chapter has one. This survey should not take more than a minute and will show the three to six core ideas around which the discussion will cluster. This orientation will help you organize the ideas as you read them later.

QUESTION 2. Now begin to work. Turn the first heading into a question. This will arouse your curiosity and so increase comprehension. It will bring to mind information already known, thus helping you to understand that section more quickly. And the question will make important points stand out while explanatory detail is recognized as such. Turning a heading into a question can be done on the instant of reading the heading, but it demands a conscious effort on the part of the reader to make this a query for which he must read to find the answer.

READ 3. Read to answer that question, i.e., to the end of the first headed section. This is not a passive plodding along each line, but an active search for the answer.

RECITE 4. Having read the first section, look away from the book and try briefly to recite the answer to your question. Use your own words and name an example. If you can do this you know what is in the book; if you can't, glance over the section again. An excellent way to do this reciting from memory is to jot down cue phrases in outline form on a sheet of paper. Make these notes very brief!

Now repeat steps 2, 3, and 4 on each succeeding headed section. That is, turn the next heading into a question, read to answer that question, and recite the answer by jotting down cue phrases in your outline. Read in this way until the entire lesson is completed.

REVIEW   5. When the lesson has thus been read through, look over your notes to get a bird's-eye view of the points and of their relationship and check your memory as to the content by reciting on the major subpoints under each heading. This checking of memory can be done by covering up the notes and trying to recall the main points. Then expose each major point and try to recall the subpoints listed under it.

These five steps of the SQ3R Method—Survey, Question, Read, Recite, and Review—when polished into a smooth and efficient method should result in the student reading faster, picking out the important points, and fixing them in memory. The student will find one other worthwhile outcome: Quiz questions will seem happily familiar because the headings turned into questions are usually the points emphasized in quizzes. In predicting actual quiz questions and looking up the answers beforehand, the student feels that he is effectively studying what is considered important in a course.[2]

Exercise 15–6. Applying SQ3R
Apply SQ3R to the same chapter you SCORE'd in Exercise 15–4. Which system do you prefer? Compare your experiences with another student's.

The LOVE System   This is a system for studing with another person. The letters stand for Listen, Outline, Verbalize, and Evaluate. This system relies on both your listening and reading abilities.

Although more than two can participate, the following description assumes two people studying together.

LISTEN

After each overviews the chapter, one reads out loud, at a moderate rate, the first chapter portion to be covered. The other listens. The reader should mark the text as he or she normally would when reading.

[2]From Francis P. Robinson, *Effective Study*, 4th ed., pp. 29–30. Copyright 1941, 1946 by Harper & Row Publishers Inc. Copyright © 1961, 1970 by Francis P. Robinson. Reprinted by permission of the publisher.

OUTLINE

The listener records key words, names, and numbers and is encouraged to ask the reader to speed up, slow down, repeat what's been read, or ask questions. The reader should make every attempt to accommodate the listener.

When a section of reading is completed (it can be one paragraph, five paragraphs, or the whole section, depending upon mutual agreement), the listener prepares a very brief outline based upon his or her key notes.

VERBALIZE

By referring to just the outlined notes, the listener now recounts to the reader what was read. The listener makes every attempt to recall all the main points.

EVALUATE

The reader evaluates the accuracy and completeness of the recounting by checking against the text. Errors are corrected as they occur. The reader should make every effort to correct and prompt during the recounting.

When one chapter section is completed, the reading and listening roles are reversed for the next section. If more than two people take part (a maximum of four is advisable), each reads a section in turn. At the end of a reading *each* person verbalizes based on his or her own notes.

When joint studying effort is completed, make sure you keep your notes. Like your SCORE notes, they are usable for review and exam preparation.

Exercise 15–7. Applying LOVE

Form a group of three. Apply the LOVE system to Chapter 14 in this text. Repeat for a chapter in another text you and your partners select. Your instructor may wish to assign another text.

Studying Nontextbook Written Materials

Your teacher may assign supplemental material to study. It is likely that such materials (encyclopedias, magazines, journals, newspapers, and microfilms) will have few or no topic headings. Also, unless you own or make copies of the publication (or are prepared to gently use an eraser), you are not in a position to mark the material as you read. Therefore, the study systems described above must be modified. Here is a system that will prove useful. It's called RORE and the letters stand for Read, Outline, Review, and Evaluate.

READ

Read the first and last paragraph in the article. Go back to the beginning. As you now read each subsequent paragraph or paragraph group, select a representative word or phrase and write it in your notebook. Continue down through the article reading and adding to your notes. This step is performed at a brisk pace. Your goal is to identify sufficient material so that a topic outline may be prepared.

OUTLINE

Construct a topic outline based on your markings.

REVIEW

Review and complete your outline by referring to the article and rereading as necessary. Continue this step until you feel you have identified all the article's main points. (See Figure 10–2 for a typical result of these first three steps.)

EVALUATE

Perform the Evaluate step as described in the SCORE system.

The RORE method of studying can also be used when you are researching material for term paper projects. Be sure to cite the source of your material on your note sheets so it may be properly cited in your report. Remember, assigned readings are usually as important or more so than your regular textbook. The RORE system will allow you to study such assignments in a productive manner.

Exercise 15–8. Applying RORE

Apply RORE to (a) the article "Out in the Cold" in Chapter 9; (b) a magazine or newspaper article you select; (c) a selection your instructor may specify.

Studying Nonwritten Materials

The only reason you are now reading a textbook is that no one has yet figured a way to package normal textbook material into an audiovisual system that is efficient, effective, inexpensive, and usable independently by the individual as a book is.

But that doesn't mean you can't get a jump on the future and at the same time add variety to your studying. How? By using nonwritten materials available in your library. Here's how to *study* these alternate materials.

Sound Recordings

If learning is your intent, listening to audio material can be an almost total waste of time unless (1) you apply the listening techniques described in Chapter 11 and (2) you are prepared to make an organized written record of what you hear.

Although you can usually stop and replay portions of the recordings, listening to audio tapes can be demanding. It's probably more demanding than a classroom lecture because the usual classroom supports (a teacher who can answer questions, other students who can help) are absent. However, recorded material does allow you access to people and ideas otherwise unattainable. Also studying a recording (especially if it's accompanied by the material in writing) may be more productive than studying the equivalent material in a textbook chapter. This is so because recordings tend to emphasize a subject's main ideas.

Here is a system for studying lectures or talks delivered via records or cassette tapes. It's called LORE for Listen, Outline, Review, and Evaluate.

LISTEN

A basic situation to deal with is that you can't first satisfy yourself as to the recording's content without, of course, listening to the whole tape. Therefore, if descriptive material accompanies the recording, read this material. It will help prepare you.

Start the recording and listen closely to the opening statements. They will usually summarize the main topic for discussion. Stop the recording and record these main topics in a manner similar to the Copy step in the SCORE system.

OUTLINE

Restart the recording. As an important statement presents itself in its entirety, stop the tape, summarize the idea in your head, and then enter a summarized version of it into your outline.

Continue in this fashion until the recording, or the portion you are interested in, is complete. As you go through this step, replay as necessary. Avoid simply transcribing what you hear word for word. This causes you to concentrate on the words and not the ideas they represent. Also, you may not be left with an outline of what is important.

If your machine has a counter, set it to zero before you start the recording. As you stop to record something important, note the counter setting and enter it on your outline next to the corresponding idea. This procedure will help you in the next step.

REVIEW

Rewind the recording to its beginning. Now review your outline notes. As you go through them, evaluate whether or not you think them complete and whether or not you understand what you heard and recorded. If you are unsure, go back to the appropriate part of the tape (refer to your counter setting) and add to your notes.

Continue this procedure until all your notes have been reviewed. When this step is completed, you have performed the equivalent of the S, C, O, and R steps in the SCORE system.

EVALUATE

Evaluate your learning by performing the appropriate parts of SCORE's Evaluate step.

Films, Filmstrips, and TV Tapes With or Without Sound

These are, more or less, a combination classroom lecture and textbook chapter in disguise. However, as with recordings, you control the presentation. There are two ways to use these materials.

1. Take notes and assemble them into the *read* step in your SCORE study system for related text chapter material.
2. Study them separately by using the LORE system.

When using LORE, the first step will be a combination of listening (if there is sound) and viewing. The Outline, Review, and Evaluate steps remain the same.

Like recordings, visual or audiovisual materials can be productive learning aids. They add interest and variety to your study efforts. Locating audio/visual materials in your library is discussed in Chapter 18.

Exercise 15–9. Applying LORE
Apply LORE to the following library material: (a) an audio tape, (b) a silent filmstrip, (c) a sound filmstrip, (d) a sound film or TV tape.
Here is a summary of the study systems described in this chapter.

Textbook	*SCORE*	*OORE*	*SQ3R*
	Satisfy	Overview	Survey
	Copy	Objectives	Question
	Objectives	Read	Read
	Read	Evaluate	Recite
	Evaluate		Review

Nontextbook written materials (journals, magazines, newspapers)	*RORE* Read Outline Review Evaluate

Nonwritten material (audio cassettes, film-strips, other media)	*LORE* Listen (and/or view) Outline Review Evaluate

Use the LOVE system (Listen, Outline, Verbalize, Evaluate) when actively studying with others.

Thematic Studying

What would you do if you found yourself in one or more of the following situations?

- You find your assigned text assumes a lot of prior knowledge. This make it difficult to read and understand.
- The text is too simple and you don't feel challenged.
- The book's scope is limited and you desire more coverage.
- The degree of detail is limited and you want to explore further.
- You have a special interest that is not covered in the assigned text.
- You find the writing style (organization, sentence structure, word choice) not to your liking.
- You find a particular idea or concept hard to understand.

The answer is to get help. Help can come from your teacher, your fellow students, and the authors of other texts and producers of audiovisual material. Learning a particular body of knowledge or studying a particular concept by using sources other than the assigned text is called *thematic studying*.

Thematic studying is helpful when you find it hard to understand the assigned text or a difficult concept within the text. Quite often you will find that looking at another text on the same subject (especially subjects related to math and science, such as accounting, geometry, statistics, chemistry, physics, engineering) will promote understanding of the material. Just as some speakers may be easier for you to understand than others, so may some textbook writers. For a variety of reasons (method of explanation, writing style, use of illustrations) other texts on the same subject can really help improve your learning. Have all the texts in front of you open to the appropriate pages. When trying to gain understanding, move back and forth between the texts. The additional texts can sometimes be obtained from a teacher but your college library is usually your best source.

The ideal thematic approach is a multi-source one that includes texts (for basic treatment and alternate viewpoints), magazines (for latest developments), audiovisual material (for basic treatment and alternate viewpoints), and people (for all considerations). Your awareness of these alternate learning possibilities will help when you encounter difficulties. When you consult these sources, use the study systems described earlier in the chapter.

Thematic studying is particularly suited for term paper assignments. Term papers are really intensive studying efforts on a particular topic. Using the thematic approach will add interest to your effort and result in a feeling that your time has been well spent.

In summary, use thematic studying for overcoming difficulty in understanding, for becoming well grounded in your major field of study, and for writing term papers.

Summary

Time spent in classroom is not sufficient for college learning. Developing competency, awareness, and flexibility requires that you spend time outside the classroom in self-directed reading, reflecting, and learning. It requires that you study.

As the manager of your own learning you have great freedom in choosing how to study. But you must choose wisely. Someone who studies 15 hours a week with the proper system can be much more effective than someone who studies 30 hours using poor study methods. For this reason *how* you study is more important than the amount of time spent studying.

Studying requires that you be physically and emotionally prepared. A good diet, proper rest, and an environment free of distractions are necessary. As a manager of your learning you can use the principles of planning, organizing, staffing, directing, and evaluating to manage each of your study sessions in a systematic fashion. Study systems should combine the learning concepts of participation, organization, and persistence. They should also be fun to use and adaptable to different subjects and situations. They should leave you with a feeling of accomplishment.

The study systems discussed in this chapter are SCORE, OORE, SQ3R, and RORE (all for studying by yourself), LOVE (for studying with another), and LORE (for studying audio/visual materials). These systems are easy to use and add interest to your study time. Their practical use will greatly enhance your learning. Thematic studying is an approach that uses more than one source of information on the same subject.

KEY TERMS

Concentrate	LOVE	Remember
SCORE	SQ3R	Thematic studying

REVIEW QUESTIONS

1. What preparations and practices should be part of your study sessions?
2. Identify the elements necessary for a productive study system.
3. Describe the SCORE system of studying textbooks. Identify and describe two others.
4. Identify six aids to concentration.
5. Describe six methods that promote remembering.
6. Identify and describe a method of studying nontextbook material.
7. Identify and describe a method of studying nonwritten material.
8. What is thematic studying? When should it be used?

CHAPTER 16

HOW TO STUDY MATH AND SCIENCE

BASIC IDEAS
- Math and science courses improve your *general* ability to think clearly and solve problems.
- Math and science courses require skill at arithmetic.

KEY POINTS
- What is most important when studying math and science?
- What is the scientific method?

The humanities and social sciences (most of the courses you study) concern how people feel, work, and behave. Math and science concern how nature works and behaves. However, the results of scientific research (e.g., the automobile, the airplane, the atom bomb, the transistor, the Salk vaccine, space flight, test-tube babies) affect people's feelings, occupations, and behavior. For this reason some study of math and science is necessary. Such study allows you to better understand and perhaps shape present and future technological, environmental, and personal change.

Mathematics includes the study of algebra, geometry, trigonometry, calculus, statistics, and business math. Science includes the study of biology, chemistry, and physics. The skills discussed in earlier chapters (thinking, vocabulary, reading, listening and note taking, writing, speaking, and studying) all apply to these subjects. This chapter discusses some special points to consider when studying math and science.

Arithmetic Review   Most problems you solve will require the repeated use of addition, subtraction, multiplication, and division. Test your ability in these areas by completing the following exercise.

Exercise 16—1. Sample Arithmetic Problems

Solve these problems. Be sure to *show all your work neatly* in your notebook. Place the answer in the space provided. Do not use an electronic calculator. Take decimals to two places. (Your instructor may wish to administer another set of problems. If so, follow directions carefully.)

1. Add 218 to 56. _____

2. Add 57 to 23 and then subtract 36. _____

3. Multiply 16 by 8 and divide the result by 4. _____

4. Reduce 15/45. _____

5. Add 2/3 and 1/10 and 1/6. _____

6. Multiply 3/5 by 6/10 and express the result in decimal format. _____

7. Convert 4/3 to decimal format. _____

8. Express 17/25 as a percentage. _____

9. If one meter equals 3.28 feet, how many meters are there in 100 feet? _____

10. A friend paid $150 for a tape recorder. This is 40% less than the normal price. What is the normal price? _____

The study of math and science is often made complicated because students lack basic skills. As a result, the inability to perform the required arithmetic is confused with the interest or difficulty level of the math or science course itself. If any of the first nine problems in Exercise 16–1 were answered incorrectly (see answers at end of chapter), then you probably need help in arithmetic. Consider doing the following:

1. Obtain a basic arithmetic self-help book. Ask your librarian for help in locating one.
2. Enroll in a basic arithmetic course.
3. Obtain a tutor.
4. Visit your college's learning laboratory, if it has one.
5. Study your math or science course with a partner who is willing to help you.
6. Above all, practice your arithmetic and adopt a positive attitude in your ability to improve.

The Classroom

Review the material in Chapter 11. But be sure to emphasize the following points in your math and science classes:

• *Take neat notes.* Teacher explanations and illustrations are particularly important. Your notes will help you to solve homework problems.

• *Concentrate on the process.* In class it is not the *answer* that is important. What is important is the *process* used to get to the answer. Avoid getting caught up in copying every arithmetic step off the chalkboard. It is much more important to listen to the instructor's explanation of the process. In this way you will understand the concept at work. It is the understanding of the process that will allow you to solve similar problems.

• *Ask questions immediately.* Since understanding the process is most important, questions become a chief classroom ally. It is better to ask a class question than to spend hours struggling with the homework assignment.

• *Keep up to date; do assigned homework.* Following the class discussion is much easier when you have first read the assigned chapter. You are then in a position to ask questions regarding the assigned material.

The Laboratory

Here is your chance to prove to yourself the material covered in the text and in class. Here are some procedures to follow:

• *Understand the assignment.* Read and study your lab manual as you would any textbook. (See Chapters 9 and 10.) Review the specific assignment before you enter the lab. Prepare a list of questions you may have and ask your instructor about them before starting work. If the assignment is a teacher-prepared handout, read it as you would any chapter. Make sure you have a firm idea of the experiment's purpose. Ask yourself, "When I have finished this lab session, what should I have accomplished and what should I have learned?"

• *Know the equipment.* Using laboratory equipment skillfully requires practice. Understand both the capability and limitations of equipment. Some equipment is easily damaged or can easily damage you. Treat equipment with careful respect.

• *Ask for help.* In a lab never proceed in ignorance about procedural steps or equipment usage. One procedural misunderstanding or one poor adjustment can void a whole session's work. Ask and be sure.

• *Record neatly and accurately.* Readable and accurate recordings are essential to scientific investigation. Be sure you are recording the correct units of measurement. Periodically check your measurements before entering them on your log sheet.

• *Prepare clear reports.* A laboratory report is a term paper for which you supply the facts. The usual format is (1) statement of purpose or phenomenon to be tested, (2) equipment description, (3) procedure, (4) results, and (5) conclusion. Include in the report your log sheets, necessary sketches, and appropraite graphs and charts.

Studying

Math and science courses rely heavily on previously covered topics. You must keep up. If you fall behind, you will compound your problems. The *ordered* and *timely* coverage of course topics is essential. It is the only way to sustain a whole term's effort.

Use the SCORE study system described in Chapter 15, but eliminate the O step since in math and science courses it is best to treat the chapter topics in their order of appearance. When studying, follow these guidelines:

• *Work the problems.* Math and science courses require large amounts of participation, organization, and persistence. It's quite possible to sit in class and follow a teacher's solution to a problem or read the text and follow an illustration. But it is quite another matter to solve problems by yourself. It's not enough to say, "I think I understand and could do a problem if I had to so I won't bother with the homework." You must involve yourself directly in the chapter exercises. You must actually work the problems to assure yourself that you are in fact competent in the subject matter. Here are approaches to use:

1. *Adopt a scientific attitude.* Unlike other subjects the exact sciences recognize only one correct (exact) answer. You must be precise and you must be correct. Two plus two can only be four, no more or no less. Recognize that science is built on fact. It will help you adopt a precise, orderly attitude toward your studies.

2. *Adopt the scientific method.* Use the following procedure when doing homework, laboratory, or exam assignments:

   a. *Define the problem.* Many students get sidetracked in problem solving because they do not understand or they misinterpret the question. Therefore, before proceeding with the problem, make sure it is understood. It helps to identify in writing (in longhand or with mathematical symbols) what you are being asked to solve.

A great aid to problem definition and solution is to visualize or sketch a model of the problem. For example, assume the question is, "What force in pound-feet per second squared must be applied at a 45=degree angle to a 10=pound steel ball to provide an acceleration of 2 ft/sec,²"? See how the simple sketch shown in Figure 16–1 helps you visualize both the problem and its solution.

b. *Gather facts.* Assemble all the information stated or implied in the problem statement.

Figure 16–1
Sketching Helps Solve Problems

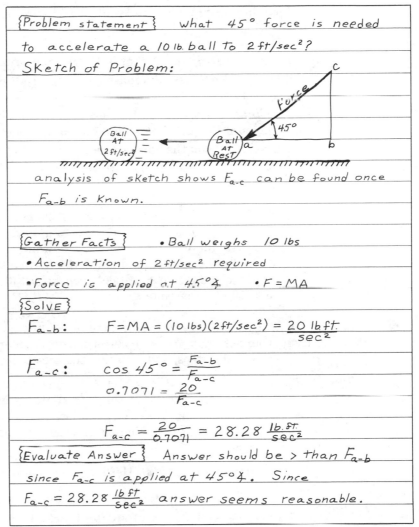

{Problem statement} what 45° force is needed to accelerate a 10 lb. ball to 2 ft/sec²?

Sketch of Problem:

analysis of sketch shows $F_{a\text{-}c}$ can be found once $F_{a\text{-}b}$ is known.

{Gather Facts}   • Ball weighs 10 lbs
• Acceleration of 2 ft/sec² required
• Force is applied at 45°⁄   • F = MA

{Solve}

$F_{a\text{-}b}$: $F = MA = (10\ lbs)(2\ ft/sec^2) = \dfrac{20\ lb\ ft}{sec^2}$

$F_{a\text{-}c}$: $\cos 45° = \dfrac{F_{a\text{-}b}}{F_{a\text{-}c}}$

$0.7071 = \dfrac{20}{F_{a\text{-}c}}$

$F_{a\text{-}c} = \dfrac{20}{0.7071} = 28.28\ \dfrac{lb.\ ft.}{sec^2}$

{Evaluate Answer} Answer should be > than $F_{a\text{-}b}$ since $F_{a\text{-}c}$ is applied at 45°⁄. Since $F_{a\text{-}c} = 28.28\ \dfrac{lb\ ft}{sec^2}$ answer seems reasonable.

c. *Solve the problem* by executing required calculations in a neat, orderly fashion. Cultivate the ability to clearly show what you are doing. Another person should be able to pick up your solution and easily follow all your steps.

d. *Evaluate your answer.* Does it make sense in light of the problem statement and the figures given? Suppose you have been asked to determine statistically the percentage of the population over six feet tall. If your answer works out to 115%, you know there is something wrong with your solution. *If* you have left an easily retraced trail, you will be able to locate your error and correct your answer.

Applying the procedure to Problem 10 in Exercise 16–1 results in the following:

1. *Problem Definition*: What is the normal price?
2. *Assembled Facts*: Purchase price = $150, purchased at 40% discount.
3. *Solution*: Let X = normal price. If it was purchased at 40% discount, the purchaser paid 60% of the normal price.

Therefore 60% of the normal price is equal to the purchase price

$$\therefore (0.60)\,(X) = 150$$
$$X = \frac{150}{0.60} = \$250$$

4. *Evaluation of Answer*: The answer cannot be less than $150, since the purchase price represents a discount. If you assume the discount was 50%, then $150 would represent half the normal price. That would make the normal price $300. Therefore, the answer must fall between $150 and $300. The answer of $250 is ∴ reasonable.

• *Study-then-solve.* As you complete reading a chapter section (1) satisfy yourself that you can perform the chapter illustrations by masking over the steps, and (2) solve the questions at the end of the chapter.

• *Do in-chapter reviews.* If the text contains in-chapter reviews after each section, make sure you complete them. In-chapter reviews are a helpful learning tool. You can check your understanding and build confidence.

• *Study with a partner(s).* Here is one student's experiences with joint studying:

I was doing poorly in a math course. I decided that I must change my approach to studying in order to do better. I then began studying with a friend who was in the same course but knew less than I did. By trying to teach him, I actually gained many insights and was motivated to learn and study more. This change in study procedure was measured by a sharp increase in my grades.

You may want to choose someone whom you feel knows more than you do. In any event, joint studying of math and science courses can be extremely helpful. Don't let your shyness hold you back from finding a partner. Take the first step.

• *Read ahead.* It is a good idea to try to keep one chapter ahead of the class pace. This promotes familiarity with what will come next. It gives you an overall view and, most important, gives you a feeling of controlling the material rather than it controlling you.

• *Use thematic studying.* See the discussion in Chapter 15.

• *Talk to your teacher.* If you have made a reasonable try and still have trouble, then do not hesitate to visit your teacher in his or her office. Teachers of math and science recognize that extra help is often necessary. They are prepared for and welcome student visits. Take advantage of this opportunity to obtain individual help.

Exam Taking

Follow the procedure for taking exams discussed in Chapter 19. Be sure your approach to problem solving includes the following:

• *Understand the question.* Be sure of what is being asked. It is not reasonable to expect credit for solving the wrong problem. Sketching a problem, as described above, is an excellent way to understand the problem and its solution. If the problem is not clear, then:

• *Ask questions.* Avoid questions like, "Am I taking the right approach?" or "Can you tell me if this question requires the use of equation X?" These are excellent questions for the classroom or in the teacher's office. In an exam concern yourself with understanding the problem as stated. Then take it from there.

• *Use the scientific method.* Use the procedure described in the preceding section: define the problem, gather facts, solve the problem, and evaluate your answer.

• *Show all work.* Answers don't just appear. In math and science the process used to arrive at an answer is often more important than the answer itself. Therefore, your teachers are just as interested in how you get an answer as they are in the answer itself. Showing all steps will also allow you to backtrack on your work. This is extremely useful should you discover your answer doesn't make sense in light of the data given in the problem.

• *Identify your answer*. Clearly show your answer by underlining or circling. If the steps leading to the answer and the answer itself are not obvious, you will more than likely lose credit.

• *Write clearly*. Remember a mark of a good scientist is the ability of another to follow one's problem-solving steps.

• *Use calculator appropriately*. The use of an electronic calculator does not relieve you of the responsibility of clearly showing all your steps in writing.

• *Set the problem up*. Sometimes time will start running out. Other times you will not recall all the steps necessary to achieve a solution. In such cases set the problem up and show how you would have proceeded. Instructors will often give partial credit if you can demonstrate process knowledge.

• *Don't panic*. If one problem gives trouble, go on to another. Often the process used to solve one problem will help solve another. If you have worked the homework problems and give yourself a chance, solutions will come.

Summary

The study of math and science allows you to better understand the world you live in. Basic skill in addition, subtraction, multiplication and division is necessary for these subjects. If you are weak in these skills, start a self-improvement program; ask for help, study with another, or do all three.

When in the classroom take neat notes, concentrate on the method or process used to solve a problem, ask questions immediately. Prepare for class by keeping up with assigned homework. In the laboratory make sure you understand the assignment, know the equipment, ask for help as necessary, record data neatly and accurately and prepare clear reports. Study in an orderly and timely fashion. Make sure you actually work out assigned problems. It is not enough to say, "I could do these problems if I wanted to." Actually working the problems is the only way to assure you do well.

Adopting a scientific attitude and using the scientific method will help you in math and science courses. Adopting a scientific attitude means recognizing that math and science are built on fact and that your solutions to problems must be correct and precise. The scientific method means first defining the problem to be solved, then gathering facts, solving the problem, and evaluating your solution.

This chapter closes by discussing several techniques for taking exams including understanding the question being asked, showing all work, and using an electronic calculator properly.

KEY TERMS

Arithmetic skill	Scientific method	Neatness
Scientific attitude	Preciseness	Study partner

REVIEW QUESTIONS

1. What is meant by a scientific attitude?
2. Describe the scientific method of problem solving.
3. What is meant by "evaluate your answer"?
4. Why is it important to read the assigned chapter before you come to class?
5. What is meant by "setting a problem up"?

ANSWERS TO EXERCISE 16–1:

1. 274	4. $\frac{1}{8}$	7. 1.33
2. 44	5. $\frac{14}{15}$	8. 68%
3. 32	6. 0.36	9. 30.49
		10. $250

CHAPTER 17 ﾞ
HOW TO STUDY CREATIVELY

Look at the palm of your left hand. Now cup your hand slightly. Take note of the following characteristics of this fleshy landscape as you observe your palm:

- The three small mounds of flesh at the base of the four long fingers.
- The large mound of flesh below and alongside the thumb.
- The many small fingerprint-like lines appearing in each mound.
- The much smaller amount of longer, more well-defined lines appearing in each mound, especially the small mounds.
- The three or four large, well-defined crevasses that are at the center of your palm (sometimes referred to as your lifelines).

Now consider the relationship between the palm of your hand and the formation of a river. The four mounds of flesh in your palm represent mountains. The smallest lines represent rivulets, the next largest represent brooks, and the largest lines are rivers. Now imagine a small storm cloud slowly moving over your hand and releasing rainwater into the palm. The falling rain enters the rivulets (the smallest lines in your hand), and the water is carried down the mountains forming small streams called brooks (the next larger lines). The brooks continue their down-mountain journey and join up with each other. They combine with other streams to form rivers (the lifelines). They may join together to form still larger rivers or find their own way to the ocean.

In this simple demonstration your hand was used as a three-dimensional representation of mountains, streams, and rivers. It represented the essential visual and operational aspects of a river system. It provided a simplified version of a real thing; it served as an abstraction of reality. In other words, your hand served as a model.

Models   A model can represent a thing, idea, or activity. There are two types of models. A three-dimensional model represents something physical. Three-dimensional models show how something will look or how it operates. Airplane and car models are examples of such models. They are usually called *test models* or *scale models*.

A two-dimensional model (a *diagram*) can be used to portray a principle, idea, concept, or activity. Like three-dimensional models, such diagrams promote understanding of the subject. These diagrams are often interesting to make. They require no special tools or artistic ability.

In the above example your hand was used as a three-dimensional model to represent a river formation. You can also draw a two-dimensional diagram that represents the formation of a river. Such a model appears in Figure 17–1.

Figure 17–1
Model of River Formation

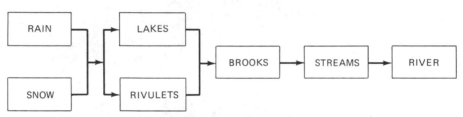

Figure 17–2 models the procedure for obtaining a part-time job. Note how the model moves from left to right. It has a starting point (the job inputs), a middle portion (the process), and last, the intended result. Look also at some of the diagrams that appear in earlier chapters (for example, Figures 2–3, 6–1, 9–1, and 11–1). These diagrammed models help promote understanding of the subject under discussion.

While viewing a model is helpful, *creating* a model provides an exciting and rewarding learning experience. Preparing a model for a particular subject helps you understand and retain the material. A study system based on model making not only promotes retention of facts and main points, it also emphasizes ideas and concepts. But before using model making as a study method, you must first learn how a model is created. This is discussed next.

Creating a Model

An Example   Look again at Figures 2–3, 6–1, 9–1, and 11–1. Notice the same pattern

Figure 17–2
Model for Obtaining a Part-Time Job

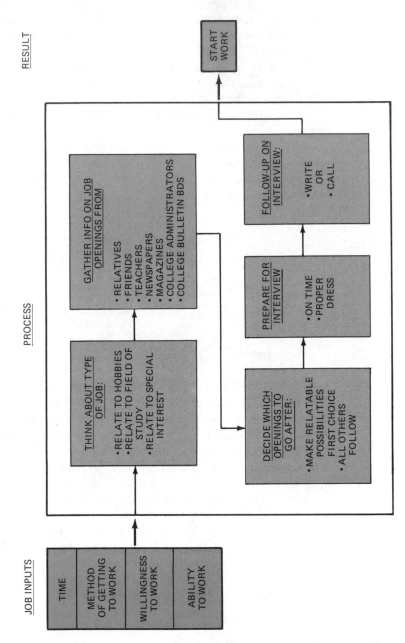

JOB INPUTS

| TIME |
| METHOD OF GETTING TO WORK |
| WILLINGNESS TO WORK |
| ABILITY TO WORK |

PROCESS

THINK ABOUT TYPE OF JOB:
• RELATE TO HOBBIES
• RELATE TO FIELD OF STUDY
• RELATE TO SPECIAL INTEREST

GATHER INFO ON JOB OPENINGS FROM
• RELATIVES
• FRIENDS
• TEACHERS
• NEWSPAPERS
• MAGAZINES
• COLLEGE ADMINISTRATORS
• COLLEGE BULLETIN BDS

DECIDE WHICH OPENINGS TO GO AFTER:
• MAKE RELATABLE POSSIBILITIES FIRST CHOICE
• ALL OTHERS FOLLOW

PREPARE FOR INTERVIEW
• ON TIME
• PROPER DRESS

FOLLOW-UP ON INTERVIEW:
• WRITE OR
• CALL

RESULT

START WORK

emerges: Input-Process-Result. This is the pattern you need to achieve when model making. Suppose you were interested in modeling an activity such as learning to play tennis. Here is how you might proceed:

RESULT

This part of the model is concerned with identifying what your model is trying to accomplish. What is the purpose of the model? Although it will appear last in your diagrammed model, the purpose or objective of the model is the first thing you must decide when creating a model. The purpose for this model (the result the model should describe) can be written as "Achieve Reasonable Tennis-Playing Skills."

INPUTS

This part of the model is concerned with identifying the items you must start with to achieve the stated purpose. In this case what will you need to achieve your desired result? You would probably identify the following necessary elements:

- Yourself	- Tennis Balls	- Money for Lessons
- Tennis Instructor	- Tennis Court	- Time for Lessons
- Tennis Racquet		

PROCESS

This middle part of the model is concerned with identifying the elements necessary to make effective use of the inputs to attain the desired result. For the tennis model it more or less asks the question, "What must I do to make effective use of the tennis racquet, ball, court, myself, and my instructor so that I may learn to play tennis?" In answering this question you would probably decide the following was necessary:

- Establish a play schedule
- Receive instruction
- Practice alone
- Practice with others
- Actually play

ORGANIZE

Having identified the model elements, you are now in a position to arrange them logically. Think of this step as simply starting with something (the input), doing something (the process), and finally ending with the result—in other words a beginning, middle, and end. This pattern is useful since it provides a basis for logical arrangement and promotes analysis. Try creating your tennis model in the space provided in Figure 17–3a. (Figure 17–3b summarizes the model making basics.)

Figure 17–3a
Tennis Playing Model

(Use this space to show your tennis model.)

Figure 17–3b
Model Making Basics

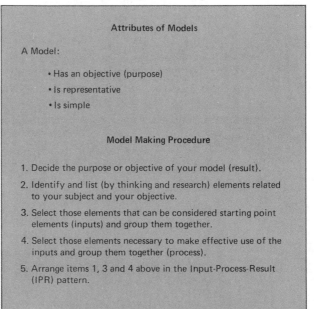

Attributes of Models

A Model:

- Has an objective (purpose)
- Is representative
- Is simple

Model Making Procedure

1. Decide the purpose or objective of your model (result).

2. Identify and list (by thinking and research) elements related to your subject and your objective.

3. Select those elements that can be considered starting point elements (inputs) and group them together.

4. Select those elements necessary to make effective use of the inputs and group them together (process).

5. Arrange items 1, 3 and 4 above in the Input-Process-Result (IPR) pattern.

How Model Making Helps Learning

It's possible that different people may think about a model for the same subject in different terms and diagram it differently. But this is not really important. What is important is that *you* develop the model and that it adequately represents the subject being analyzed. Why is this important? An educational aim of yours is to develop the ability to think at various levels. The ability to comprehend when matched by an ability to apply, analyze, evaluate, and create is often the mark of a self-directed person who can act and think for him or herself. Developing such an ability is a main reason for attending college.

Figure 17–4 summarizes these learning points and illustrates why studying based on model making is a powerful learning experience. Each step in the ladder represents a more advanced level of thinking. The Creative Study Method (CSM), which is based on model making, requires that you think your way up the ladder. As you do, you sharpen your general thinking skills as well as learn the material you are studying. The primary aim of CSM is to promote understanding of concepts and relationships in course material. Retention of facts is promoted, since the nature of CSM provides many opportunities to

Figure 17–4
Studying and the Higher Levels of Thinking

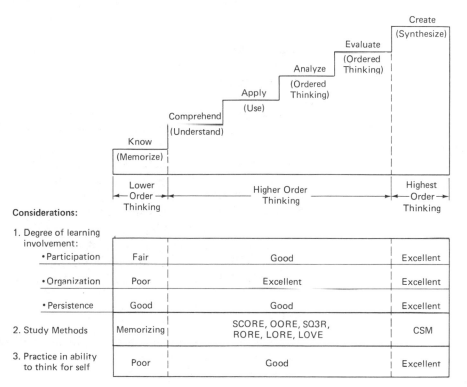

Considerations:	Lower Order Thinking	Higher Order Thinking		Highest Order Thinking
1. Degree of learning involvement:				
• Participation	Fair	Good		Excellent
• Organization	Poor	Excellent		Excellent
• Persistence	Good	Good		Excellent
2. Study Methods	Memorizing	SCORE, OORE, SQ3R, RORE, LORE, LOVE		CSM
3. Practice in ability to think for self	Poor	Good		Excellent

participate, organize, and persist. CSM requires practice. But once it is mastered, you will learn more in a given amount of time. You will wonder how you ever studied a college subject without employing CSM or something like it. It is a rewarding system to use. When you look at your model, you will feel a large degree of satisfaction in having created something that didn't exist until you came along.

You may now be asking, "Just what is CSM and how can I apply it to my studies?" As you read the following section for the answer, keep in mind that the model-based CSM is really nothing more than a special kind of topic outline, one you write out horizontally instead of vertically.

| **The Creative Study Method** | Here is a general description of how the model-based Creative Study Method works. |

PHASE A

1. Review the chapter (or chapter section) to gain overall familiarity. Do this by reading first any paragraphs that precede the first main topic heading, then the summary, and finally the topic headings in between. Then prepare a topic outline based upon the topic headings. Use the headings as they appear. Do not turn them into questions. Using the outline as a basis, answer one of the following questions:

   - What is the chapter trying to accomplish?
   - What am I supposed to learn from this chapter?

   The answer to these questions can often be found in the chapter heading itself, the first few chapter paragraphs, or in the chapter summary. Write out your answer in one simple sentence. This sentence establishes the *result* portion of your model.

2. Now look at the topic outline and select those elements you think may be starting point elements (*inputs*). They should be related to the identified result. Group them together.

PHASE B

3. Now select those elements necessary for making effective use of the inputs so the result can be achieved (the *process*). Group these elements together.

4. Now arrange your result, input, and process information in the IPR pattern. You should consider your first try a tentative arrangement. It will most likely change as you more fully read the chapter. This step has special learning value since it requires you to analyze the chapter elements and organize them in your own fashion. You are stepping up the ladder in Figure 17–4.

5. When your diagram has been sketched, proceed to read the chapter as you would any textbook chapter. Transfer marked information from your textbook to the corresponding part of the model. When this step is complete, you will have a complete model that reflects the major chapter points. Keep in mind that elements may shift between input, process, and result as you read. This is actually a good sign since it indicates you are really thinking about and analyzing the material.

PHASE C

6. Periodically evaluate your grasp of the chapter material by (a) attempting to recall your model in writing or (b) describing your model to another.

Figure 17–5
The Creative Study Method

PHASE A (Decide Objective)	PHASE B (Sketch Model)	PHASE C (Evaluate Learning)
• Review chapter to satisfy yourself as to its contents. • Prepare topic outline based on chapter topic headings. • Decide the primary purpose (objectives) of the chapter's material.	From Topic Outline: Select those elements that can be considered starting point elements (inputs) and group them together. Select those elements necessary to make effective use of the inputs so the result can be achieved and group them together. These elements represent the process portion of your model. Arrange input, process, and result elements in IPR pattern. From Textbook Chapter: Read chapter to identify and mark major points. Transfer essential markings to appropriate portion of model. Revise model as necessary.	Evaluate grasp of chapter material through: 1. Attempting to recall model in writing. 2. Describing your model to another.

Application of CSM tends to change all material, regardless of its original thought pattern, into a sequential-based thought pattern that is process oriented. The result of such a change is to promote understanding. The CSM is as much an attitude toward what you study as it is a systematic procedure for comprehending what you study. Through practice you will find CSM one of the more interesting mind games you can play. Figure 17–5 summarizes the CSM procedure.

Before adopting CSM as a study method, it is helpful first to become adept at the SCORE system described in Chapter 15. This practice will help you adjust to the processes required for using CSM.

Applying CSM

CSM is designed for studying a total chapter or a chapter section. However, practice at the paragraph level will help sharpen your model making skills.

Paragraphs, regardless of the overall chapter pattern of which they are a part, all basically follow one of two thought patterns. These are:

Deductive (whole to part—main idea followed by details)
Inductive (part to whole—details leading to main idea)

These patterns are particularly suited to model making because of the model-like thought flow they represent (the paragraph's main idea represents the result portion of a model). With this observation and with your new model making knowledge, see if you can construct a model for the paragraph that appears in Figure 15–2, part (c).

Figure 17–6
Modeling a Paragraph

This is a model of the paragraph in Figure 15-2, part (c).

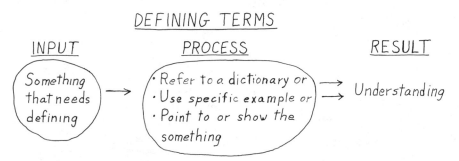

DEFINING TERMS

INPUT — Something that needs defining

PROCESS — · Refer to a dictionary or · Use specific example or · Point to or show the something

RESULT — Understanding

Now compare your model with the one shown in Figure 17–6. It's not necessary that your model exactly reflect this figure but it should be a general approximation.

It is not always possible to construct an adequate model at the paragraph level. The paragraph may be too short or it may not completely follow the normal inductive or deductive pattern or it may be unsuitable for other reasons. However, as mentioned, practice at the paragraph level is instructive.

Applying CSM to a Chapter Section

Economics is know as the "dismal science." But studying economics doesn't have to be dismal. Figure 17–7a contains a chapter section from a well-known economics textbook. As you read the passage, mark it to reflect those portions that you feel relate to input, process, or result. (Don't be afraid to change your mind.) Now, in the space provided in Figure 17–7b, sketch a model that you feel reflects the material. Remember, there are *many model possibilities* and there is no one right answer.

When you have sketched your model, compare it with that shown at the end of this chapter. Do you think yours is better? It's possible it is. Did the fact that you were studying economics make any real difference? The chances are it didn't—because you became interested in seeing how your model would turn out. This feature adds to the attractiveness of CSM.

As you will see in the next section, the availability of topic headings makes applying CSM easier.

Applying CSM to a Chapter

Assume your assignment is to study Chapter 10 in the text *Biological Science* by William T. Keeton. (This is a popular text found in many college libraries.) It would be helpful if you had a copy of this text but it's not necessary in order to follow this discussion. The procedure described in Figure 17–5 will be used to create a simple yet powerful model of the main chapter ideas.

PHASE A: DECIDING THE OBJECTIVE

The chapter title can sometimes provide help in determining what basic point the material will cover. In this case the chapter heading is *Nervous Control*. This heading is not totally descriptive since it doesn't indicate what is being controlled and to what end. However, a review of the *first few chapter paragraphs* and *the topic outline* (which you prepare in this phase) makes it clear that the chapter material is aimed at describing how animals control their physical actions through control of their muscles. This then becomes the objective,

Figure 17–7a
Sample Chapter Section

Demand to a purely competitive seller You will recall (Chapter 22) that a purely competitive market entails a very large number of producers selling a standardized product. Because he offers a negligible fraction of total supply, the individual competitive seller exerts no perceptible influence on market price. Price is set by the market, and the individual firm can sell as much or as little as it chooses at that price. Stated differently, the demand schedule is perfectly elastic to the individual competitive firm.

But let us digress here for a moment to voice a word of caution. We are not saying that the *market* demand curve is perfectly elastic in a competitive market. Indeed, it is not, but rather, it is typically a downsloping curve. . . . As a matter of fact, the total-demand curves for most agricultural products are quite *in*elastic, even though agriculture is the most competitive industry in our economy. We are saying that the demand schedule faced by the *individual firm* in a purely competitive industry is perfectly elastic. The distinction comes about in this way. For the industry—that is, for all firms producing a particular product—a larger volume of sales can be realized only by accepting a lower product price. All firms, acting independently but simultaneously, can and do affect total supply and therefore market price. But not so for the individual firm. If a single producer increases or decreases his output, the outputs of all other competing firms being constant, the effect on total supply and market price is negligible. The single firm's sales schedule is therefore perfectly elastic, . . . This is an instance in which the fallacy of composition is worth remembering. What is true for the group of firms (a downsloping, less than perfectly elastic, demand curve), is *not* true for the individual firm (a perfectly elastic demand curve).

Columns 1 and 2 of Table 23–3 show a perfectly elastic demand curve where market price is assumed to be $131. Note that the firm cannot obtain a higher price by restricting output; nor need it lower price in order to increase its volume of sales.[1]

Figure 17–7b
Model for a Chapter Section
(In space below show model based on above material.)

[1]From R. Cambell McConnel, *Economics,* 6th ed. (New York: McGraw-Hill Book Company, 1975), p. 477.

purpose, or result of the model you are in the process of creating, namely: "Control of Muscles in Animals." This is quite a distance from simply "Nervous Control." Nevertheless it's been drawn from information contained in the second paragraph of the chapter.

PHASE B: CREATING THE MODEL

By reviewing the chapter topic outline (the actual outline for this chapter can be found in Chapter 9 in this text), you can make an initial attempt at identifying the model's input and process elements. The result might look like this:

Input Elements	Process Elements
Sensory Receptors	Nervous Pathways
	Transmission of Impulses
	Control by Brain

Note that in this case it was possible to identify the model elements by referring only to the chapter's five main topic heading ideas. Also note that the material that will appear first in your model (Sensory Receptors) comes almost at the end of the chapter. Figure 17–8 shows the completed model.

Figure 17–8
A Model of Nervous Control in Animals

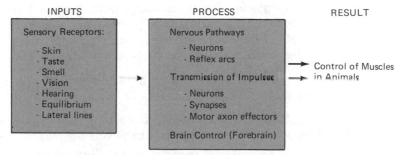

This represents an initial attempt at model making. Detailed reading of the chapter may result in your modifying the model. Note how the model, simple as it is, promotes an understanding of the subject matter that is often hard to achieve through straight reading. The model allows you to stand back and analyze the material. Because the model is patterned, it promotes recall of the chapter's basic ideas and its attendant details. Your ability to adequately respond to class and examination questions is enhanced.

With a firmer model-based idea of the chapter's ideas, you can now proceed to read the chapter. Knowing how the chapter parts relate will help you to enter the chapter at a point that appears either interesting or important. Any reading you now do will be more easily understood since you will be able to place the vocabulary, structure, and emphasis in context. At this point you read the chapter much as you would in the SCORE system Read step. Instead of transferring important markings to your outline, you can enter them in the appropriate area on your model. During this Read step you can decide to create additional models for particular chapter subdivisions.

PHASE C: EVALUATING YOUR LEARNING

Periodically evaluate your grasp of the chapter material through written recall of the model or by describing the model to another person. If you take some care and produce a neat, simple diagram, it will be easier to picture the model in your mind when you attempt to recall its features.

Your ability to create models will grow as you practice the technique. To become familiar with the process described above, it is a good idea to start not with a whole chapter but with a smaller portion that stands by itself (see Figure 17–7a). You can then progress to the point where you feel confident to model a total chapter.

CSM
Pointers

Recognize the following regarding CSM:

• CSM is basically nothing more than a topic outline that is laid out horizontally instead of vertically. The only real difference is that CSM *always* follows an inductive part-to-whole pattern and it *always* has three majors parts: input, process, and result. Into these parts you logically fit appropriate ideas and facts. If you can create a topic outline, with practice, you can study with CSM.

• Using CSM for a single paragraph may bring mixed results. Use it for material that represents at least a chapter section.

• Some chapters or chapter sections will be more difficult to model than others. There are several reasons for this:

—The material may not include information that addresses each of the three model elements of input, process, and result. In such cases you can still complete the model by supplying the missing material based on your own analysis of what is logically needed.

—The overall material structure, as reflected by its topic headings, may be (infrequently) vague and not easily identifiable. In such instances delay attempts at model making until you have read more of the chapter.

—The material as written may be unclear, thus preventing analysis. However, there will most likely be few such cases.

• Use model making as part of the Evaluate step in the SCORE study system (see Figure 15–2e). Use of models in this fashion is an interesting method of testing your understanding and retention of material you study.

• The left-to-right model-drawing pattern is useful because it is simple and promotes understanding. However, you can adopt other pictures that suit your taste or reflect your imagination. As long as the three elements of input, process, and result are present, you can use any sort of model representation. For example, consider using circles within circles, boxes within boxes, floors in a three-story building, or rooms in a three-room house. You can even select something associated with your subject. For example, instead of the approach used in Figure 17–8 you could enter the same information on a rough sketch of a human body. These approaches can add more interest and fun to model making. But remember that the CSM emphasis is on thinking your way up the Figure 17–4 thought ladder and on identifying input, process, and result.

• As with outlines, expect to revise your model until you hit upon a right combination. This revision process contributes to your understanding and retention of the material.

The CSM is a more than suitable substitute for any of the study methods described in Chapter 15. It promotes interest in what you study, provides a reward for your efforts, and allows you to think at more advanced levels. CSM helps you understand and makes it easier for you to remember. The key to using CSM rests in gaining, through practice, confidence in model making. This useful learning tool has application in college as well as out.

Exercise 17–1. Practice in Modeling Paragraphs

Review the material in this chapter on modeling paragraphs. Recognize that a paragraph's topic sentence is the "result" part of a paragraph-level IPR model. Now do the following:

a. Create an IPR model for each of the four paragraphs shown in Exercise 9–2. Remember that some paragraphs do not lend themselves to model making. Also some paragraphs are easier to model than others. Paragraphs 1, 3, and 4 should present no modeling problem. Paragraph 2, because it is rather short and a bit vague, may present a problem, but you can add any missing information.

b. Prepare a model for the first full paragraph that appears in Figure 10–1.

Exercise 17–2. Practice in Creating Models

Before completing these exercises, review the model making procedure summarized in Figure 17–3b.

a. Prepare an IPR model for the material in Figure 17–1.

b. Prepare IPR models for each of the following:

(1) Washing your hands	(6) Making a studio music recording
(2) Combing your hair	(7) Surfing
(3) Learning to drive a car	(8) Obtaining a loan
(4) Learning to sail a boat	(9) Studying a text
(5) Going on a diet	(10) Listening

c. Prepare an IPR model that represents the activity of being a college student. Now compare your model with Figure 2–3.

Exercise 17–3. Applying CSM to Chapter Sections
Before completing this exercise, review the Creative Study Method summarized in Figure 17–5.

Apply CSM to:

a. The section entitled "The Term Paper Writing System" in Chapter 12 of this text.

b. A chapter section in one of your current texts. Pick a text associated with the subject you like best.

c. Repeat *b.* above using a text for a subject you least like.

Exercise 17–4. Applying CSM to Chapters
Repeat Exercise 17–3 above but this time model the complete chapters.

Summary

One truly understands only what one can create.

Giambattista Vico

Many students find studying uninteresting because they see it only as a memorizing act. Simply trying to memorize things not only is boring, it takes the fun out of studying. The resultant grades you receive may not be related to your actual understanding.

The study systems described in Chapter 15 are designed to promote interest in what you study while helping you understand and retain the material. A system that is also interesting and rewarding is the Creative Study Method (CSM). CSM is for you if (1) you want a study method that emphasizes concepts and relationships, (2) you enjoy being creative or would like to learn how to become so, (3) you really want to become expert in a particular field of study, or (4) you want to answer the question, "How can I get the most out of college and still satisfy the cumulative average pressure that is built into the system?"

Model	Process	Inductive	CSM
Input	Result	Deductive	

REVIEW QUESTIONS

1. What is a model?
2. What is a two-dimensional diagrammed model?
3. What are the attributes of a good model?
4. What thought patterns are predominant in model making?
5. Describe the model making procedure.
6. Describe the CSM study system.

Note: Figure 17–9 represents *one* possible approach for modeling the material in Figure 17–7a. *It is not the only right answer.* Your model may be different but it may also be better. The factors of objectivity, representativeness, and simplicity should be used to evaluate your model.

Figure 17–9
An Answer for 17–7b

INPUT	PROCESS	RESULT
• Competitive market (large # of companies selling a standard product)	• Market sets price • For <u>Industry</u> to increase volume price must be lowered • But since <u>Single</u> Company's market actions are negligible, it can raise/lower volume at will with no price change • ∴ a single company can raise or lower it's volume with no effect on product price	Although in a competitive market, individual company can act independently

CHAPTER 18

THE STUDY PALACE: HOW TO USE THE LIBRARY

BASIC IDEAS
- A library represents the intellectual artwork of mankind.
- A library can help make you what you want to be.
- Librarians are the nicest part of a library.

KEY POINTS
- How can you use your college library to advantage?
- What are the four basic ways of finding library materials?
- Do you know how to make your college library a resource for your specific curriculum?

As a college student you are apt to ask the questions: "What can the library do for me? How can I find what I need when I need it?" This chapter will help answer these questions.

What Can the Library Do for You?

The library is an intellectual time machine. It allows you to understand the past and present so you can better enter the future. The library is a silent meeting that comes to order when you ask a question of a librarian, open a book, listen to a tape cassette, or watch a filmstrip. The library is a study palace. You can meet with yourself or, through multimedia resources, with thousands of other people. Each will have his or her own knowledge allowing you the opportunity to comprehend, apply, analyze, evaluate, and synthesize. The word college means a group of people gathered together for a common purpose. You can find no greater gathering than that in your college library.

Studying in the library can reduce distractions and promote concentration. The library also has other uses:

- A place *to be quiet* and just think or daydream.
- A place *to meet and study* with others in assigned study rooms.
- A place *to find* people (*librarians*) interested in helping you.
- A place for *thematic studying:* a source for alternate textbooks and/or multimedia material to achieve comprehension of course material.
- A place simply *to browse and explore.*
- A place *to find and use* different forms of *educational materials.*
- A place *to keep up to date* through latest issues of newspapers and magazines.
- A place *to conduct research* for term paper and other assignments.
- A place *to complete "reserve reading" assignments.* Your instructor may assign readings outside your textbook and may have arranged for the materials to be available by putting them "on reserve" for you in the library.

Perhaps most important, the library allows you the opportunity to engage in self-directed study. The ability to help yourself learn by using the library should be one result of your college experience. The people and the materials in your college library are ready to help you achieve this independence.

Among the nicest people you will find on campus are those in the library. They include college librarians, library technicians, and assistants. They are all specially trained. Librarians are apt to hold advanced degrees in Library Science and/or a special field. They may also teach classes in library use. They all have one thing in common: an interest in helping you use the library's resources. Like your teachers, they are your guides in achieving competency, awareness, and flexibility.

A librarian without a question is like a cassette tape with no listener or a book with no reader. Librarians thrive on questions. They can do their best for you when the question is specific. While always prepared to act on requests such as, "I need a book on economics," they can respond much more directly if the request is, "I need a book on Adam Smith's theory of supply and demand." The point is, the more thinking you can do regarding what you need (i.e., the better you define the problem) the more efficient and effective will be your assistance.

What a Library Has and How It's Organized

The Resources

College libraries used to be simply collections of books. They no longer are. As the world's knowledge has grown and diversified so have the methods of classifying, storing, and retrieving what the world knows. The material in today's library can be categorized as follows:

- Printed material that is directly readable.
- Printed material that is readable through machine assistance.
- Spoken material.
- Visual material.
- Visual and spoken material.

Figure 18–1 shows the book and nonbook material often available in today's modern college library. While not all libraries will have all the resources shown, many will have most of them.

Figure 18–1
The Study Palace

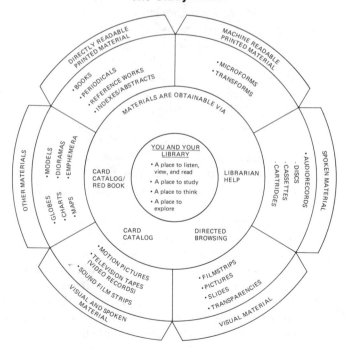

Here is a description of the nonbook materials mentioned in the figure:[1]

Microform. A miniature reproduction of printed or other graphic matter which cannot be utilized without magnification. Microfilm (a roll of film) and microfiche (a sheet of film) are examples of microforms.

Transform. Information coded by methods that require transformation from one form (i.e., a book) to another form (i.e., a punched card) and which requires the use of a machine (usually a computer) for translation. Examples include files stored on magnetic tape, punched cards, and punched paper tapes.

Audiorecord. A recording of sound. Cylinders, discs, rolls, wires, and tapes (open reel-to-reel, cartridge, and cassettes) are included under this heading.

Filmstrip. A roll of film containing a succession of images designed to be machine-viewed frame by frame, with or without sound.

Slide. A small unit of transparent material containing an image, mounted in rigid format and designed for use in a slide viewer or projector.

Transparency. An image produced on transparent material designed for use with an overhead projector.

Videorecord. A recording designed for television playback. Video tapes and discs are included in this category.

Globe. A sphere with a representation or a map of the earth or the universe. Relief globes indicate different heights of land forms by means of a raised surface.

Model. A three-dimensional representation of an object, either exact or to scale, a mock-up.

Diorama. A scene produced in three dimensions by placing objects and figures in front of a representational background.

Emphemeral Materials. Newspaper clippings, pamphlets, single unmounted pictures and sketches, charts, and plans of curricula or local interest are included in this category. Such material is usually not specifically cataloged and is usually stored in file cabinets.

---

[1] With the exception of the term *transform*, the definitions below are drawn and/or adapted from J. R. Weihs, S. Lewis, and J. MacDonald, *Non-book Materials, The Organization of Integrated Collections* (Ottawa: Canadian Library Association, 1973).

THE CARD CATALOG

Library materials are arranged to facilitate a library's basic responsibility of classifying, storing, and retrieving materials. The basic method for locating the resources shown in Figure 18–1 is use of the card catalog. The card catalog shows what the library has. It indexes most of the library's book and nonbook materials. The cards are arranged alphabetically by subject, by work title, and by work author. Using the catalog is about the same as using a textbook's index. The purpose of the card catalog is to provide you with a specific reference number, referred to as the *call number,* for the material you seek. Knowledge of the call number allows you either to request the book or to proceed directly to that section of the library where the material is stored. Figure 18–2 illustrates typical catalog cards.

THE CALL NUMBER

The call number that appears on the card also appears on the book or nonbook material. These call numbers represent a means of classifying material so it can be identified and located.

There are two basic classification methods: one is the Dewey Decimal System, the other the system of the Library of Congress. It is very likely that your college library will use one or the other of these systems. Some college libraries have their own classification system. The Library of Congress System is more adaptable to in-depth collections than the Dewey System and is therefore more popular with large college collections. The two classification systems are outlined below.

A Summary of the Dewey and Library of Congress Classification Systems

Library of Congress Letter	Subject	Dewey Decimal Number
A	General Works	000
B–BJ	Philosophy	100
BL–BX	Religion	200
C	General History, Archaeology, Biography (Biography of individuals related to subjects will classify with the subject.)	900, 920
D	World History, History of Individual Countries	930–999

Figure 18–2
Examples of Card Catalog Cards

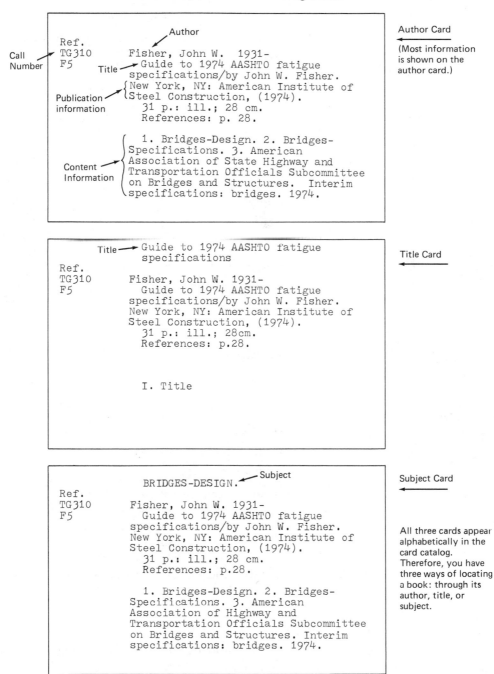

Author Card

←

(Most information
is shown on the
author card.)

Title Card

←

Subject Card

←

All three cards appear
alphabetically in the
card catalog.
Therefore, you have
three ways of locating
a book: through its
author, title, or
subject.

Library of Congress Letter	Subject	Dewey Decimal Number
E	United States History	970–973
F	U.S. History, by States	974–979
G	Geography, Anthropology, Customs, Recreation	390, 790, 910
H	Sociology and Economics	300, 330
J	Political Science	320
K	Law	340
L	Education	370
M	Music	780
N	Fine Arts	700
P	General Language and Literature	400, 800
PR	English Literature	820
PS	American Literature	810
P	Pure Science	500
R	Medicine	610
S	Agriculture	630
T	Technology	600
U	Military Science	350
V	Naval Science	350
Z	Bibliography and Library Science	016, 025

As you can see, the Dewey System relies on numbers as its primary means of classification and the Library of Congress System (LC) primarily on letters. The Dewey System has been shown out of numerical order to facilitate comparison with the LC System. To provide for more detailed levels of classification, the Dewey System subdivides its numbers while the LC System uses numbers after its letters.

CALL NUMBERS AND CURRICULUM

From a curriculum viewpoint the library would probably be less imposing if its materials were cataloged by curriculum. You could then proceed directly to "your" part of the library and avail yourself of the materials. As a matter of fact, that's how college libraries actually started out. Individual collections of books by professors and later by departments were the first college libraries. While some colleges do have separate libraries for certain curriculums, the basic trend is to a central library housing all materials. This centralization tends to make it more difficult to find *all* the book and nonbook material that relates to your special interest. Wouldn't it be helpful if you could identify your material by curriculum? Well, you can and it's really rather simple.

How to Find Library Materials

There are four basic ways to find the library's materials.

1. *Ask a librarian.*
2. *Use the card catalog.*
3. *Use the card catalog red book method.* Next time you find yourself near the card catalog, look for two large red volumes on or in the vicinity of the catalog drawers. They represent the *Library of Congress Subject Headings*. They make it possible to gain a greater view of the materials your library holds.

Here is how they work. Suppose you are interested in the subject of marketing. Ordinarily you would go to the subject card catalog, pull out the appropriate drawer, and find the cards indexed under the heading "Marketing." But if you stopped there you would receive a very narrow view of the potential library holdings on the subject of marketing. If, instead of going directly to the card catalog, you were to first look up the subject heading "Marketing" in Red Volume 2, you would find a list of topics that includes the following:

Market hunting
Market segmentation
Marketing management (HF54151)
Marketing of livestock
Marketing research
Marketing research as a profession
Markets (HF5470-5475)

But the reward doesn't end there. Under each of these headings the red book contains still more subclassifications. For example, if you happened to be concerned with the heading "Marketing Research," you would find the following subheadings listed:

Figure 18-3
The Curse of Emot Koob

Market surveys

Marketing research

Motivation research (Marketing)

Consumer panels

Interviewing in marketing research

Retail trade-research

Sales forecasting

Research

Research, Industrial

Simulation methods

Statistical methods

Vocational guidance

Notice most of these headings do not start with the letter M. You would not be aware of them if you had simply consulted "Marketing" in the alphabetically oriented card catalog. While the card catalog *may* cross-reference some of these subject headings, it by no means will cross-reference all of them. The red book holds those subject heading combinations that unlock the card catalog and the library as well.

Note that the red books do not tell you what your library has. What it does do is tell you where to look in the card catalog for subjects of interest. If your library has material on the subject, you will find a corresponding index card.

4. *Engage in directed browsing.* If you already have the title of a work or the name of its author, you should consult the card catalog directly. If your library carries the work, you will find a card showing its call number. Sometimes, however, you don't have a specific reference but want to know what may be available on a given subject. In such situations pulling books straight from the shelves (directed browsing) can be interesting and helpful.

Look again at the summary of the Dewey and Library of Congress classification systems. You will notice the material is curriculum oriented. The library is really an assemblage of small collections, each of which concerns a particular field of study (curriculum). This information forms the basis for the call numbers used in identifying library materials. Knowledge of call numbers, as they relate to curriculums, can help you see the library not as a large collection of seemingly unrelated material but as a mosaic of knowledge that can be looked at to suit your special interests. On the following page is an example of curriculums and their assigned Library of Congress call number designations. When your aim is to explore generally, such information will prove valuable.

Selected Curriculum	Selected LC Subject Heading	Associated LC Code Letters
Advertising Art and Design	Advertising	HF5801-6191
	Posters	NC1800-1855
	Lithography	NE2250-2570
Business Administration	Accounting	HF5601-5689
	Finance	HG201-9970
Education	Educational Psychology	LB1051-1091
	Types of Education	LC1001-1091
Engineering	Chemical	TP155-156
	Electrical	TK
Nursing	Physiology	QP
	First Aid	RC86-88

If you wish to determine where "your" books (and other materials) are located, ask a librarian for or send for a copy of a slim blue booklet called the *LC Classification Outline* published by the Library of Congress. It's free and a copy can be obtained by writing to Card Division, Library of Congress, Building 159, Navy Yard Annex, Washington, D.C., 20541.

If you have not as yet selected a curriculum, directed browsing can provide direct exposure to the materials in a field you may be considering. By reading a book's Table of Contents and reviewing some of its material, you will be able to tell if the book fits your needs. This sort of direct review is just not possible when using the card catalog. Aside from talking to people, there is no better way of directly learning about and gaining exposure to new material.

Reference Books

Reference books contain concentrated groupings of information regarding specific subjects. Here are examples of some reference books for the curriculums mentioned above.

Curriculum	Selected Dictionaries, Encyclopedias, Handbooks
Advertising Art and Design	*Encyclopedia of Advertising; Art Dictionary*
Business Administration	*Financial Handbook; Accountants Handbook; A Dictionary for Accountants; Office Management Handbook; Production Handbook*
Education	*Dictionary of Education; Encyclopedia of Educational Research; Handbook of Research in Teaching*

Engineering	*Chemical Engineers' Handbook; Electrical Engineers' Handbook; Mechanical Engineer's Handbook*
Nursing	*Encyclopedia of Nursing; Facts About Nursing*

Other curriculum-related reference material can be found by consulting:

- Constance M. Winchell, *Guide to Reference Books,* 8th ed. American Library Association, Chicago, 1967.
- Mona McCormick, *Who-What-When-Where-How-Why Made Easy,* Quadrangle Books, Chicago, 1971.

Periodicals, Indexes, Abstracts

A *periodical* is a continuing publication that usually appears at least once a year. Since thousands of periodicals are published, you are sure to find some that relate to your curriculum. Here are three useful guides which can tell you the names of periodicals that relate to your curriculum or subject of interest.

- *Ulrich's International Periodicals Directory,* 16th ed., 1975–1976, R. R. Bowker Co., New York, 1975.
- *The Standard Periodical Directory 1970,* 3rd ed., Oxbridge Publishing Co., Inc., New York, 1969.
- Bill Katz, *Magazine for Libraries,* 2nd ed., R. R. Bowker Co., New York, 1972.

An *index* is a publication that catalogs (by subject and magazine) all articles that have appeared in a given set of periodicals. An *abstract* goes one step further and summarizes an article's main point. Indexes and abstracts are available for many specific curriculums. Here are some that are general in nature.

Social Sciences Index
Humanities Index
Public Affairs Information Service Index
Readers Guide to Periodical Literature
Christian Science Monitor Index
New York Times Index
Science Abstracts
Abstracts for Social Workers

Bibliographic Research

Bibliographic research involves consulting a library's resources for information. At one time the term referred to books only, but, as Figure 18–1 shows, a library may contain many different types of material. Today the term *bibliographic research* refers to consulting any material (book and nonbook) that is stored.

When researching it is necessary to keep a running record of material you consult. You should record information on 3 by 5 cards. Write out complete references to the source as well as passages you intend to quote. Such cards provide the information you need to support your term paper effort and prepare footnotes and a bibliography. Here are some examples of how to prepare bibliographic research cards and footnotes for term papers:

For a signed newspaper (or magazine) article:

General Subject
  Author
  Headline
  Newspaper
  title, date, and
  article location

```
Selecting College Electives
Wristen, Dr. Henry M.
""Education Without Longing for Cookie-Cutterism''
The New York Times (December 11, 1977)
page 23
```

For a book:

General Subject
  Author
  Title
  Publisher
  location and name,
  date, pages used

```
Preparing term papers
Turabian, Kate L.
Student's Guide for Writing College Papers, 2nd ed. rev
Chicago: University of Chicago Press, 1969
pp. 22–31
```

The aim of using a card is to record information in such a way that you do not have to refer to the source again. Here are some guidelines to follow:

- Write your cards out as you consult the source. Use one card per source. Write on one side only.
- Record only what is absolutely necessary. Summarize important points in your own words. If you copy passages word for word, use quotation marks. Make sure your notes are accurate. For each point summarized or quoted, cite the source page number on the left side of the card. Write neatly.

- If you must use several cards for the same source, code and sequence the cards.

Figure 18–4
Library Resource Guide—
A Curriculum-Specific View of the Library

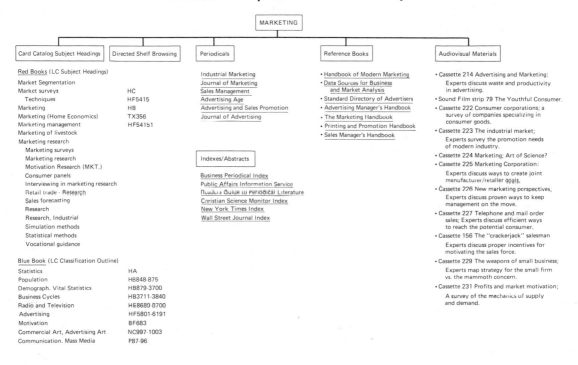

Putting It All Together Figure 18–4 is an indication of what *you* can create for that portion of your own curriculum that interests you.

It is a result of using the four basic methods of finding library materials as well as reviewing references, periodicals, and nonbook materials. Such a curriculum-oriented guide puts a library's resources at your command, aids thematic studying, and is of great help in preparing term papers.

Exercise 18–1. The People in the Library
Complete this table for those entries that apply to your college library. You will find the completed table a useful aid in your studies and assignments.

Name of Facility	Location	Person to Contact	Phone Number
1. The Reference Section	_____	_____	_____

Name of Facility	Location	Person to Contact	Phone Number
2. The Periodicals Section			
3. The Pamphlets Section			
4. The Government Documents Section			
5. The Reserve Section			
6. The Audiovisual Section			
7. Study Room Section			
8. Reading and Learning Laboratory			
9. Audio Studio Section			
10. Viewing Rooms			

Exercise 18–2. When You Were New

Look up a newspaper for the date you were born or a magazine for the month and year you were born. Prepare a one-page summary of the major articles discussed.

Exercise 18–3. Bibliographic Research

Prepare a bibliography card for a book you select. Include a summary of an idea in the book as well as a quoted passage.

Exercise 18–4. A Library Resource Guide

Create a Library Resource Guide (use a format similar to Figure 18–4) for one or more of the following: (a) a specialty within your curriculum, (b) a subject that especially interests you, (c) a subject you don't like or are not doing well in, (d) a hobby of yours.

Assembling Your Own Library

Here is a list of books to consider obtaining for your own personal use. They will prove helpful throughout your college career regardless of your particular field of study.

DICTIONARIES (Any of the following will serve you well.)

- *The American Heritage Dictionary of the English Language*
- *Funk and Wagnall's Standard College Dictionary*
- *Thorndike-Barnhart Comprehensive Desk Dictionary*
- *Webster's New Collegiate Dictionary*

REFERENCES

- Mona McCormick, *Who-What-When-Where-How-Why Made Easy*. Chicago: Quadrangle Books, 1971. This book describes itself as "a guide to the practical use of reference books with many helpful hints for the perplexed student." It is.
- William J. Strunk and E. B. White, *The Elements of Style*. New York: MacMillan Company, 1962. Available as an inexpensive paperback, this book can turn you into a better writer. Parts II and V are particularly helpful.
- Kate L. Turabian, *Student's Guide for Writing College Papers*, 2nd ed. rev. Chicago: University of Chicago Press, 1969. A helpful guide that emphasizes format techniques.

Consult *Home Reference Books in Print: A Comparative Analysis* for additional information on dictionaries and references.

GENERAL WORKS

- Stuart Chase, *Guides to Straight Thinking*. New York: Harper and Row, Publishers, 1956. This book describes itself as "an entertaining readable and instructive book on how to improve your thinking and avoid being fooled by others." The examples used are dated, but the book will really help you think straight.
- S. I. Hayakawa, *Language in Thought and Action,* 2nd ed., New York: Harcourt, Brace & World, Inc., 1964. A book on the meaning and use of language that will improve your ability to communicate with yourself and with others. Chapters 1, 3, and 10 are particularly helpful.

Summary

College libraries are often imposing structures. The shear amount of material they house can quickly overcome your good intentions. Is there a way of breaking through the curtain of catalog cards a library appears to put between you and its resources? Is there a way of having the library reveal its treasures to you?

The answer to both these questions is yes. And the answer is built on recognizing the extraordinary learning opportunities available in today's college library as well as knowing how to avail yourself of the library's resources. This chapter presents a broad yet curriculum-oriented view of the library, its resources, and how they can help make you a complete college student. It also discusses the preparation of bibliography cards.

Spending time in your college library should be a weekly feature of your study schedule. Frequent use of the library will greatly assist you in becoming competent, aware, and flexible.

KEY TERMS

Librarian	Reference books
Library resources	Periodicals
Card catalog	Indexes
Call number	Abstracts
Red books	Bibliographic research
Library Resource Guide	Bibliography card

REVIEW QUESTIONS

1. Describe the key terms above.
2. Identify and describe five different uses of the library.
3. What are the two main systems used to organize library materials?
4. List six nonbook materials that can be found in a library.
5. Identify and describe four ways to find library materials.

Evaluating Your College Experience

When you complete this part you should be able to accomplish the following:
1. Know and apply the techniques of exam preparation and taking.
2. Analyze exam results to improve future performance.
3. Apply the self-management method to special college situations. (This objective is repeated from Part I to emphasize the self-evaluation aspects that accompany both Chapters 4 and 19.)

PREVIEW OF CHAPTER

Chapter 19, How to Take and Use Exams, tells how to prepare for, take, and use the results of examinations. This chapter provides detailed exam preparation instructions, discusses how to manage exam taking itself, shows how to answer different types of exam questions, including essay questions, and tells what to do if exam results are poor—or good.

Teacher-administered classroom exams usually evaluate only course competency. Competency as a manager of your overall college career and in the educational aims of awareness and flexibility must be evaluated by yourself. Chapter 4, presented earlier in the text to encourage development of self-management skills, shows how to evaluate these other aims.

CHAPTER 19 ❧

HOW TO TAKE AND USE EXAMS

BASIC IDEA
- Always ask the best of yourself.

KEY POINT
- Most exam scores are determined before you enter the examination room.

When giving an exam a teacher is doing a simple thing. She or he is attempting to find out how much you have learned (how competent you are) in a given subject. Exam results have little to do with anybody other than yourself. Your performance is a highly personal affair for which you are directly responsible.

An exam is for *you*, for these reasons:

- Results show to what extent you are learning the course material.
- Results allow you to identify weak areas that may need special attention.
- Results allow teachers to assign you a grade or certify your skill in a given area.

Good results, in addition to providing a sense of satisfaction and motivation, indicate that your study program is working well. Poor results indicate the opposite.

How well you do on current and future exams is directly related to (1) how well you managed your study program prior to the exam, (2) how well you are able to manage the actual test taking, and (3) how well you use test results to better control future performance. The following discussion covers all three of these points.

Preparing for Exams
You do not achieve competency as a result of taking an examination. An exam measures the degree of competency you bring to the examination room. To be sure you arrive prepared, do the following:

Far in Advance of the Exam
Good exam performance is a function of good study management prior to the exam. Therefore:

1. Establish and adhere to a study schedule.
2. Ask questions in class and in your teacher's office to clarify material.
3. Employ a systematic study method such as SCORE. The specific method you use is not important; just make sure you use one you are comfortable with (possibly one you have adapted) and one which includes the learning concepts of participation, organization, and persistence.
4. Engage in periodic review of your notes.

The periodic review should begin several weeks before an exam is scheduled. At the end of each normal study period take out your previous study notes and spend about 20 mintues reviewing them. During this review stage, try to reduce the several pages of notes that will usually result from a study session to no more than a page of key words, phrases, and facts. This will make subsequent review efforts less imposing, and will also prepare you for the week-before review discussed below. Here a note of caution is in order. Exams are important, but if you drop all your other study concerns because of an impending exam, you will only put yourself behind for the next round of exams. Exam taking is a normal aspect of taking college courses. Preparing for them should be part of your normal study program.

A Week to Ten Days Before the Exam
Your teacher will most likely provide you with information in the following areas. If not, you should ask about them.

The topics to be covered. Although you may have covered many topics in the preceding time period, it is not likely that you will be tested on all of them. An exam that covers all the material would usually take too long. Therefore, your teacher will probably select those topics considered most important. Ordinarily a teacher will share this information with you.

The topics to be emphasized. Within a selected group of topics the teacher may choose to emphasize one or two of them. Try to determine if this is the case.

The type of questions to be asked. The type of questions can provide a clue as to how you should prepare for the exam. If you are to be asked mostly fill-in or true or false questions, it is likely that the questions will concern mostly factual or definitional information. Essay questions usually mean more of an emphasis on concepts and their application to different situations. Multiple-choice questions may mean an emphasis on facts, but you can't always be sure. You will have to get used to each teacher's approach. Knowing the type of question will help you focus your exam review efforts.

Teachers often reveal quite a bit about an upcoming exam. However, students don't always take advantage of these previews. If a teacher has given you a list of course obectives, it is clear not only what you should be studying but also what you can expect on an exam. Additionally a teacher may briefly review what's to be covered by discussing in class the three areas indicated above, usually without having to be asked. If you make a note of these comments, you will be able to establish an effective review plan.

The Last Few Days Before the Exam

With as much of the above information as it is possible to obtain, you can then engage in your final review sessions. At this stage the emphasis is on reviewing previously studied material. Attempting to learn new material during this final stage is usually very difficult and tends to increase your anxiety level. Adequate preparation ahead of time will preclude the questionable practice of cramming, which unfortunately is sometimes a mistaken substitute for a meaningful college education.

Here are several review methods. Gather the notes resulting from use of the SCORE (or similar) system. These notes, along with any summaries of these notes you may have made, represent what is important. At this stage use the text only as a reference to clarify or review some point. In reviewing, use one or more of the following approaches:

- Look at the key words or topic headings in your notes and recite to yourself (silently or out loud) associated material. Another approach is to have someone read you key words or phrases, from your notes, with you supplying the details.
- Recall in writing the outlines or models you created as a result of your study sessions.
- Review material with others interested in preparing for the exam. These sessions can be systematic reviews of notes or they can be free-wheeling sessions where questions are put to each other in no particular order. These "study parties," if planned for and if conducted with *some* but not a lot of foolishness, can be fun

and very useful. If conducted far enough in advance of the exam (at least three days), they can provide you with valuable information on gaps in your grasp of the material. Such gaps can be filled in the remaining time.

Day of Exam

Have a good rest the night before and a good breakfast in the morning, Arrive at the exam room on time. Rushing through traffic or across campus can only heighten the anxiety you may already feel. Find a seat away from potential traffic flow caused by departing students and away from potentially distracting friends. Make sure you have any necessary materials such as a slide rule, pen, pencil, eraser, ruler, reference tables, and similar items the exam may require.

Avoid detailed last-minute discussions with friends or frantic fumbling through the text. All someone has to do is mention some obscure fact and your brain can be destroyed. At this point the question no longer is, "Do I know the material?" but rather "Can I be calm enough to allow myself to show what I know?"

Exam Questions

If exam results are to be useful in evaluating your competency *and* enabling you to assess and perhaps adjust your study program, then the exams themselves must be valid, that is, they must test what the course covers. You can rely on your teacher to give valid tests, but from your standpoint it is not enough that the tests be valid. You must take the exam in a manner that allows you to fully reveal your competency. Otherwise the results will not be a true measure of your ability or of the effectiveness of your study program. To achieve test validity: (1) you must be aware of the *types of questions* encountered on exams and (2) you must effectively and efficiently *manage the exam taking* itself. This section discusses exam questions, the next exam taking.

There are basically two types of exam questions you will encounter: in one type the answers accompany the question and you select or recognize the answer you think correct; in the other type you provide the answer. The first type is called an *objective question* because there is generally thought to be only one acceptable answer. Thus your answer can be objectively assessed as either right or wrong. The second type is called an *essay question* because you are required to create an answer in writing.

Objective Test Questions

Included in this category are true or false, matching; and multiple-choice questions.

TRUE OR FALSE

Questions of this type present a statement and you decide whether the statement is true or false. For example:

T   F   The total number of students attending college is less than 5 million.
T   F   Lack of money is the main reason for dropping out of college.
T   F   It is a fact that there will be a United States presidential election in the year 1988.

As with all questions, it is important that you first understand the question before answering. Misreading the question is always possible. This is especially so with true or false questions, since there is a tendency to move rapidly from one question to another.

MATCHING LISTS

In this type of question two columns of words or phrases are listed and you answer by correctly matching the entries in each column. Here is an example:

Column A	Column B
____1. The first step in the management process.	A. Creating
____2. The lowest form of learning.	B. Evaluating
____3. Your most important resource.	C. Memorizing
____4. The highest form of learning.	D. Money
____5. The last step in the management process.	E. Organizing
	F. Planning
	G. Time

Next to each item in Column A is a blank space. In these spaces you write the letter from Column B that best matches the statement in Column A. Note there are more answers than questions. This technique is sometimes used to decrease the possibility of your guessing correctly. Also, sometimes the same answer may apply to more than one statement. The Column B is usually arranged in alphabetical order (as above) or in numerical order (if the responses require numbers or dates), so don't waste test time trying to figure out whether the statements are matched by some special coded arrangement.

It is best to proceed using the process of elimination. That is, match the ones you're sure of first. This will usually eliminate some possible answers. Proceed to the statements you are less sure of and select from the now reduced set of responses.

MULTIPLE CHOICE

Here a statement or partial statement is made and attached to it are usually four or five answers which support or complete the statement. There are two types of multiple-choice questions. One is called correct answer and the other best answer. The *correct answer* questions usually address matters of fact. They ask who, what, when, and where questions that relate to names, numbers, terms, dates, and places. Here is an example:

What percentage (approximately) of junior college students drop out before graduation? (A) 15% (B) 25% (C) 50% (D) 65% (E) 75%

The *best answer* questions usually address matters of understanding, application, and analysis. They ask which, why, and how questions that relate to concepts, principles, procedures, and methods. Here is an example of the best-answer type:

Which of the following is most apt to ensure graduation from college? (A) Availability of money (B) Attending an out-of-state college (C) Motivation for courses (D) Use of a systematic study method (E) No part-time job

Several of the above choices are *acceptable* answers, but only one of them is the *best* answer. For such questions you must not only think through to the best answer, but also answer the question in the context of the course you are then taking.

Use the following approach when answering either type of multiple-choice question:

- Answer those you know first.
- Return to the unanswered questions and analyze the possible answers using a process of elimination. Cross out those answers you are sure are not correct. Then choose the best of the rest.
- If you are still not sure, mark the question in the margin and leave it. Return to it when the other questions have been answered. This will allow you time to think. Also, information contained in other questions may refresh your memory or provide a clue for answering.

Essay Questions

Included in this category are short-answer, restricted-response, and extended-response questions. Unlike objective type questions, which supply you with answers and require only that you recognize which is correct, an essay question requires that you supply the answer. Essay questions (in particular the restricted-response and extended-response types) are usually used to measure your understanding of course material as opposed to simply measuring your knowledge of facts. The essay question (and the best-answer multiple-choice question) is designed to have you think above the first level of the thought ladder shown in Figure 7–17. While facts may be important to your answer, the emphasis is on measuring your ability to apply, analyze, and evaluate material.

SHORT ANSWER

The short-answer or fill-in type presents a question or an incomplete statement. You answer by supplying a word, phrase, or number as appropriate. For example:

- What was the name of the *type* of vehicle that first landed men on the moon? (_____)
- A person who continues college study after receiving a bachelor's degree is said to be engaging in (_____).
- If X = 2 then $X^2 + 3X - 2$ is equal to (_____).

Strictly speaking the above questions do not require an essay (a short literary composition) to answer. Since they require essentially factual responses, short-answer questions can be thought of as objective type questions.

RESTRICTED RESPONSE

This type of essay question is used to restrict what you say and how you say it. The questions contain conditions that you must follow to obtain full credit. They ask you to list, identify, or describe. Here are some examples:

- List the five activities associated with the management process.
- Identify the three main aims of a college education. Select the aim you think most important. Support your selection in a brief paragraph.
- Describe, step by step, the procedure for taking a patient's blood pressure.

Use the following procedure to answer a typical restricted-response question.

The Approach. Answering restricted-response essay questions requires that you: *Read* the question carefully and recognize the use of key words such as list, identify, and indicate. *Pay attention* to length restrictions. *Use* the question itself as a basis for organizing your answer. *Review* your answer to make sure that it is responsive to the question and that it is neatly and clearly written.

An Example. Here is an example that applies the approach to the following question.

> Identify the three main aims of a college education. Select the one you think is most important. Support your selection in a brief paragraph.

Note that the question has three parts and each part has a key word. In this example the key words are *identify*, *select*, and *support*. Your answer should follow the pattern established in the question. Note also the length restriction. Based on this analysis here is how you might answer this question.

College Aims

1. The aims of a college education are to achieve:
   a. Competency
   b. Awareness
   c. Flexibility
2. I believe awareness is the most important aim.
3. Here is why I chose awareness. When I graduate college it will mean I have demonstrated my competence and flexibility in a particular field. What then becomes important is the ability to work with other people in applying what I know. This is best done by being sensitive to the feelings and ideas of other people. Therefore the need to work with others is why I feel awareness is most important.

EXTENDED RESPONSE

This type of question allows you more freedom in responding. The questions contain terms that ask you to analyze, evaluate, create, explain, compare, or contrast. An extended-response essay question usually requires you to write at least several paragraphs and sometimes several pages. How can you tell how much to write? A clue can be found in the phrasing of the question (e.g., explain, evaluate) and in the amount of time allowed for answering. Assume you are given an hour test with 25 multiple-choice questions worth 50 points and two essay questions worth 25 points each. You should then plan on spending about 15 minutes (25 percent of the time) answering each essay question.

A major difference between a restricted-response and an extended-response essay question is responsibility for organizing the answer. The phrasing of a restricted-response question more or less provides the organizational approach for answering (see example above). Extended-response essay questions may require you to do your own organizing. The following shows how to answer a typical extended response question.

The Approach Answering extended-response essay questions is very similar to writing a mini term paper. Both require you to respond to a given topic with appropriate analysis and relevant facts. Both require the preparation of a logically arranged, well-written response that promotes reader understanding. These factors must be present for you to receive a favorable evaluation. Here is a system to use.

Make sure you first understand the question, and be sure to place the question in the context of the course. Then do the following:

1. Prepare a simple statement that describes your answer. Try to limit this statement of intent to one sentence and base it on the question being asked.
2. Sketch a brief outline of the points you will cover. Work with and revise the outline until it reflects a logical, comprehensive response.
3. Next to your outline topics note any special points you will make, examples you will use, or facts you will cite. All of this information will, of course, be based on recall; so give yourself some time to reflect. As sources of information you can recall any outlines or models you may have made while studying. You can also review the previous questions and your answers as possible sources of information.
4. Now write your answer based on the outline. Use clear, simple sentences. Be sure to write or print neatly. Start a new paragraph for each main idea in your outline. Consider using simple sketches or graphs if they are appropriate and if you think they will promote understanding. Remember that your outline represents the essence of your answer so your prime concern at this stage is to promote reader understanding of your answer.
5. Review your answer to make sure that it is free from error and that it contains the two qualities you started out to achieve:
   a. A responsive answer
   b. A well-written, neat answer

An Example. Here is an example that applies this system to the following question.

Describe what is meant by a perfectly competitive market and explain how a company operating within such a market can (within limits) approach monopolistic practice.

(**Step 1** Prepare descriptive statement)

This essay will describe a perfectly competitive market and explain how the nature of elastic and inelastic demand allows a single company within this market to operate monopolistically.

(Notice how the statement of intent is built around the question asked while also including the basic answer you intend to give.)

(**Step 2** Sketch brief outline)

I. Describe perfectly competitive market ←————— *Many buyers + Many sellers*
    · Discuss demand to industry ←——— *inelastic*
    · Discuss demand to one seller ←——— *elastic*
II. Describe monopoly
III. Show connection ←——— *both can sell what is produced*

(**Step 3** See arrowed comments above)

(**Step 4** Write answer)

This essay will describe a perfectly competitive market. It will explain how the nature of elastic and inelastic demand allows a single company within this market to operate as if it had a monopoly.

A perfectly competitive market has many buyers and many sellers. The action of any one seller in increasing or decreasing supplies has little or no impact on market price. This also means that while the demand curve to an industry may be inelastic, the demand curve (i.e., sales) for an individual firm within this industry can be elastic. This is so because an industry facing an inelastic demand cannot sell more than a certain amount. But a single company within this industry can sell at the market price all it can produce since all it produces is negligible when compared with the rest of the industry.

A monopolistic market has many buyers and one seller. The firm holding the monopoly directly controls supplies. Such a firm can sell (within limits) all it produces.

This then is the connection. A firm in a purely competitive field can sell all it produces because it's supply actions have a negligible impact on the rest of the industry. A firm holding a monopoly can also sell (assuming elastic demand) all it produces because there are no other suppliers.

(**Step 5** Review answer)

At this point review your answer to make sure it follows what you promised to say in the first paragraph. Also check to make sure your answer is easy to understand and that it is neatly written.

Open Book Questions

Open book exams are usually given when your teacher is interested in evaluating how well you can apply what you have learned. If you are to be given such an exam, don't waste your time memorizing facts or formulas. They are in your text or your notebook. It is much better to practice working out problems that require you to demonstrate understanding and application. Don't be misled: open book exams can be among the hardest you will take. Chances are such exams will emphasize various types of essay questions that will require you to analyze problems or situations and create an answer. Be sure you are familiar with your text and its problems. Concentrate on application, not memorization.

Taking the Exam

Regardless of the type of questions asked, follow the exam-taking procedure described in this section.

Exam Overview

Enter your name on the exam answer sheet. Do not start answering questions right away. Just as you first become familiar with a chapter before you study it, you should first become familiar with an exam before you attempt to answer questions. Becoming familiar can save you time and, if done methodically and with a sense of confidence, can serve to reduce nervousness. You can become familiar by doing the following:

At the beginning, determine the test conditions by reading the directions. Must all questions be answered? If not, what is the basis for choosing? Must the questions be taken in order? Is there a penalty for guessing?

Next, review the exam and note the type of questions presented, their relative value, and the type of subject material covered. On the basis of this, decide the sequence in which you will answer and determine roughly how much time you will allow yourself to spend in each section. You will, of course, budget your time in accord with the designated point value.

At this stage it is probably a good idea to write down on the back of the question sheet some basic notes (key words, an outline, a model). You can refer to such notes when answering questions. This tends to ease you into the exam and relieves the pressure of having to carry around all that information in your head as you answer questions.

Answering the Questions

- When answering multiple-choice and other objective questions:
  —Answer those you know first.
  —When not sure of an answer, use the process of elimination.
  —If stuck, leave the question and come back to it later.

- Answer essay questions as previously indicated.

- Proceed to answer by first making sure you understand the question and second, answering the easy ones first. Avoid either spending too much time on an answer you know (because you may have more to say) or too much time on an answer you don't know (because you may become momentarily stubborn or upset at yourself for not being able to answer). Since most objective questions are usually worth the same, it is simply good management to answer those you know first. You can then go back and take those you initially skipped, in order of least difficulty. Also follow the easy to difficult approach with essay questions.

- When you have responded to all the questions, go back and review your answers. Avoid the impulse to change an answer unless you have first satisfied yourself that your original approach to answering the question is definitely wrong.

- Regardless of the type of question, it is best to take them at face value and in the context of the course. It is a waste of time to assume that a question is a trick or that something else is actually being asked. You may encounter vague questions but there will be few of those. They occur not because the teacher intended them as such but simply because the question was phrased poorly. (It happens, and most teachers will appreciate your calling such cases to their attention should you discover any.)

- Nervousness is a normal condition. While you can't eliminate it, you can take steps to prevent it from disabling you. Try these approaches:

  —Make a sort of ceremony out of reading the directions and reviewing the exam. Be deliberate. Spend several minutes familiarizing yourself. This will give you something to do with the test as well as prepare you for what is to come.

—Count slowly (and silently) to ten and then begin again. Close your eyes and concentrate on silently pronouncing the numbers as perfectly as possible.

—Allow yourself to go limp in your chair. Take the tension from your shoulders and have your arms droop lazily at your sides. Maintain this position for 15 to 20 seconds, straighten up and repeat. (Be careful you don't fall asleep.)

—Breath deeply several times in succession; stop and repeat.

• Sometimes exams are combinations of different type questions. As previously mentioned, it is good practice to manage your time in accord with the point value of the questions. In such a situation, first review the total exam. Note next to the essay questions key words or points you will make when you prepare the full answer. Then go back and answer first the objective questions and then the essay questions you are sure of. This approach builds confidence. Spend the remaining time answering those questions (regardless of type) you are most nearly sure of. Sometimes when time is short it is better to outline an answer to an essay question that is worth many points than to ponder answers to objective questions worth fewer points. Your teacher is apt to provide partial credit if you show you at least know the basic approach.

• If you are completely blank and cannot recall the answer, try thinking of some idea or activity that has absolutely nothing to do with the question. Do this for several minutes. Then go back and try again. This will help you relax and promote recall of material associated with the question.

• Spend any remaining time checking your answers.

• An answer that cannot be read is an answer that cannot be evaluated. Illegible handwriting is an invitation to the teacher to downgrade you. Poor handwriting will often lead to negative assumptions about your ability to think clearly and your aptitude as a college student, and in most cases the teacher will be justified in thinking so. If you can't write legibly, then get help so you can. In the meantime consider printing your answers. If you are worried about appearing immature—forget it. It's better to print your words and prove you know the material than to use unreadable longhand and have the teacher conclude you don't. Besides, a combination of print and script is a perfectly acceptable method of writing.

Unauthorized Assistance   This sounds like it might almost be legal. But, of course, it isn't. The pressure to perform or the fear resulting from unpreparedness can sometimes cause a student to depart from his or her normal code of behavior.

Cheating is the ultimate trick a student plays on him or herself. Aside from the primary point of making an absolute mockery of the purpose of a college education, there is also the fact that there is no way a student can avoid being found out—there is at least one person who will always know about it.

What to Do When Exam Results Are Good (marks consistently 80 or better)

"You mean there's something I should do even when my exam results are good?" Yes—and here they are:

- If you have not yet chosen a major field of study (and maybe even if you have), determine whether the course represents a field that holds career potential. Try to be aware of what is happening to you while it is happening. This is a way of becoming sensitive to your interests and abilities.
- Consider making the field represented by the course your minor field of study.
- Become a tutor. This is an especially good idea if you are thinking of becoming a teacher.
- If you did *very* well on the exam, consider reducing the time spent studying for this course. You may find you can reduce the time and suffer little or no exam performance loss. The extra study time you now have can be spent on other courses that may require more attention.
- If the course holds a special interest for you, ask the instructor for special reading references.
- Make a point of (modestly) letting present or potential employers know of your achievements.
- Write a letter or tell family and friends how good you are (again modestly).
- Reward yourself.
- Hope you won't have to refer too often to the next section.

What to Do When Exam Results Are Poor (Marks of 70 or less—75 or less if the course is part of your major)

A failure or poor performance on an exam (or several exams) does not mean a student is worthless or incapable of doing college level work. There are countless students who at one time did poorly but nevertheless went on to graduate. They turned it around very simply; they resolved to better prepare themselves for the next exam. Blaming the teacher, the college, the faulty pen used, the student in front of you with the nervous head snaps, or the bird that crash dived against the window may provide temporary emotional relief, but it won't help improve your exam scores.

To improve a student must know what went wrong and why. Here is what to do. First try to determine the main reason for the poor results. Is it (1) faulty exam-taking procedure, (2) repetition of previous errors, or (3) poor study management?

If you did poorly because you misread the directions or misunderstood the questions, then you have found out something about yourself. You have allowed your nervousness, and the resultant haste, to trip you into making mistakes. Read the suggestions above under "Taking the Exam" and next time make it a point to slow yourself down and make a conscious effort to relax.

It is not enough to know what questions were answered incorrectly. You must know *why* your answer was incorrect. Otherwise you are bound to repeat your error. This point is especially important for questions that deal with ideas instead of facts. Facts don't change; if you have a fact wrong, you can easily correct the error. However, it may not be so easy to correct a misunderstanding or a misuse of an idea or principle. Wrong facts lead to single errors, but misunderstood ideas can lead to many errors in the same exam and a repetition of these errors on future exams. What can you do about incorrect answers? Analyze the nature of the questions and your errors. If they are errors of fact, get the right information. If they fall into the "misunderstood idea" category, then restudy the material and/or get help. Although it is highly desirable to do this in all your courses, it is essential for math, science, and engineering courses since these courses build on what has gone before. Methods of gaining new understanding include individual restudy, studying with another, thematic studying, asking questions during in-class exam reviews, and seeking individual help from your instructor. Instructor assistance is mentioned last but it will save you a lot of time if you employ it first. Analyzing the nature of the questions and the errors has at least three benefits:

1. You won't repeat errors based on misunderstanding.
2. You will be able to evaluate the nature of the questions and determine which part of the thinking scale (see Figure 17–4) the questions seem to reflect. If the questions stress application of ideas rather than simply recall of facts, then you will have a clue as to how you should study and prepare for the next exam.
3. You will be able to determine which questions reflect class work and which text assignments. If they are more class oriented, then your class notes will have to be very good and your study efforts will have to reflect their importance.

Weak exam performance due to poor study management is a special cause for concern. It must be decided whether the problem is a lack of interest, lack of self-control, poor study skills, or some combination. Parts 1, 2, and 3 in Figure 4–1 will help you decide and help you take appropriate action. If you haven't already done so, you might try answering the series of questions that appear in Chapter 1. Your answers will help direct you to that part of this book which most concerns you.

Cramming

One way to evaluate a student's view of college is to evaluate his or her study efforts. You may know someone whose studying consists solely of cramming, that is, attempting to condense four or five weeks of systematic study into three or four hours of agonizing memorization a few days or hours before an exam. It is likely they have a terribly distorted view of education and college. They see college as basically a test factory, a place to rush through and get over with as quickly as possible. They don't see college as probably their one formal opportunity to take giant intellectual steps. They seem not to recognize that college can help them grow into a person capable of making a better world for themselves and those around them. Is this stating the case too strongly? Perhaps. But to the extent that cramming is always used to prepare for exams there is not much margin for another viewpoint.

Cramming is not the answer to a lack of systematic preparation. There is no answer to such a lack. In fact cramming itself can cause fear and anxiety. The student knows he or she lacks preparation and tries to compensate by cramming. This only reveals the degree of unpreparedness, which in turn provokes more anxiety. The result is that the student appears at the examination room with a long face, tumbling stomach, and twitching eyebrows.

Is cramming ever justified? Are there times when it is the only reasonable solution? Yes to both. When you have been ill, or you have been forced to devote a large amount of time to another subject, or personal or family circumstances or problems occur, cramming may be unavoidable. The only valid reasons for cramming are those relatively few instances when circumstances interrupt your academic efforts and threaten course success. Under such circumstances you *should* make your best effort to avoid still further academic complications.

To get the most out of your shortened study effort, do the following:

- Take your class notes or, if you have none, obtain those of another student. Summarize only the main ideas on a separate piece of paper.
- Use the SCORE study system described in Chapter 15 but limit the Read step to a chapter's introduction, summary, topic

headings, and topic sentences. Prepare a separate summary sheet that shows the main chapter ideas along with the main ideas from the class notes.

• Review this summary sheet repeatedly as you approach the end of the cram session.

Cramming may help you memorize enough to get by. But cram only when circumstances prevent you from otherwise learning the material through use of a systematic study program.

Other Ways to Evaluate Your College Experience

For the most part classroom exams measure only how competent you are in course material. But *awareness* and *flexibility* are also aims of a college education. How can you evaluate your progress in these areas? See items 4 and 5 in Figure 4–1. They will help answer this question.

Summary

Exams are important. Results show your competency. They provide evidence to you and your teacher that you have learned a particular subject. Exams allow your college to ultimately certify to society that you are in fact competent to practice in a particular field or learned in a particular field of knowledge.

This chapter shows how to prepare for, take and use the results of exams. Exam preparation includes the use of systematic study systems as well as periodic review leading up to the exam. Taking an exam requires knowledge of question types and application of test-taking skills. There are two types of questions: objective and essay. Objective questions require that you choose from supplied answers and include true or false, multiple choice, and matching lists. Essay questions require that you create an answer and include fill-in, limited-response, and extended-response questions. Test-taking skills include first reviewing the exam to determine its requirements, budgeting your time, answering easier questions first, and using a process of elimination when selecting answers to questions.

Using exam results—good or bad—is important in ensuring good results on future exams. If you do poorly on an exam, use the exam results to control your future study actions and to prevent the pattern from repeating itself. Exams are one of several important measures of competency, a measure that allows you to evaluate course competency and your ability to manage your college education. Exam results allow you to evaluate your study program and make necessary changes. The result is that you directly control the exam scores you achieve.

| Preparation | Essay questions | Poor results |
| Objective questions | Exam overview | Good results |

REVIEW QUESTIONS

1. Describe the four steps associated with exam preparation.
2. What is: (a) an objective question? (b) an essay question?
3. Describe three types of objective questions.
4. What is the difference between a correct-answer and a best-answer multiple-choice question?
5. Describe three types of essay questions.
6. (a) What is the procedure for answering: (i) a restricted-response essay question? (ii) an extended-response essay question? (b) What characteristics must essay answers have?
7. Identify three things you can do to relax while exam taking.
8. Identify five important factors for answering exam questions.
9. Describe how to use good exam results.
10. Describe the three approaches for dealing with poor exam results.

DISCUSSION QUESTION

1. Form a group with one other person. Separately answer this question:

   Identify the five basic activities associated with the management process. Select one you think is most important. Support your selection in a brief paragraph.

   When answers are completed, swap them. Evaluate and assign a grade to your partner's answer. Each describe to the other why you evaluated the answer as you did.

APPLICATION QUESTIONS

1. Answer the question in the Discussion Question above as an individual assignment.
2. Identify the four basic learning skills. Rank them in order of importance. Write a brief paragraph supporting your ranking.
3. Identify the steps in the learning ladder. Select three you think most important and support your position.
4. Justify the value of a college education and summarize your particular reasons for attending.

ANSWERS TO OBJECTIVE QUESTIONS CONTAINED WITHIN CHAPTER

- *True or False:* F, F, F
- *Matching Lists:* F1, C2, G3, A4, B5
- *Multiple Choice:* E, C
- *Short Answer:* Lunar module; Post-graduate study; 8

Note: Answers to questions dealing with dropping out and graduation percentages are based on F. Newman et. al., *Report on Higher Education,* U.S. Department of Health, Education, and Welfare, Washington, D.C., 1971.

~§APPENDIX?~

Choosing Your Curriculum

This appendix gives specific instructions on how to manage your choice of curriculum and elective courses. It recommends tests that will help you discover your current interests and aptitudes. If you are concerned with what major field you should be studying, you will find this material particularly interesting and helpful.

Curriculum Selection Basics

How can you achieve a high level of motivation for your courses? One way is to turn your interests and abilities into a curriculum choice that reflects your characteristics. How do you do this? By using a systematic decision-making approach, to identify curriculum possibilities from which you may choose. The curriculum you select should be something you achieve through clear choice and not from confusion about available options. To make a good choice you need information about how to make decisions, about yourself, and about curriculums. The following discusses all three areas.

The Decision-Making Process

Have you ever worked one of those pencil and paper maze puzzles? A maze continually presents the questions of where am I and where do I want to go? Selecting a course of study can be as confusing and uncertain as finding your way through a maze. The kind of questions that occur are: What am I good at? What will I be good at? What are the job prospects in a given field? How can I find out things about myself? What if I make a mistake and choose wrongly? If I change my major, is all that time wasted? The questions can go on and on—but you can't. If you are to achieve competency, awareness, and flexibility, somehow at sometime you will have to make a curriculum decision.

All managers are faced with decisions. A manager doesn't always have all the information that might be desirable. Additionally the amount of time for deciding is often limited. It is surprising, however, that many managers would keep with their basic initial decision, even if they had more information and time. This does not mean that snap decisions should be made; it does not mean that decisions are made with no valid information. It means that the basis for making a decision often includes an element of judgment (i.e., hunch, feel, emotion) of what the correct course should be.

This kind of decision-making situation (limited information, limited time, the exercise of judgment) approximates the conditions you face when selecting a curriculum for study. Just as you can never state the largest number (someone can always add 1), you can never really have all available information. In fact it is not necessary and may not be possible to have all the information. What is needed is a reasonable amount of representative information. How do you know if you have reached this point? That's where your judgment comes in. At some point in the decision-making process, you will stop and say, "I believe I have enough information; I think a decision can now be made."

The Decision-Making Process and the Management Functions	What can you conclude from all these considerations? One conclusion is that a systematic decision-making approach can certainly be of help. Such a system can increase the chance that your curriculum selection decision will be valid for you. Does the phrase "systematic decision making" sound familiar? It should remind you of the five management functions we covered in earlier chapters. Here now you have a good opportunity to apply the management process to curriculum selection. (For this discussion the term *control* is used in place of *evaluate* since it better fits the decision making process.)

The Self-Management (S-M) Method of Curriculum Selection

Figure A–1 illustrates a method you can use to arrive at a curriculum selection. Here are the steps:

Planning

Planning is deciding in advance what you want to do. In this case you are to decide which curriculum to register for. Your objective can be described as, "Which curriculum shall I choose?"

Colleges require that you identify your curriculum choice by a certain date. This date (minus maybe a week or two for uncertainties) then becomes your target date. Establishing a date will allow you to focus your activities toward some specific end point. It will also allow you to determine when necessary information must be made available. This will guide you and others whose assistance you may enlist.

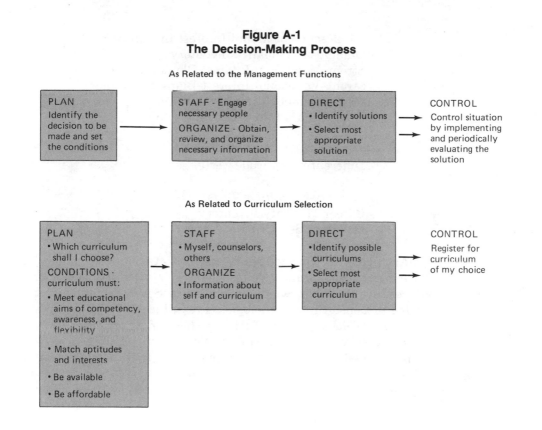

Figure A-1
The Decision-Making Process

As Related to the Management Functions

PLAN	STAFF - Engage necessary people	DIRECT	CONTROL
Identify the decision to be made and set the conditions	ORGANIZE - Obtain, review, and organize necessary information	• Identify solutions • Select most appropriate solution	Control situation by implementing and periodically evaluating the solution

As Related to Curriculum Selection

PLAN	STAFF	DIRECT	CONTROL
• Which curriculum shall I choose? CONDITIONS - curriculum must: • Meet educational aims of competency, awareness, and flexibility • Match aptitudes and interests • Be available • Be affordable	• Myself, counselors, others ORGANIZE • Information about self and curriculum	• Identify possible curriculums • Select most appropriate curriculum	Register for curriculum of my choice

Organizing and Staffing At this point you gather information about yourself and available curriculums. Listed below are some sources of information.

INFORMATION ABOUT YOURSELF

- Personal journal
- Hobbies
- Other people
    - Parents
    - Teachers
    - Friends
- Tests (See high school or college counselor or company personnel department.)

    Interest Tests
    - Career Assessment Inventory (CAI)
    - Kuder Preference Records (Vocational, Personal, and Occupational)

- Minnesota Vocational Interest Inventory
- Omnibus Personality Inventory
- Strong-Vocational Interest Blank for Men
- Strong-Vocational Interest Blank for Women
- Strong-Campbell Interest Inventory
- Occupational Interest Inventory (OII)

Aptitude Tests
- Differential Aptitude Tests

Interest and Aptitude Tests
- Career Maturity Inventory
- Holland's Self-Directed Search

Arrange with your college counselor to take one or more of the above interest and/or aptitude tests. (If the services of a counselor are not readily available, send for Holland's Self-Directed Search by writing to Consulting Psychologists Press, Inc., 577 College Avenue, Palo Alto, California 94036. Enclose a check or money order for $2.50. You can take and score this simple test by yourself.) When testing is completed, make a list of the four or five jobs that most interest you.

This job list together with these materials:

- *The Dictionary of Occupational Titles*
- *The Occupational Outlook Handbook*
- *The Curriculum Summary Table*

will help you choose a curriculum as well as decide on elective courses.

INFORMATION ABOUT CURRICULUMS

The Dictionary of Occupation Titles. The major tool used for conducting further research is a federal publication called *The Dictionary of Occupational Titles (DOT)*. The DOT lists over 21,000 jobs that people practice in the United States, each job having its own code number. Assume that as a result of an interest/aptitude test you have selected the job of Journalist-Reporter for further investigation. By referring to DOT, you can read the following description of that job:

"131.267-018 REPORTER (print. and pub.; radio & tv broad.)
Collects and analyzes information about newsworthy events to write news stories for publication or broadcast: Receives assignment or evaluates leads and news tips to develop story idea. Gathers and verifies factual information regarding story through interview, observation, and research. Organizes material, determines slant or emphasis, and writes

story according to prescribed editorial style and format standards. May monitor police and fire department radio communications to obtain story leads. May take photographs to illustrate stories. May appear on television program when conducting taped or filmed interviews or narration. May give live reports from site of event or mobile broadcast unit. May transmit information to NEWSWRITER (print. & pub.; radio & tv broad.) for story writing. May specialize in one type of reporting, such as sports, fires, accidents, political affairs, court trials, or police activities. May be assigned to outlying areas or foreign countries and be designated CORRESPONDENT (print. & pub.; radio & tv broad.) or FOREIGN CORRESPONDENT (print. & pub.; radio & tv broad.)"

This type of DOT description exists for most every job in the United States. In reading the description you gain understanding of the nature of the work and the kind of preparation necessary to perform the work.

The Occupational Outlook Handbook. The Handbook is another source of curriculum information. It contains the following information for more than 800 occupations.

- Nature of job
- Places of employment
- Training, other qualifications, and advancement
- Employment outlook
- Earnings and working conditions
- Sources of additional information

While all this information can be useful to you, that portion dealing with "Training, other qualifications, and advancement" (together with the DOT entry) can be of special help in identifying curriculum-related information.

(*Note:* Both the DOT and the Handbook are usually available in your college or community library. Your high school or college counselor or your company's personnel department may also have these publications.)

The Curriculum Summary Table. At this point in the information-gathering step you will have:

Identified (as a result of a test) a job that interests you and for which you may have an aptitude.

Read about the job in *The Dictionary of Occupational Titles* and in *The Occupational Outlook Handbook.*

To conclude the information gathering you must organize your data in systematic fashion that will help you analyze the information and arrive at a choice. Remember you are striving to identify possible curriculum choices. The instrument for organizing your data is called the Curriculum Summary Table. The following example has been completed for the job of Journalist-Reporter, DOT code 131.267-018.

Curriculum Summary Table

Job Name	DOT Code	Associated Curriculums	Associated Courses
Journalist-Reporter	131.267-018	Journalism Liberal Arts	*Journalism* Reporting, Copyreading, Editing, Feature writing, History of journalism, Typing *Liberal Arts* English, Writing, Sociology, Political Science, Economics, History, Psychology, Speech

With the information obtained from the appropriate pages in the DOT and the Handbook, a table can be constructed for each job that may interest you. Notice that completing the table for the job of Journalist-Reporter has resulted in the identification of two curriculums. Which then do you choose? If as a result of your research you have decided that a reporter's job is really what you want, then (if it's available) you will choose your college's journalism curriculum. If, however, you are not quite sure about becoming a reporter or perhaps think yourself interested in other related jobs, you might then choose the liberal arts curriculum. Does this mean you abandon journalism-related courses? No. It means you use your research to advantage. You can use the courses in the Associated Courses column in the table to pursue your journalism interest and also help gain career flexibility by:

- Choosing these courses as electives
- Auditing a course
- Using the subject matter as topics for term papers
- Considering the areas as possibilities for part-time or summer jobs

Remember, little of what you learn as a consequence of employing a systematic curriculum selection procedure will be wasted. You will either determine what you do like or determine what you don't like.

Directing
Having gathered and organized your data, it now becomes a matter of actually making a decision. Which curriculum shall you choose? From your curriculum tables, you will choose that curriculum that best fits the realities of your particular situation. Counselors can provide information on job availability, length of academic preparation, potential earnings, and advancement in curriculum-related jobs. You may also want to ask yourself some questions. Top among these will be: Despite what aptitude and interest tests may show, what research may reveal, and what advice I may receive, do I actually feel comfortable with the curriculum at the top of my list? Earlier in this discussion it was mentioned that a large degree of subjective, sometimes emotional judgment may enter the decision-making process. It is at this point that you exercise your judgment. Other considerations that will enter into your curriculum selection are:

- *Special Abilities.* Is there some special ability required that you don't believe you possess? All tests attempt to screen out such conflicts, but they are, after all, only guides.
- *Finances.* Can you afford to follow your choice? Can you obtain help?
- *Availability.* Is you curriculum choice available in the college you are planning to attend or are now attending?

Controlling
The element of control is actually present throughout the total decision making process. You must make sure that you, and those that may assist you, obtain the actual data you need. You must also decide in a timely fashion. It is important that you control the tendency to make a hasty decision before acquiring the necessary data. If you have established a curriculum selection schedule, then you should not allow yourself to be panicked into deciding. Your curriculum choice can have a profound effect on your life. It is obviously something you want to consider very carefully.

Control also involves following through once your decision (via registration) has been implemented. Is the curriculum what you expected? Are you doing the most to make it a successful venture? Are you giving yourself and the curriculum a fair chance? These are the kinds of questions you should periodically ask yourself. They will help you keep control of your college career.

Selecting Electives   Because this appendix emphasizes career education, it has concentrated on selecting a curriculum on which to base career competency. But, as you know, competency in a particular career is not the only educational aim. You can treat elective courses as opportunities to release talents and explore interests. Here are some approaches to consider:

1. Treat all of your courses as opportunities to achieve not only competency, but also awareness and flexibility.
2. Use the Associated Courses column of your Curriculum Summary Table as a base for selecting electives. If you have had to choose between two attractive curriculums, consider using the courses in the unchosen one as electives.
3. Reverse the Chapter 5 procedure for completing the Management-By-Motivation Chart. This time start with what you would like to know (the objectives) and then find a course that fits the bill. Avoid taking no for an answer if people tell you that administrative procedures will prevent you from taking a particular course for which you possess prerequisites. Calmly explain your reasons. Your chances of succeeding will increase if you try hard enough.
4. Seek permission to audit a course you believe may interest you. Although you are more or less a guest, auditing can be very stimulating and rewarding.

If You Should Change   What happens if you discover your curriculum is in fact not for you? The possibility of this occurring appears pretty high since it is commonly believed that about half of all students change their major at least once. What can you do?

THE INITIAL DECISION

Decisions arrived at lightly or in a haphazard manner are often not very good decisions. A well-thought-out decision has a better chance of holding up. That is one reason this appendix has emphasized decision making and has provided you with a specific system for curriculum choice. It is not necessary that you use the particular curriculum selection method described in this appendix. What is important is that you at least closely approximate a systematic approach. If you do, the chances are you will have sought counselor assistance when necessary, asked the right questions, gathered helpful information, and identified workable solutions. The chances of your having to change curriculums will have been minimized simply because you will have initially employed a reasonable decision making method.

ELECTIVES

One of the benefits of the S-M method of curriculum selection is the listing of potential elective courses in the Curriculum Summary Table. If you choose your electives to match your other interests, you will find that redirecting your studies may not be a difficult thing to do.

TIMING

The actual change action you take will depend upon where you are in your college career. If you are starting your last semester at a junior or senior college, then it seems reasonable that you should complete your studies as planned. If conditions (time, money, responsibilities) permit, you can then decide what other studies to pursue. If you are not already attending evening college, you may want to consider doing so to supplement your original college work.

If you are halfway through your first junior college year or third senior college year, you can probably switch with little penalty. If you are sure you want to switch, then you should. But being sure doesn't mean only knowing what you dislike. If you are going to switch, do it because there is something you like better, not just because you don't like your present program. Unless you have identified an alternative that matches your new interest and abilities, you may just go from one poor situation to another.

Summary

Dr. Henry M. Wriston, Past President of Brown University, in writing about his own college days said:

I have resented the misguided ignoramus who first sought to give a dollar value to a college degree. True education is intrinsically . . . valuable . . . no two members of (my) class followed the same pattern in any respect, choice of vocation, social life, place of residence, degree of success or lack of it. In sum, all that rigid standardization in high school and college was, happily, defeated. We proved we were individuals, not robots. Our education was a success.[1]

You may want to consider Mr. Wriston's comments when you go about choosing your curriculum and electives.

[1]"Education Without Longing for Cookie-Cutterism," *The New York Times,* December 11, 1976, p. 23.

Index